Navigating White News

Navigating White News

Asian American Journalists at Work

DAVID C. OH AND SEONG JAE MIN

Rutgers University Press

New Brunswick, Camden, and Newark, New Jersey

London and Oxford, UK

Rutgers University Press is a department of Rutgers, The State University of New Jersey, one of the leading public research universities in the nation. By publishing worldwide, it furthers the University's mission of dedication to excellence in teaching, scholarship, research, and clinical care.

Library of Congress Cataloging-in-Publication Data
Names: Oh, David C., author. | Min, Seong-Jae, 1974– author.
Title: Navigating White news : Asian American journalists at work / David C. Oh and Seong Jae Min.
Description: New Brunswick : Rutgers University Press, [2023] | Includes bibliographical references and index.
Identifiers: LCCN 2022019278 | ISBN 9781978831421 (paperback) | ISBN 9781978831438 (hardback) | ISBN 9781978831445 (epub) | ISBN 9781978831452 (pdf)
Subjects: LCSH: Asian American journalists. | Journalism—United States—21st century. | Reporters and reporting—Social aspects—United States. | Asian Americans—Ethnic identity. | Asian Americans—Race identity. | Asian Americans and mass media. | Mass media and race relations—United States. | Asian American professional employees. | United States—Race relations—21st century.
Classification: LCC PN4867.2 .O4 2023 | DDC 071/.3—dc23/eng/20220706
LC record available at https://lccn.loc.gov/2022019278

A British Cataloging-in-Publication record for this book is available from the British Library.

rutgersuniversitypress.org

Manufactured in the United States of America

The book is dedicated to Asian American journalists,
who make our communities visible in all of their complexity.

Contents

Preface

This is a project grounded in cultural studies work on media production and on identification. It is committed to radical contextualism, exploring identities and lived experiences of individuals in depth. As such, it also requires a discussion of the standpoints and experiences of its authors. We describe our personal identities and experiences to discuss how and why we wanted to write this book.

David C. Oh: I identify as both a second-generation Korean American and Asian American. Though there are overlaps, these identities are also marked by differences in ethnic and racial meaning. As a second-generation Korean American, it means I identify as part of the diaspora in the United States. My identity is informed by the ways heritage meanings are valuable to my experience. As scholars of diaspora note, transnational meanings from the homeland are adopted insofar as they provide everyday meaning in the local home. I speak Korean in my household with my spouse and children, eat Korean food frequently (though not every day), and view popular media of South Korea. However, I do not identify as Korean. I have lived in Korea and interacted with Koreans enough to know that my presence is always contingent. I have to earn my place because my habitus and the ways I perform my identities are not sufficiently Korean. I am, as Stuart Hall claims, located in an in-between space of *new ethnicities*. I am not sufficiently culturally Korean, and my racially Asian body marks me as physically alien in the United States, despite being culturally U.S. American.

Like most Asian Americans, my own racial identity was crafted in relationship to my lived experiences with racism. As such, being Asian American is not a cultural identity but a political identity, one that seeks community with other Asian Americans as a way of collectively resisting our shared experiences of marginalization. Sometimes, this is an active political project of antiracism that finds solidarity with other communities of color, and, sometimes, it is merely a desire to be around and with people who understand my experiences, who do not require explanations, and who see me as fully human. It is, as such, a reactionary identity that is formed in opposition to White supremacy's marginalization of Asian Americans as an alien presence, as a threat, or as socially awkward *model minorities* that are used as a wedge to divide Black and Asian Americans, as noted by many scholars of Asian American studies. That does not mean, however, that new meanings are not created through it. It leads to pan-ethnic community among Asian Americans with various identities—different ethnicities, mixed race, adoptee, mixed ethnicity, different generations—without the specific commitments and knowledge of ethnic identities and within the specific sociocultural context of the United States.

It is in this context that my own racial awareness is formed. It started slowly as I fully bought into colorblind ideologies of post-racism. It took a lifetime of racial slights, from microaggressions to overt racist bigotry and physical threats, and years in Seoul as an adult where I saw a glimpse of a life in which I was not racially marginalized (although newly marginalized for linguistic and cultural deficiencies). Throughout that time, I had graduated with a minor in journalism, earned a master's degree in broadcast journalism, interned at WTVH, a local TV station in Syracuse, New York, and worked at Arirang TV, a Seoul-based English-language cable network, in its news division. I did not work long enough in the United States nor have the racial consciousness to recognize the ways in which news itself and newsrooms are organized with the logics of White subjectivities; rather, this awareness occurred during my doctoral studies in which I studied race and media and reflected upon my previous training. As a scholar of race and media now, I have studied mediated representations of race in news and popular entertainment, and I have studied the ways Asian Americans construct racial, ethnic, and diasporic identities through media. It is through this lens that I turn toward understanding how Asian American journalists produce news and navigate racialized newsrooms, especially as our identities have become more salient with the COVID-19 pandemic. My purpose is to not only understand Asian American news workers but to also lift up their voices and perspectives in order to build upon a nascent body of theory about journalists of color and to also, hopefully, decenter journalistic practice from its White moorings.

Seong Jae Min: I have a bit different life trajectory from David, the first author. I was born and raised in Seoul, Korea, and most of my identities were informed by the Korean context. I spent all of my youth and early adulthood in Korea, studying and working there. I grew up in an upper-middle-class family and received a good education. I was a cisgender male in a largely patriarchal and racially homogeneous Korean society. I have socialized with people who were mostly like me in terms of socioeconomic background. "Marginalization" wasn't really a word that entered my lexicon of life. I believe I had what today's Americans call "White privilege" while in Korea.

As I first came to the United States for graduate school in 2000, I slowly noticed that things were different. I kept saying "sorry" for my less-than-ideal American English, and even for the very Asian-sounding name most Americans had difficulty in pronouncing (hence I changed mine from "Seong Jae" to "SJ"). I learned that Asian American men were not desirable dating partners. Worse, I was not aggressive enough and outgoing, traits many Americans find valuable. As these realizations happened, I tried harder to be in the mainstream, the way I used to be back in Korea. One way to do so was to purposefully try to avoid the issue of identities in life. I generally did not believe in Asian American racial consciousness, and, even when I did, I saw it as something of an underdog mindset. I maintained a colorblind perspective for a while, internalizing what some scholars called the White gaze, in which Asian Americans see things through the eyes of White people. In studying media and communication, I also eschewed critical and cultural perspectives, subscribing to the objective, positivist research paradigm. I downplayed "Hallyu," or Korean wave in media, as a one-trick pony.

I am not sure how it happened—it may be a slow accumulation of microaggressions and subtle racism I experienced; it may be the interactions I had with critical and cultural studies scholars and texts I have read over the years; it may be the tidal waves of #BlackLivesMatter and racial awakenings occurring across the United States and the world, but I increasingly got involved in studying the issues of individuals' identities including race, gender, and sexuality. After all, I realized, I cannot avoid the issue of identities, the core of individuals, both shaped and constrained by the cultures and communities we live in. So, rather than avoiding the issue of identities, why not embrace it head on? Becoming an Asian American in the United States, for me, was a process to understand the social context, history, and power dynamics of society and how they influence my identities.

Journalism and media institutions play powerful roles in (in)forming individual identities. They have become primary institutions of socialization and control societal discourses. It is thus vital to understand how power and discourses are produced *within* these institutions, not just their overt products. That is why we study journalists—Asian American—and how their identities matter in navigating the news spaces predominantly occupied by Whites. David started from the critical studies tradition and studies journalism, because journalism matters. I began from journalism studies and tackle the issue of identities, because identities matter. We hope that this book can contribute to furthering the discussion of journalism, identity, and how one sees the world.

Navigating White News

1

Introduction

• •

In the early spring of 2020 as the seriousness, scale of death, and disruption from COVID-19 became inescapable, former President Donald J. Trump and some ordinary U.S. Americans turned to Sinophobia and a generalized racist blaming of East Asian Americans. Former President Trump had been fomenting resentment and mistrust against news media, its institutions and workers, creating a newly dangerous environment for journalists. There were already trickles of stories about attacks on Asian Americans,[1] and, later, hate crimes intensified across the United States, including cases like the Atlanta mass shooting that claimed the lives of several innocent Asian American women. As Asian Americans ourselves and as former reporters, we wondered what it meant for Asian American journalists to be in the field when both their racial and professional identities were targeted for abuse. Did this lead to cognitive dissonance as norms of journalistic objectivity invalidated the value of their lived experience as racialized others under threat? How did they emotionally protect themselves? In ordinary times, what does it mean to be a racial other in the newsroom? How does their racial diversity matter in the construction of news—story choices, source choices, framing, prominence of stories—or do the institutional norms of journalism supersede their intersectional identities? It is these questions that this book explores.

Thus, the purpose of this book is to investigate the ways in which Asian American reporters' racial and ethnic identifications intersect with their professional identification as journalists. We are interested in understanding with greater clarity how intra-racial identification practices matter in their views of news, their commitments to covering Asian American communities, their understanding of the racial politics of their newsrooms, and what they hope to change. As critical scholars of race and news, we are oriented toward understanding power—its flows, differentials, and beneficiaries. We are committed to social equity through our scholarship, centering the experiences of the marginalized (Boylorn and Orbe 2014). As such, we are not neutral observers, but we study Asian American reporters' experiences with the implicit goal of greater social equity. As such, it is our hope that the understanding produced through the research in the book can advance conversations that can lead to social change in newsrooms. However, the book does not make specific policy suggestions or make arguments for structural change. Instead, we center the voices of Asian American reporters in order for people in the industry and in journalism schools who are positioned to create change to consider the inequities and challenges the reporters raise. We hope for greater equity in the coverage of Asian American communities, and we hope for greater equity for Asian American reporters (as well as other reporters of color), but the goal is not explicitly to argue for how these changes can be wrought. Rather, it is to bring light to the ways in which Asian American reporters make sense of news and news practices amid the Whiteness of the profession.

To the best of our knowledge, this is the first book-length treatment of Asian American journalists and the ways that they make sense of and navigate newsrooms.[2] We argue that this is important for several reasons. First, although there is an abundance of research on news coverage of race, there are only a few ethnographic studies of journalists of color. Perhaps because of the time and difficulty of gaining access to reporters or because of the greater theoretical interest in effects or content, the object of study has typically been on representations, discourses, and news users. For instance, there is only one book-length project, by Don Heider (2000), that examines White journalists' news practices and meanings. Although the book is highly important, there also need to be book-length treatments of journalists of color that explore the sociology of newsrooms. To date, there are a few historical books and journalistic accounts such as *Rugged Waters: Black Journalists Swim the Mainstream, Within the Veil: Black Journalists, White Media,* and *Race News: Black Reporters and the Fight for Racial Justice in the Twentieth Century*; however, these are not scholarly, ethnographic studies of race and the newsroom for journalists of color, let alone Asian Americans. This is despite the recommendations of the 1968 Kerner Commission to have more investments in training, coverage, and hiring of journalists of color (Byerly and Wilson 2009). With this in mind, the American Society of Newspaper Editors[3] (ASNE) adopted in 1978 the goal to have newsrooms' racial diversity match the communities they cover by the year 2000 (Delaney 2018). More than 50 years later after the Kerner report, there have only been minor improvements to newsroom diversity, and it appears that ASNE will miss its revised target date of 2025 as only 16.6 percent of journalists are people of color, according to a 2017 ASNE survey (Delaney 2018). Indeed, only 12 percent of radio reporters are journalists of color, only 17 percent of news staff for online and print media, and only 25 percent of news staff for television (Arana 2018). This is despite the fact that many of the largest markets are in majority minority cities and despite the fact that the United States is set to be a majority non-White country in 2045 (Arana 2018).

So, why does this book address Asian American journalists, specifically? This is, in part, because our own identities, professions, and lived experiences help inform an analysis of Asian American journalists' work and the meanings they construct. We are first- and second-generation Korean Americans who worked as reporters before entering academia.[4] We understand newsroom culture, have experienced firsthand White-normative journalism pedagogy, and have struggled against structural racism and microaggressions in our everyday lives and current professions. The first author is a second-generation Asian American and scholar of Asian American studies and media diversity, who recognizes the vital role of journalism in shaping societal discourses. The second author is a first-generation Asian American and a scholar of journalism and political communication, who came to the realization that his Asian American identity matters in how he perceives and studies news. In this book, we bring together our overlapping yet varied intellectual standpoints to explore the issue of race in journalism. We hope that our work might legitimate Asian American journalists' experiences and elevate their voices—storytellers whose own stories are worth hearing.

Beyond our own standpoints, studying Asian Americans is meaningful because it complicates binary notions of race, i.e., the Black-White paradigm (Kim 1999b; Lipsitz 1998; Eng and Han 2018). This better reflects the multiracial constitution of the United States and the complexities of power. For instance, Bonilla-Silva (2004) argues that a Black-White model is an increasingly inadequate model of racial difference as the United States is moving toward what he argues is a three-category racial hierarchy that is more similar to the way race is understood across Latin America; this includes categories that he calls "White," "Honorary White," and "Collective Black." Expanding beyond a Black-White paradigm also contributes to what Claire Jean Kim (1999a) refers to as racial triangulation. This means understanding how Asian Americans fit within a cultural mapping of race in which people of color are marginalized in co-constitutive ways to advance White supremacy. Perhaps, best known are the ways in which Asian Americans have been positioned as a racial wedge through the model minority stereotype (Kim 1999a; Hamamoto 1994; Fong 2008) and how Asian Americans are constructed as unassimilable "aliens" (Lee 1999; Ono and Pham 2009; Kim 1999a). Although our analysis does not study other racial groups directly to understand racial triangulation, we talked with Asian American reporters about how they understand their racialized positions against the dual backdrop of COVID-19 and the Black Lives Matter protests. We also hope that the study contributes to a larger, burgeoning body of literature that begins to trace co-constitutive racial contours in newsrooms and news practice.

Finally, it is important to study Asian Americans at this time because of the omnipresent pandemic of COVID-19, which has been a dual contagion of disease and racial animus. Like Asian Americans employed in essential work, some Asian American reporters continued to be in the field, covering news and confronting racist abuse. A number of journalists have experienced harassment, such as CNN reporter Amara Walker, who described three incidents of verbal abuse in a single day; CNN reporter Kyung Lah, who was called a racist slur while preparing for a live shot with Jake Tapper; and CBS reporter Weijia Jiang, who was racially singled out during a press conference with former President Donald Trump when he told her to "ask China" in response to her question about the administration's response to the United States's COVID-related deaths. These are among just a few instances of Asian American reporters and of Asian Americans, more broadly, who have been assaulted verbally and physically, as well as killed, by people motivated only by their racist association of COVID-19 with Asian Americans. The anti-Asian American harms depend on a cultural logic of racial lumping in which all Asian Americans act as stand-ins for China and on an elision in which Asian Americans are not seen as U.S. American but as a foreign, alien presence. Indeed, during times of health crisis, Asian Americans have historically been associated with unnatural disease (Le et al. 2020).

Race and News

In a quote that is widely attributed to former *Washington Post* president Philip Graham, journalism is argued to be "the first rough draft of history" (Shafer 2010). The authors of these drafts, the women and men who cover news, thus have an outsized role in shaping our understanding of the past. They also shape our present through the news's agenda-setting function (McCombs 1997) and their framing of the stories they select (Entman 1993). Thus, it is problematic that journalism has historically been a White-dominated profession because its cultural and political power have largely been consistent with White-masculine norms.

Outside of Connie Chung, who retired nearly two decades ago, and, to a lesser extent, Ann Curry, who was summarily dismissed from *Today*, there has not been an Asian American journalist who has been a household name. Arguably, there is not a single Asian American anchor with this degree of visibility today. Indeed, the public would have difficulty naming an Asian American journalist beyond their local markets. In addition to prominence, there are also simply too few Asian Americans in mainstream U.S. newsrooms. This reflects a larger pattern in the profession as it is Whiter and more male-concentrated than other occupational fields (Grieco 2018). Although pipeline issues are a contributing cause, particularly because the usual entry points of unpaid internships require some degree of family wealth (Arana 2018), it is also likely that journalists of color leave because of the lack of mentorship and frustration with arguably White-centric professional norms that sustain the field (Kil 2020). In newsroom settings, Asian American journalists and journalists of color, more generally, are marginalized. For Asian American journalists during most of the twentieth century, they were concentrated in ethnic media outlets. Since the late twentieth century, however, the proportion of Asian American journalists has somewhat increased, but they are still underrepresented,[5] particularly considering that Asian Americans are the fastest-growing racial group in the United States (Budiman 2020).

Diversity in newsrooms, however, does not necessarily guarantee better coverage of communities of color or increased sensitivity toward race-related issues (Liebler 1997). As Sui et al. (2018, 1092) write, "Unless there is a specific reason to do so that is driven by the broader needs of the news organization, minority reporters may lack sufficient incentive to focus more on race-related issues." Through education in journalism schools, training on the job, and socialization in newsrooms, journalists of color are assimilated into dominant newsroom culture as a way of fitting in and furthering their careers (Alemán 2014). This socialization disciplines journalists of color to eschew reporting from their racialized subjectivities because doing so is seen as insufficiently professional (Nishikawa et al. 2009; Newkirk 2000). Therefore, it is important to understand how traditional journalistic norms and culture operate vis-à-vis journalists of color in contemporary newsrooms.

In addition to studying journalistic norms and culture, it is important to be aware of what is happening across the journalistic landscape. There has been high volatility in the profession in recent years because of the threat of the internet to print news' business model, the role of social media as a distribution vehicle for news, increased workload for journalists who remain in the newsroom, and blogging and social media that have created space for citizen journalists, who have ushered in new journalistic practices. Once a totem in journalism, objectivity has been challenged by new norms such as transparency, interactivity, participation, and even advocacy (Min 2018). Objectivity has also been challenged by recent social movements such as #BlackLivesMatter, which has increased racial consciousness in newsrooms and has allowed journalists to more openly report from a point of view. For Asian American journalists in particular, the COVID-19 pandemic has brought unique challenges, as the disease was ethnoracialized in the United States due to its reported origin in Wuhan, China. Unfortunately, this tied into historical discourses of Asian Americans as embodied signifiers of disease, an all too frequent association of Asianness with contagion (Kim and Shah 2020; Leong 2003; Oh 2020). This ethnoracialization of the disease in American society has elicited important responses from Asian American journalists concerning their work norms and practices, such as guidance from the Asian American Journalists Association (AAJA).

Despite these dynamic changes, we know very little about how journalists' race and racial identities matter in their professional work, and, in turn, how the newsroom and larger social environment shape their personal and professional identities. This book is an attempt to address this. It is an investigation of how Asian American journalists' personal and professional identities operate in newsrooms as well as in the larger U.S. American social system. It seeks to reveal the lived experiences of journalists of color and explore how they navigate the White-normative world of news. In doing so, this book provides some unique and important perspectives to the study of race and media.

First, it argues that journalists' racial identities matter in their experience of predominantly White newsrooms and in their understanding of what counts as news. In addition, we go further than other studies of race and newsrooms by understanding that their ascribed racial identities alone are insufficient as an explanation of their experiences in the newsroom but that their avowed racial identities matter, too. In other words, it is not only how they are seen as racially different but how they make sense of that racial difference. Racial difference is a starting point, but understanding intra-racial articulations of identity provides further clarification. In contrast, classic studies in the "sociology of news" tradition have paid relatively little attention to journalists' personal identities. Instead, they explore how structural factors such as journalistic norms and culture, economics, and organizational work routines shape individual journalists' beliefs and behaviors. Sociologists such as Herbert Gans, Gaye Tuchman, Michael Schudson, and Todd Gitlin produced foundational texts in which they examined journalism's professional ideologies, cultural practices, daily routines, and newsroom bureaucracy to illustrate that what we call news is a socially constructed practice arising from complex institutional dynamics. For example, Tuchman (1978) demonstrates that within news organizations, reporters follow routines that tell them where to look for news and how to gather it efficiently. Her notion of the "news net" was deeply influential in the understanding of journalistic routines, but it did not consider journalists' identities as part of the fabric of the net. For instance, journalists' standpoints and experiences shape whom they know, whom they trust, and what they understand as newsworthy.

Gitlin (1980), on the other hand, shows that issues pertaining to racial minorities are less likely to be covered and that the agency of journalists of color is compromised in profit-driven mainstream news organizations whose personnel as well as main audience is predominantly White. In both cases, they examine how news structures impact news coverage by individual journalists. We are interested in how individual journalists' racial identities matter in their perception of news structures, norms, and processes. Although their conclusions are undoubtedly important, what is lacking in such a large, structural perspective is how individual journalists enact agency within structural constraints, thereby making visible micro-level negotiations of their personal and professional identities within newsroom structures and journalistic norms. Focusing on the journalists' perceptions and practices of news provides a different vantage point and a counterweight to the prevailing perspective that depicts individual journalists as impotent agents vis-à-vis larger structures.

Second, it decenters the scholarly gaze from White journalists to journalists of color. In Heider's (2000) book *White News: Why Local News Programs Don't Cover People of Color*, he concluded that "incognizant racism" in newsrooms is a powerful institutional force that leads to minimal and stereotyped coverage of people of color. He writes: "[Incognizant racism] is the result of dozens of daily decisions, of years of training and practice, of decades of cultural orientation, and of a well-documented history of systematic and institutionalized neglect . . . Neither news organizations as a whole, nor the news workers as individuals had the desire to change coverage to be more inclusive" (Heider 2000, 52). Two decades later, it is still a relevant and powerful observation, but its White-centric focus inadvertently reinforces Whiteness and White perspectives. For instance, as we will describe in this book, Asian American journalists certainly do not experience the Whiteness of newsrooms as incognizant or inadvertent. Our work suggests that journalists today are well aware of racism that is present in news work and in some cases attempt to exercise their agency to address it. Because of this gap and because of the two-decade absence of news on the sociology of race and news, it is important to return to this question given the racial, technological, and economic transformations that have shaped news in recent years. This book is an analysis of journalists' identities, negotiations, and understanding of what constitutes good journalism in this conjuncture.[6]

Third, this book is the first major study of Asian American journalists' newsroom experiences. Even though Asian Americans are the fastest-growing racial minority in the United States, Asian American journalists have rarely been studied in the literature on race and the sociology of news. As noted earlier, work on race and media in the United States has been positioned along what is referred to as a Black-White binary paradigm (Omi and Winant 1994; Perea 1997). This is understandable considering the pernicious nature of anti-Black racism in U.S. racial formations, but studying race and racism by complicating and triangulating differently racialized experiences provides a deeper understanding of how racism functions and how people of color, including journalists of color, navigate race in the United States as suggested by critical race scholars (Gonzalez-Sobrino and Goss 2019). By studying Asian American journalists' experiences, it points to areas of similarity and overlapping interest among journalists of color. These shared experiences both demonstrate the ways in which White supremacy takes on similarly patterned hegemonic responses as well as provide the possibility for interracial alliances that might disrupt the newsroom status quo. Our work expands the discourse of critical race studies by exploring the unique experiences of Asian American journalists, a group that has received little attention in media research.

Of course, there are existing studies on Asian Americans in media. But the vast majority of them are about representation, media effects, or audience interpretation. That is, the most popular studies in this area are about how Asian Americans and other people of color are stereotypically portrayed in the media and how such biased representation may lead to negative social consequences such as increased racial bias. Studies about race and newsrooms are no exception. The most well-known conclusion about race and newsrooms is that the intractable lack of diversity in newsrooms leads to problematic coverage of communities of color. While this is undoubtedly a critically important topic— this book addresses it, too—reversing the lens to consider how covering news matters for journalists is an area that is rarely studied. This book's main approach is to focus on Asian American journalists' identities and roles rather than effects on coverage. It attempts to understand Asian American journalists' nuanced subjectivities present in their news work and their negotiation of personal and professional identities. As journalism is critical for the healthy functioning of democracy and for social progress, we want to analyze U.S. news structures and practices through the lens of Asian American journalists.

In-Depth Interviews of Asian American Journalists

Due to our own personal identities and orientations, we are sympathetic to the experiences of Asian American journalists interviewed in this book. Though some critics might argue that the work is not "objective," we do not claim objectivity as a norm for humanistic, critical scholars. Rather, what is important is the rigor of the work, the theoretical insights gained, and the credibility of interpretations. Our personal identities and subjectivities are precisely the standpoints that allow us to better understand the rich and nuanced lived experiences of our participants, and, thus, it is a strength of the project. In fact, some of our participants told us that our background in journalism and our shared identity as Asian Americans helped build rapport and that it provided shared understanding with them. Together with the participants, we attempt to situate ourselves in relations of power and explore how we may have been subject to forces of dominant professional and social norms in U.S. journalism. Privileging subjectivity and examining power relationships in society are consistent with the tradition of critical/cultural studies, a theoretical framework that informed our analysis. Following Stuart Hall (1991), we understand journalism as a cultural practice, a negotiated site of meaning where hegemonic control and manifestation of individual agency are taking place at the same time.

Over the course of six months in 2020, we interviewed twenty East Asian American journalists in major newsrooms across the United States. With the exception of one producer and one columnist, the participants are frontline reporters who engage in the daily work of news gathering and reporting. They bring a range of unique experiences with variation across gender, age, geographic location, ethnic and immigration background, and news organization type. Twelve of the twenty are women; their ages ranged from the early 20s to early 60s; and the majority of them are print reporters, but we also interviewed radio, online, and television reporters. About half work in national news organizations, while the other half work in local newsrooms. The coasts were somewhat over-represented, but we also interviewed reporters across the South and Midwest. Many of them are second- or third-generation Asian Americans, with two who might be identified as "1.5-generation" U.S. Americans because they immigrated as children. Despite these variations, they all self-identify as "Asian American." It should be noted that because the study was, in part, focused on how racialization mattered with COVID-19, we only interviewed Asian Americans who would be racially associated with the disease. That is, we only interviewed Asian Americans with heritage ties in East Asian nations because of shared physiology and dominant culture's flattening of East Asian difference as monolithic. Our use of the label "Asian American" does not presume that East Asian American is conceptually equivalent to Asian American; it is simply because East Asian Americans also belong within the larger category of Asian American. As such, the criteria used for the study are self-identification as Asian American with East Asian heritage ties and their active employment as newsroom reporters.

The timing of the interviews also came at a historically consequential moment. They were conducted during the peak of the COVID-19 pandemic in the spring and summer of 2020 but prior to the publication of stories about anti-Asian hate crimes against Asian American elders, so anti-Asian sentiment was not yet experienced as bodily threatening for most reporters. In the pandemic, it also required the use of video interviews via Zoom and WebEx platforms. Though we would have preferred to interview in person, video interviews seemed appropriate given the ways that many reporters, and much of the general public, have been working during the pandemic times, and they allowed us to overcome restrictions based on distance. Although not the same as being in person, video interviews allowed us to see our participants and to gauge nonverbal communication. Each unstructured interview lasted around an hour and an hour and a half, but a few stretched passed two hours. We asked general questions about the participants' understanding of their racial and professional identities and how they approach journalism, and then we let them talk freely about their experiences, feelings, and views of news. Unstructured interviews such as this give more depth, complexity, and agency to the participants, and are more effectively able to reveal sincere, honest, and nuanced thoughts from participants (Kvale 1996).

In order to maintain confidentiality, the participants have been assigned pseudonyms, and identifying information has been removed. In writing the analysis, we referred to them only by broad association, saying, for example, "Amy [pseudonym], a reporter on the West Coast." Regrettably, this also means that we are unable to include specific stories that carry the richness of their experiences. This is because these stories are still largely searchable online, and, as such, would violate confidentiality. Reporters are publicly visible, so greater caution must be taken to protect their identities. Making these promises assured reporters that they could speak more openly. Discussing experiences of racism, discrimination, and microaggression can be traumatic, and the conversations can also be fraught. Because criticism of their own news organizations, colleagues, and work settings is also uncomfortable and risky, it was important to establish our respect for their confidentiality. By building rapport between interviewers and interviewees and by guaranteeing confidentiality, we believe we accessed feelings and beliefs with depth. Further, in the reporting of data, we transcribed quotes directly so that the reporters' language, spontaneity, and emotion is visible, although we did remove verbal fillers, e.g., um, when their inclusion did not change the meaning of the quote. The only other changes are the inclusion of brackets to flatten details that might point to their identities. For instance, if they said they grew up in Euless,[7] a suburb of Fort Worth, we would say they grew up in [a suburb]. Finally, we adhered to research ethics by gaining informed consent prior to the interviews.

Table 1 shows the list of the Asian American journalists we interviewed and their brief profiles. Again, their real names are replaced and they are only broadly identified: print includes newspapers, wire services, and digital-only publications; broadcast includes both television and radio stations.

Our analysis followed the principles of grounded theory. Grounded theory is often utilized as a tool of humanistic, ethnographic methods as a way for researchers to inductively and qualitatively conceptualize what has been taking place in the lives of study participants. In grounded theory, data exploration and theory building occur at the same time (Strauss and Corbin 1998). Through the interviews, we attempted to not only conceptualize the interview data but to also explore relations among conceptual categories to specify the conditions under which theoretical relationships manifest (Glaser and Strauss 1967). This inductive interviewing and theory building process is the most

Table 1
Participants by gender and type of news outlet

Name	Gender	Organization type
Amy	Woman	Broadcast
Brian	Man	Broadcast
Clara	Woman	Print
Dana	Woman	Broadcast
Ethan	Man	Print
Felix	Man	Print
Gwyneth	Woman	Print
Hannah	Woman	Print
Ivan	Man	Print
Jennifer	Woman	Broadcast
Kate	Woman	Print
Larry	Man	Print
Mark	Man	Print
Nina	Woman	Print
Olivia	Woman	Print
Paul	Man	Print
Quinn	Man	Print
Rose	Woman	Print
Sophie	Woman	Print
Tara	Woman	Broadcast

preferred method for understanding ethnic identity (Phinney 1996). Following grounded theory, which does not have a hard separation of phases between data collection and analysis, we transcribed and open coded immediately after each interview, using the NVivo qualitative research software application. As interviews were conducted, we engaged in an iterative process of constant-comparison to develop themes in what is described in grounded theory as axial coding. In this inductive process of analysis, we attempted to find emergent themes and construct categories that explain and synthesize the data. Eventually, this was integrated into a theoretical framework that specifies causes, conditions, and consequences of the studied processes (Strauss and Corbin 1998). The flexibility inherent in in-depth interviewing is a good fit for grounded theory strategies for increasing the incisiveness of the analysis (Charmaz and Belgrave 2012).

Preview of Chapters

The following chapter provides an explanation of the literature on Asian American racial identity formation and discusses the participants' varied understanding of their racial identities and the life experiences that have informed them. It argues that the participants cluster into three primary interpretive communities, which we understand as identity positions. It also examines the different critical exposures that produce racial reflexivity. This chapter is not specific to their news work or journalistic identities, but it provides context to understand the diversity of Asian American experiences in order to understand how their standpoints shape their views of their role as news workers. It also provides a basis for the following chapters as it is apparent that racial reflexivity that produces distinct racial identities also leads to eventual questions about the nature of news—its structures and values.

In chapters 3 and 4, we explore the ways that Asian American reporters understand newsrooms and news practices as White news. We argue that even for Asian Americans who are largely unbothered by their racial socialization into Whiteness or who believe their own newsrooms are racially progressive, there still is a recognition that newsrooms, generally, are defined by Whiteness. The chapters discuss how Asian Americans navigate these spaces and the everyday frustrations and microaggressions they experience, how some participants resist in order to transform their newsrooms, and the role of racial activation in motivating their resistance.

In chapter 5, we explore how Asian American journalists' racial standpoints shape their views of news itself. In particular, the chapter addresses participants' skepticism, ambivalence, and mild endorsement of objectivity as a professional news norm. We discuss the roles of racial activation and gender and their relationship to a skepticism about objectivity, in particular. The chapter, then, discusses how the negotiation of racial identities and attendant meanings interacts with journalistic norms to which they are socialized, demonstrating that in their discursive challenges to objectivity, they connect to other mainstream journalistic values, such as fairness, truth-seeking, and accountability for the powerful.

In chapter 6, we show how the journalists' racial identifications and ambivalence about news norms shape the stories they cover. We find that many have a desire to elevate the voices of Asian Americans and cover more community stories. While this was true across all racial identifications, racial activation matters in the commitment to pitching and finding stories about the Asian American community or relying more frequently on Asian American sources in stories that are not specifically about Asian Americans. It is an attempt to normalize Asian Americans as U.S. American. That said, the hope is to represent Asian Americans with more complexity, not as flatly "positive" stories but ones that may include their human failings, community flaws, and other newsworthy qualities of human life. Depending on their status and the newsroom in which they work, journalists sometimes have to struggle against the logics of White newsrooms by acting strategically to have the stories get told.

In chapter 7, we discuss the specific conditions of COVID-19 on Asian American journalists' news work. The chapter argues that structural conditions have minimized some harms of racist abuse but that there is also a general tendency to resist victimization narratives as a means of fitting into the masculinist norms of the newsroom, which require having a "thick skin." When reporters do speak about relatively subtle harms, there is also a gendered response in which men only address external harms, e.g., racial microaggressions, while women include external harms but also internal harms, e.g., increased anxiety, fear, or depression. This willingness to self-reflect on internal harms produces more motivation to uplift Asian American voices through their work as news workers.

In the epilogue, we bring the findings of the various chapters together to make a theoretical argument for racial activation as the primary trigger that leads to skepticism of news practices as White news and which generates the affective space and moral vision to push back against White news practices. We also point out that this move is incremental rather than radical as it works within existing systems and does not fundamentally challenge White racial hegemony in news, although it may have the potential, along with other changes in the news landscape, to alter the meaning of professional news values and practices. This could itself be a radical shift.

2

Asian American
Reporters' Racial and
Ethnic Identifications

● ●

To provide context to Asian American journalists' varied understandings of news practice, we begin by discussing the meanings that the reporters give to their racial and ethnic identities. It is too often the case that race research inadvertently implies racial similarity by not examining intra-racial difference, or it individualizes differences that do not fully take into consideration the ways in which identities are constituted within discourse (Hall 1996a). As Fish (1976) points out, people belong to interpretive communities that produce shared understanding, and as Hall has said, our beliefs are never our own but are constructed within existing discourse (Hall 2003). For this reason, this study begins by analyzing the interpretive communities and meanings that Asian American reporters produce. This understanding matters for this study because, as later chapters indicate, Asian American reporters' different perspectives on news and their newsrooms are articulated through the meanings given to their racial identities.

Though this chapter does not directly address the specific purpose of the book, it provides necessary background. Specifically, we investigated how Asian American journalists understand their racial identities and how their lived experiences were formative in these interpretations. To organize the chapter, we begin by constructing a theoretical framework about racial identity based in Hall's (1996a) concept of identification, which we connect to interdisciplinary studies of Asian American racial identity. We then discuss three different identity positions—interpretive communities—for the reporters. This includes a non-salient racial identity that is marked by a lack of affective investments in Asian American identity, identities that are situated primarily in ethnic meanings and communities, and racial identities that draw together pan-Asian meanings.

Theorizing Asian American Identification and Discourse

To begin, it is important to note that cultural studies, the theoretical perspective guiding this book, rejects the tendencies of social psychology to understand identity, personal and ethnic, as a stable, core sense of self (Erikson 1968; Phinney 1996; Cross 1978). Instead, cultural studies argues that identities are not essentialized nor fixed but, rather, relational, context-specific, and marked with contradiction (Woodward 1997; Gilroy 1997). Stuart Hall (1996a) eschewed the concept of "identity" in favor of identification, noting that identities are a process of becoming rather than a state of being. It is not a core, stable self but multiple, fragmented identifications that are continuously renewed and constructed in a process of meaning-making that is in relationship to others and that is produced differently across social contexts. "Identification is, then, a process of articulation, a suturing, an over-determination not a subsumption" (Hall 1996a, 3). Thus, there are four primary conclusions: (1) identifications change in a process of becoming; (2) identifications are multiple and fragmented; (3) identifications are articulated within cultural discourse; and (4) identifications are activated and shift across social contexts.

We synthesize these conclusions with the available literature in Asian American studies, ethnic studies, and psychology, and it is for this reason that we use the concept of identification rather than identity from this point forward. Although Hall (1996a) argued that work on *cultural* identification should be joined with psychoanalytical research on the formation of individual identities, we connect cultural theories in sociology and ethnic studies with contemporary social psychological research because of its more productive work on Asian American racial identity as a way of elaborating upon Hall's aforementioned three points about identification. First, as a process of becoming Asian American, scholars note that those who are raised in predominantly White neighborhoods often express a desire to assimilate into dominant White society (Oyserman and Sakamoto 1997). However, as psychologists conclude in their work on Asian American ethnoracial identity formation, Asian Americans develop racial identities as they realize full inclusion is not possible (Tse 1999; Iwamoto et al. 2013). Although awareness of being racialized can also problematically encourage a tendency to avoid their own ethnic and racial group (Woo et al. 2020), it also catalyzes a process in which Asian Americans reject internalized blame for their marginalization and turn that blame toward dominant culture instead. Tse (1999) argues that during this process Asian

Americans explore their ethnic heritage culture to find belonging but that this, too, is incomplete as they realize they are not fully accepted in their ethnic heritage societies because of their U.S. American cultural and linguistic habitus.[1] Eventually, accepting this middle space, they seek pan-ethnic racial identity as a specific formation (Tse 1999).

The point is to emphasize that identifications shift as understanding about individuals' relationships to others and to society changes. That said, this account is too tidy and too normative for a critical approach. Although ethnic identification is important to habitus (Song 2003), habitus is more fungible than social psychological accounts proffer. Indeed, instead of understanding ethnoracial identity development as normative stages, we believe it is better understood as identity positions, meaning that among Asian Americans, there are a number of ways in which they articulate their identifications based on available discourses (Oh 2015). These identity positions are constitutive of the interpretive communities in which they belong and inform the standpoints through which they interpret the world around them. Woodward (1997), for instance, notes that positions taken within discourse constitute our identities.

Returning to Hall's (1996a) second argument, identifications are articulated within discourse. Articulation understands that people have agency to select meanings that make sense to themselves but that it is expressed within discourse means that it is not simply an individual decision. Rather, identification is an interaction between our individual beliefs about ourselves and the discourses that exist in culture about who we are (Espiritu 1992; Tuan 1998; Song 2003). In other words, becoming Asian American is always shaped and constrained by the cultures and communities in which people live. Specifically, in this case, we refer to multiple-generation Asian Americans because the experiences of the immigrant generation differ in important ways as the immigrant generation has direct, lived experiences in the ethnic homeland culture. Indeed, the difference between first- and second-generation is a major dividing line between the ways Asian Americans understand themselves in the community, particularly for younger people (Oh 2015; Park 2008). As multiple-generation Asian Americans, they often avoid associating with Asian American immigrants and "insist that uniquely Chinese American, Japanese American, and even Asian American cultures have developed in this country and it is within these hyphenated spaces where their true authenticity lies" (Tuan 2002, 211). As such, their commitments are to what Hall (1996b) refers to as "new ethnicities," new spaces for identification that lie between the dominant host culture and the homeland culture. It is a specifically hybrid and diasporic formation (Chong 2017).

The discourses from which Asian Americans can draw include wider cultural discourses that construct Asian Americans as inferior, and, sadly, it is oftentimes the uncritical starting point for Asian Americans who are raised in predominantly White suburban neighborhoods. For these Asian Americans, experiences of subtle racism and alienation is typical, although most do not understand their experiences as racist discrimination (Tuan 1998). Rather, it leads to feelings of inferiority and a desire for White acceptance and for the benefits of White privilege (Chong 2017; Trieu 2018). It leads to an internalization of the White gaze, where Asian Americans see themselves through the eyes of White people and view themselves as lacking (Osajima 2007). Even for those who grow up in more diverse neighborhoods, they still interact with the images of popular culture. As Kellner (1995) notes, media culture provides the discourses from which people construct their identifications. Particularly common is the idea that Asian Americans do not belong and are not genuinely American (Song 2003; Tuan 1998; Kibria 2002a). This is much of the fuel that is driving the recent spike in anti-Asian hate crimes as Asian Americans are blamed for COVID-19's origins in Wuhan, China (Mallapragada 2021).

During their childhood socialization, Asian Americans are taught to understand that U.S. Americanness is synonymous with Whiteness (Cheryan and Monin 2005). One common, troubling strategy for Asian Americans to resist their racialization and to seek inclusion from White Americans is to mock their own racial and ethnic groups in order to be found acceptable to White people, providing a sense of agency to tell the joke and to evoke laughter; this strategy is dehumanizing and incomplete, however, as it is based in a rejection of immutable, visible racial difference (Song 2003). Other discursive choices are to assert their belonging in the United States by referencing knowledge of U.S. popular culture, by eschewing co-ethnic and co-racial friends, and by performing other behaviors that read as White American (Cheryan and Monin 2005). It is important to note that while there is agency to articulate identifications, these are constrained by dominant cultural discourses about Asian Americans. For Asian Americans, there is often resentment that White Americans can discard their ethnic ties while beliefs about Asian Americans' foreignness are nearly impossible to shake (Espiritu 1992; Min 2002; Tuan 2002).

Outside dominant culture, ethnic communities and households as well as pan-Asian communities provide symbolic materials to articulate in ways that are more empowering. Articulating as specifically ethnic, e.g., Chinese American, can resist racialization by opting out of U.S. racial logics (Kibria 2002a; Lowe 2007). Ethnicity rather than race also is sometimes chosen to eschew hierarchies in the Asian American community that privilege East Asian Americans, especially Chinese and Japanese Americans (Chong 2017). Unfortunately, choosing ethnicity while rejecting race is not entirely effective as identifications and meanings are constrained by articulation within cultural discourse, which racializes Asian Americans and lumps together people with otherwise little in common. Nevertheless, ethnic identity continues to be quite salient. It is a strategic resource that can provide cultural, symbolic resources that provide a sense of meaning, belonging, and different perspectives (Espiritu 1992).

For this reason, most Asian Americans develop parallel identities that are simultaneously specifically ethnic and broadly pan-Asian (Kibria 2002a), although affective commitments to ethnic identification tend to be stronger than racial ones (Min 2002). Before addressing this further, it is important to differentiate between a generalized racial identification and a pan-Asian racial identification. The former implies a singular group identity whereas the latter is a coalition of various communities who are racially lumped together. Kibria (1997) argues that there is a current racial formation underway in which the coming together of Asian Americans has created a sense of shared identity; this is based in perceived similarities around cultural values such as the importance of family, hard work, and respect for elders, or everyday practices such as taking off shoes before entering a home (Chong 2017). However, when Asian Americans are asked what cultural similarities they share, they often struggle to define shared culture even while asserting that there is one (Park 2008). Instead, many Asian Americans are more comfortable identifying as belonging to a heterogeneous community that allows for cultural sampling from multiple cultures to construct identifications (Park 2008).

This points to the third major argument about identifications—that they are multiple and contradictory (Hall 1996a). Because identifications shift based on the sociocultural context in which they are articulated (Hall 1996a, Grossberg 1996), Asian Americans may shift between their ethnic identity, a pan-Asian identity, a U.S. American national identity, or a politically (re)active racial or multiracial identity during times of crisis or harm. This should not be understood as inauthentic but, rather, as the contemporary condition of Asian Americanness—heterogeneous, hybrid, and multiple (Lowe 2007). It is too simplistic to have a singular notion of what Asian American means (Espiritu 2002), and the different articulations of Asian American identification co-exist without tension except when specific contexts create friction between different positionings. For the participants in this study, the meanings emerged inductively during the interviews as it became apparent that the reporters' meanings of Asian American as a racial identity are multivariate.[2] However, this is not to say that these identifications are entirely fluid. Participants in the study might shift identifications across contexts, e.g., interviewing a co-ethnic business owner and covering a pan-Asian protest against anti-Asian hate crimes, but because they are articulating into cultural discourse, their identifications fit into a habitus in which they usually perform their Asian American identifications, which we refer to as their identity positions.

Asian American Reporters' Identity Positions

In the study, Asian American reporters tended to settle into three different articulated positions: lack of salience or disinterest in Asian American identity, ethnic-centered construction of Asian American identity, and pan-Asian construction of Asian American identity. Drawing upon available discourses in dominant culture, their ethnic communities, and pan-Asian communities, the identity positions are a suturing of themselves within these discourses. These should not be understood solely as individual choices but, rather, fitting themselves within interpretive communities. Because of their different lived experiences, knowledge, or motivations and capability for self-reflection, they come to multiple standpoints. It is important to emphasize again that unlike the social psychological literature, we do not make normative judgments about which identity position is preferable for individuals; however, at a meso- or macro-level, social justice is more likely to be achieved with racial awareness and racially conscious choices. To the extent social equality or social justice matters to Asian American reporters or not, racial identifications could matter. To organize this section, we discuss the different identity positions of our participants and their fits within them.

Non-Salient Racial Identification

Four of the participants—Paul, Kate, Felix, and Larry—identify as Asian American but did not view this identity to be salient to their everyday lives. Paul, a mixed-race White Asian American, claimed that he identifies primarily as mixed-race and that his racial identity only matters to the extent that he is treated differently. As Spickard (2007) points out, mixed-race Asian Americans practice "situation ethnicity" that adapts to circumstances and seeks community-building with other mixed-race Asian Americans, who more fully understand their specific life experience. Kate noted that as an adoptee who was raised by White American parents, she feels "very much American," repeating this specific phrase twice, thus not only linking her identity to her parents but linking U.S. Americanness to Whiteness. To understand herself in the family, she said that she "happens to be Asian," taking on a colorblind view of racial difference that is aligned with the dominant discourse of race, namely post-racialism (Prashad 2001). Thus, her identity not only is unimportant to her, but it is a liability when claiming a role in the family *and* in the nation. Though Kate's specific upbringing is not clear, Shiao (2017) argues that White adoptive parents often socialize their children toward building affective commitments to Whiteness, such as discouraging their children from dating Asian Americans. Louie (2009) also finds that most White parents of transnational Asian adoptee children frequently interpret their children's experiences with racism as individual acts of ignorance rather than as indicative of a White supremacist system. This, in turn, discourages adoptee children from talking to their parents about their experiences with racism (Docan-Morgan 2010).

Felix and Larry were both raised in predominantly White neighborhoods, and while they recognize the problems of structural racism, they are generally comfortable in White American spaces, and their racial identifications are generally not salient and are only activated occasionally. It is also important to note that it is mostly Asian American men whose racial identifications are less salient. It is possible that internalizing assimilation may be more prevalent among Asian American men because of the hyperfeminization of Asian/Americans in U.S. dominant culture (Espiritu 2004; Oh 2012) or possibly because of the ethnic family and household-centered meanings for Asian Americans (Kibria 1997). It could also be because Asian American men process harms by externalizing them as a psychological defense mechanism (Liu 2002; Kuo 1995) and are less likely to use active coping strategies to deal with racism (Liang et al. 2007; Kuo 1995). For this specific group, the reasons are not known, but it has implications not only on how they see themselves, but as we explore in later chapters, how they view and practice news work.

Ethnic-Centered Racial Identification

Most of the reporters in the study value their ethnic heritage culture and identification, but what differentiates individuals in this identity position is that they understand their Asian American identifications primarily through the prism of their ethnic heritage identity, thus they articulate an ethnic-centric understanding of race. We intentionally use "ethnic-centered" rather than "ethnocentric" in order to avoid the connotations that are often given to ethnocentrism—discrimination, hierarchy, and other problematic formations—because this is not what is being observed in this chapter. Indeed, as Asian American scholars point out, ethnicity can be a resource to resist White supremacy and its racial lumping (Kibria 2002b). In the case of our participants, however, it does not appear that these are intentional choices to resist racialization but simply reflective of the habitus from which they identify as Asian American. Perhaps because Asian American identifications are crafted largely in the household—food, traditions, and holiday rituals (Chong 2017), the reporters in this study were not reflecting a tactical choice to challenge racialization but, rather, a personally meaningful identification. In some cases, there is a conflation of ethnicity with race such that questions about what Asian American as a racial identity means to them were answered with ethnic specificity, e.g., heritage language or cultural practices. Even when the difference was clarified, it sometimes led to confusion as Asian American racial identity was understood so strongly through an ethnic prism that the other available meanings for Asian American were not visible. Of the participants, there are only four reporters who are positioned in this way, but it is notable that most of them are men and all of them are first- or second-generation Asian Americans with either direct ethnic heritage ties and/or immigrant parents.

Tara identifies specifically as her heritage ethnic identity rather than Asian American, and she slips between the labels—Taiwanese American and

Asian American, which indicates not that they are interchangeable but, rather, that Asian American essentially refers to her ethnic identity. In one instance, she said, "They always say that, she's so Asian, and she's so proud, and, and even my husband says that; he's like, you're so, you're like, you're so Taiwanese." As the quote indicates, she moves between Asian and Taiwanese fluidly. As an ethnic identity situated and heavily invested in cultural practice, it is largely stripped of a political charge, having little to do with resisting White racial hegemony. This does not mean that the conflation happens across all contexts. She has a pan-Asian friend community and differentiates Asian American as a pan-Asian label to describe communities or groups but not to describe her own personal self-identification. Unsurprisingly, unlike those who are disinterested in their racial identity, she claimed that spending "so much time there . . ." provided her with the symbolic resources to "fall in love with the country that my parents and grandparents and great grandparents came from."

Like Tara, Brian and Ethan were raised in communities with a critical mass of Asian Americans, and it seems these ethnically specific lived experiences provide more ethnic resources to be able to make the choice to identify ethnically primarily. This does not mean that living in ethnic enclaves or ethnoburbs is determinative of the ways Asian Americans articulate, but it appears to provide resources that make it possible to do so. When Brian was asked about his racial identity, he answered in ethnically specific ways, demonstrating an understanding of race that is conflated with ethnicity. He is clearly aware of the difference, but it is not how he habitually articulates this identification. For instance, he said: "I am aware of my identity as an Asian American as a Chinese American specifically, and I'm very, very proud of that heritage, and I think that, like, I try to keep myself grounded within that community as much as I can, but, you know, life is what life is." Thus, Brian's grounding in Asian Americanness is ethnically inflected. Ethan had even more access to ethnic resources as he was born and raised in his homeland country until late childhood and later immigrated to the United States, where he lived in a neighborhood with a majority Asian American community. Unsurprisingly, he also identifies primarily with an ethnic, rather than racial, identification.

Quinn, on the other hand, lived in a predominantly White neighborhood, and most of his friends were White, but he spent substantial time in his homeland country, which may be the reason he also views being Asian American through a primarily ethnic lens. Quinn believes his ethnic identity is so similar to other Asian Americans that he can understand their life experiences through his own. Put another way, he does not need to understand their ethnic specificity because he assumes their similarity. This is also situated in an understanding of Asian American identity as primarily cultural rather than coalitional or resistive. In Quinn's case, he does not conflate Asian American identity with ethnic identity, but he views the latter as more salient: "I definitely see myself as both, but I identify myself as more Korean than Asian. I think that's the right way to put it. Yeah." Thus, he does not conflate Asian American identity with ethnic identity, but the former holds less meaning as Asian American is understood as a cultural identity that is fully accessible through his ethnically specific articulation of identity.

Pan-Asian Racial Identification

A little more than half of the reporters identify racially and find it to be a salient identification apart from their ethnic heritage identity. Gwyneth and Rose identify more strongly with ethnic identity, but their recognition of structural racism propels pan-Asian identification. Dana, Jennifer, Sophia, Ivan, and Mark, on the other hand, identify strongly with both ethnic and racial identifications, suturing together multiple Asian American identifications (Lowe 2007). This parallel identification resonates with Kibria's (2002a) point that ethnic and racial identities are often parallel, multiple identifications. Finally, Amy, Clara, Hannah, Olivia, and Nina identify more strongly with a pan-Asian racial identity because their standpoints make this a more accessible form of connection. This is the clearest demonstration of identifications as articulated within particular social contexts (Hall 1996a). Although there is heterogeneity in this group, their standpoints are unified by an understanding and experience with reflexive racialization that has pointed to the importance of racial identification in the United States.

What differentiates Gwyneth and Rose from participants with an ethnic-centered racial identification is that in the latter group, while they understand that racism exists, their own understanding of Asian American as an identity conflates or slips between ethnic and racial meanings. For Gwyneth and Rose, however, although they strongly identify with their heritage identification as the primary lens through which they understand their Asian American experience, they also recognize the harms of systemic racism to the extent that they form pan-Asian racial identifications that are separate enough from their ethnic identification that it leads to the kind of shifting, multiple identifications that Hall (1996a) refers to in his theory of identification and that Lowe (2007) describes as central to Asian American identification practices.

When Gwyneth was asked what being Asian American means, her response was shaped by ethnic specificity—shared language with parents, ethnically specific practices, and co-ethnic socialization: "There'll be like major events like, you know, in Lunar New Year, so everybody gathers at some gathering place, whether it's a church or community center, and everybody brings food, and then, of course, you have your own familial gatherings of several families during holidays, and, um, you know, you can tell what was the Chinese house in the block because it'd be so loud from the street, but I, this is an environment that is very comfortable for me." As such, Gwyneth locates many of her ethnic meanings to the space of the home—the private sphere. Kibria (1997) points out that for many Asian Americans, the home and family are the most salient sources of ethnic meaning for second-generation Asian Americans. Having meaningful relationships with parents, then, is critically important for the desire for and the necessary resources for ethnic meaning. Because of the ethnically specific meanings given to Asian Americans, Gwyneth also assumes that other Asian Americans are similar to her own ethnic American household. Yet, she is differentiated from participants in the ethnic-centered identity position because her criticisms and awareness of White racial hegemony produce a distinct racial identity position, particularly in her understanding of the operation of news, which is discussed in chapters three and four.

Like Gwyneth, Rose was also raised in a predominantly White suburb and described her childhood as alienating, saying that she was "a little bit isolated because I was one of the few Asians in a White community." As scholars of ethnic identity formation note, this can produce feelings of internalized racism and a desire for White acceptability (Trieu 2018), seeing Asian American selves through White people's eyes (Osajima 2007). This produced conflicts as she negotiated her ethnically specific home with her socialization in a White neighborhood. Yet, Rose maintained heritage ties because of her frequent childhood visits to her diasporic homeland. It was these trips that also provided critical exposures that could resist a normative White standpoint.

> I think going every year kind of helped me understand that just because my hometown, or people in my hometown might look and act a certain way, doesn't mean the whole world operates by those rules. So, when I took those trips, it really helped me understand that, you know, being Asian, isn't, you know, like it doesn't necessarily mean you are a minority. It just means that you're Asian, and if you happen to be in a minority in this community, that's not inherent to being Asian, so I think when I got older, and I started thinking about, oh, you know, like there's a whole, there are whole continents where people look mostly like me and not like the people that I grew up with. That really helped.

By engaging in reflexivity and having lived experiences in a different cultural space that normalized Asian lives, this provided symbolic resources that allowed for the development of ethnic meanings that challenge the racial lumping and normative White meanings that otherwise marked her childhood experience. Her development of a racial identity was furthered when she attended a college that had a critical mass of Asian American peers. Despite this racial awareness, however, like Gwyneth, her understanding of Asian Americanness is ethnically centered. She said, "I think I would say that I feel, I feel more specifically Chinese. Um, but I do think there are a lot of commonalities in a lot of East Asian communities." The primacy of her ethnic identification may be because of the central role ethnic homeland experiences played in her development of a racial consciousness.

Dana, Jennifer, Sophia, Ivan, and Mark—they, too, have a strong sense of ethnic identity, while having salient pan-Asian identities and community connections. As such, they differ by degree rather than type. Jennifer and Ivan, for instance, both are ethnically identified while also recognizing the limitations of newsrooms that have a White vantage point, activating a racially meaningful response. Ivan, for instance, sees racial inequality through a historically informed and structural framework. Their thoughts on racial meanings are especially elucidated in their thoughts on news work, to which conversations shifted; thus, there is less known about their ethnic and racial identification practices outside the newsroom.

Dana was raised in a predominantly White community, and after sustained self-reflexivity, she has become more assertive in understanding her racial identity. "But as I came into my own as, as a grown-up, you know, and then I'm surrounded by more. Right now, I'm very proud, sort of to be who I am, but also to have community and to seek community among other Asians and Asian Americans." Indeed, her increasing awareness and criticism of White racial hegemony has meant recognizing that her visible difference marks her as other. Because of this, not only does she identify strongly as Asian American but she identifies cross-racially with other communities of color, particularly when it comes to issues of social equality and justice. "When I, when I think about, like my politics, I actually would lump into a larger group, right? I would lump in, I would lump in with the Latinas or Latinx people, and other people who are related to immigrants and refugees, and, so, I think the political identity then gets actually wider than just Asian American." This is primarily a coalitional rather than a cultural identity. It is her specific Chinese American identification that provides the cultural practices that vitalize her self-identity as Asian American. "Culturally, I still, um, there are cultural practices that link me to my, sort of, motherland. You know, we celebrate Chinese holidays and respect some traditions, you know, like burial traditions, so, yeah, I maintained a tie to, like, in my heart, I guess to Asia, China, and that's important to my identity." Indeed, although she identifies with a pan-Asian racial identity, she finds greater affinities with East Asian societies because she views them as having cultural overlaps. Thus, her ethnic identification deeply informs her notion of Asian Americanness because it is the site from which cultural practices and ancestral ties emerge, but it also narrows her scope of who is drawn into closer community and diminishes the ethnogenesis of racial identity, i.e., giving cultural meaning to racialized Asian Americanness.

Sophia, likewise, was expressive about understanding Asian Americanness as a "racial construct" as the racialization of the pandemic had ossified a burgeoning racial consciousness. As Tran and Curtin (2017) argue, experiencing indirect or direct racism often produces an awareness of structural racism and galvanizes collective identification. As a child growing up in predominantly White neighborhoods, where she experienced frequent microaggressions that marked her as foreign and insufficiently U.S. American, and where she interpreted her mother's teasing about her less-than-fluent use of her ethnic language as punitive, Sophia emotionally disidentified with her ethnic heritage identity, yet she remained connected with her ethnic community because of her family's religious participation in an ethnic church.

> Yeah, so that was probably the only thing that kept me from being completely, like, Americanized was the fact that I still once a week or twice a week in some cases, I still went to, was still exposed to other [co-ethnic] kids and, and so, you know, that, I think was very, in hindsight that was actually, really one thing that enabled me to preserve some of that, some of my identity was just having, you know, having my parents and now it's more of a case of just obviously my parents are more comfortable going to a church where they spoke in their [heritage language] as opposed to English.

As an adult, she has attempted to recover her heritage language despite knowing that it will have little everyday, pragmatic social importance. As such, her story is similar to ethnic identity formation models in which awareness of racism becomes a trigger to seek ethnic communities and commitments (Tse 1999).

Whereas Sophia is developing her racial consciousness and reconnecting with ethnic identification, Mark has a well-defined understanding that points to engaged self-reflexivity. For Mark, pan-Asian racial identification, ethnic identification, and cross-racial identification are all important expressions of his multiple articulations of Asian American identity. These are shaped by his experiences growing up in communities of color that were different from his own and his annual childhood trips to his ethnic homeland. As such, his ethnic resources form a meaningful part of his life, while his lived experience produces an awareness of "being a non-White person in the U.S." His identifying practices point to Asian Americans' construction of their identifications as specific, hybrid formations (Chong 2017). Mark said:

> And then, eventually, whether it be, I would like, in high school, probably in college that I was just really like, oh, you know, when you talk to a lot more Asian Americans and you share kind of experiences together you kind of realize that well, there's, there's a new identity that there's a shared Asian American identity and once I kind of, that light bulb flipped in my head that,

that really kind of I felt like I knew who I was, you know, like, you know, I'm the child of immigrants. It's a very common, there's a, there's a very shared identity among many other Asian Americans, sometimes not even just Asian Americans, but, like knowing that, and knowing that that's who I am and, and that I'm not like, sell out by not knowing Mandarin that well or, you know, the sense of belonging, a sense of like who, who I was.

This points to a U.S.-specific articulation of Asian Americanness that is directly about being multiple generation in the United States (Park 2008) and to a diasporic understanding that Hall (1996b) refers to as "new ethnicities," a cultural space in-between dominant culture and ethnic homeland culture. His understanding of this common, emergent culture is shaped in the immigrant experience. He said, "There is a shared kind of common cultural experience, whether our parents come from, you know, Iran, India, or Japan, or Korea. There's a shared kind of commonality that's very particular to the Asian American experience, especially in the time that we live in." Thus, Mark is articulating a pan-Asian racial identification that is not marked by perceived similarities across homeland cultures but, rather, a specific U.S. American experience for people racialized as Asian. These local constructions, then, also produce cross-racial affinities as Mark considers his identification as Asian American to be linked with other communities of color. Though he did not state it directly, it is reasonable to argue that this is because of a belief in their shared inequality in a society structured by White racial hegemony.

For the other five participants, Amy, Clara, Hannah, Olivia, and Nina, their articulations were primarily racially centered with ethnic identification being somewhat peripheral. Of course, it is important to remark on the gendered nature of this identity position. It is only women in this study who identify in this way, but the reasons for this are unclear. There was not a common lived experience that was articulated that would explain this, as the reasons for racial identification appear to be activated with different catalysts. For instance, Amy was raised in a mixed-ethnicity, pan-Asian household with a mother and father having different ethnic heritages. This is becoming increasingly more common as Asian Americans seek to marry one another although not necessarily within the same ethnic group (Chong 2017). Being in a mixed-ethnicity household leads to a necessarily pan-Asian identification, and because Amy's father is a racially conscious, second-generation Asian American, she was also socialized to understand anti-Asian racism from her childhood. Despite her father's "hyper vigilance about racism," her own racial identification was primarily pan-Asian as a synthesis of multiple Asian American cultural practices and friendships: "I would say I didn't have a lot of close friends in high school, but, uh, the three or four Asian women that were in my grade, I was friends with them, and I definitely, there's a level of maybe of comfort in speaking with them, and yeah, I don't know when I think back to it, I didn't have a lot of White, I don't have a lot of White friends, so I don't know where that hits in the identity." As Tuan (1999, 119) notes, "Those with predominantly Asian-American friends claim to share a special bond or sense of kinship with them which they do not necessarily experience with non-Asians." It was not until experiencing racism in newsrooms that Amy began to develop a racial identification that was linked to her father's anti-racist positioning and the assertion of collective belonging that has undertones of a socially conscious desire for equality and remedy.

Likewise, Clara was raised in Asian American communities, but it was after a move and the experience of daily microaggressions that her racial identification shifted. Eventually, the weight of the microaggressions became harder to ignore, and she eventually developed a desire to talk back. As bell hooks (1984) points out, shifting from silence to speech is a form of defiance that heals and makes growth possible. Whether growth was achieved is unknowable, but it is clear that Clara has valued this shift. She said, "And then, I guess it just occurred to me, you know, why am I shrugging it off? I shouldn't. I should not be afraid to speak up." Despite her coursework in Asian American studies at college, it was not until her lived experience matched the marginalization she had learned about that it catalyzed a more defiant, empowering racial identification that voices recognition and defiance of everyday harms.

Of all of the participants, Nina has the deepest family roots in the country as both of her parents were born in the United States. As Tuan (1998) argues, when generations deepen beyond the second generation, Asian Americans are more likely to racially identify because parents do not have the same ethnic resources to pass on to their children (Tuan 1998). This means for Nina, she does not practice her heritage language or ethnic traditions, so her ethnic identification is less salient than her racial identification, which she describes as deeply meaningful. She said, "I mean, definitely like being Asian American is, I mean, it's who I am, it's part of me, and it's shaped my worldview in the way I probably don't even realize, so I am very passionate."

Unlike Amy, Clara, or Nina, Hannah grew up in a predominantly White community and disidentified as Asian American. This is fairly typical for Asian Americans who are socialized into predominantly White neighborhoods as children. Arguably, this is because of a desire for White acceptance (Osajima 2007; Trieu 2018); however, this is only a partial explanation. Hannah also felt frustrated with co-ethnic comparisons and the restrictiveness they produced. She said, "There just wasn't like a lot of room for you to, like, be a very, like, complete self because you're constantly being held up against the other Asian in the room." This changed when she attended college and saw heterogeneous Asian Americans from multiple backgrounds and generations and with varied interests. This has liberated her views of who can be U.S. American and how she can articulate what Asian American means. Thus, Hannah has adopted a racialized, second-generation Asian American identification that is meaningful to her because it avoids ethnic expectations and restrictions. "I do definitely identify more towards the Asian American just because I think it's a little, I think it's a little, I don't know if simpler is the right word, but I do think it's a little more, I think inclusive, just like, inclusive of a certain experience in the states, and I like feeling like part of something bigger, I think [laughs]." There are two important points to deconstruct. First, as Song (2003) writes, belonging to an ethnic group carries cultural expectations that must be performed to demonstrate inclusion, and these can be experienced as restrictive and undesirable. Pan-ethnic identifications free Asian Americans from learning and performing their specific ethnic group practices, norms, and beliefs (Tuan 2002). Second, most Asian Americans prefer second-generation, hybrid identifications (Park 2008; Chong 2017). This is likely because it is more reflective of their lived experience as "new ethnicities" (Hall 1996b), but it is also because it avoids associations with first-generation immigrants and the stereotypes of Asian Americans as perpetual foreigners.

Finally, Olivia differs from most of the other participants as a mixed-race Asian American. Unlike Paul, she reads as more clearly East Asian, which likely shapes her experiences of her racial difference, as people often treat mixed-race Asian Americans by how they are racially marked (Spickard 2007). For her, being Asian American is an important identification. She said, "Like, I was raised with the very strong sense of, like, being Asian American and with, like, a lot of role models who were activist, the academics who were Asian American, and so it wasn't like I didn't have exposure to that." However, unlike the other participants, she attended a school with a sizeable Black American student body, which informed a racial identification that is also deeply connected to cross-racial commitments and community. As she notes, "I guess I've kind of felt like that in a lot of ways, in terms of my racial identity, like being someone that is very much like most of my friends are Black, not as many of my friends are Asian." As such, she calls into question Asian American complicity in the reification of anti-Black racism. Her desire for social equality is also focused more squarely on remedying the harms of anti-Black racism.

Clearly, Asian American reporters are not a monolith, and their articulations of identity differ as they draw upon available discourses to construct their sense of self. Because they live in culture, they also coalesce around identity positions. These should not be understood as categorical positions but, rather, as differences in degree and emphasis. All of them identify as Asian American, even if a couple are ambivalent about what this means; all of them understand their visible racial difference and how it disadvantages them, and most of them claim at least some connection to their ethnic heritage cultures. We want to take care to not overstate the case of identity positions as rigid and categorically different but to identify a clustering of identity positions. That would be antithetical to our understanding of identification as a process of becoming that is multiple and shifting. These identity positions capture the participants' habitus as described in our interviews during this particular point in their lives. That said, the identity positions matter not only in terms of their worldviews and everyday lives, but as we discuss in the later chapters, identity positions are important standpoints through which journalistic norms and newsrooms are understood.

Racial Reflexivity and Racial Identity

Trieu and Lee (2018) argue that "critical exposures" are necessary to break away from White normative worldviews and to center Asian American identities and meanings. As such, racial identification is often predicated upon racial reflexivity, usually because of experienced racial harms but also because of Asian American-centric lived experience. We refer to the response to critical exposures as *racial activation*. Racial activation produces meanings outside ethnic and dominant cultures, stimulating pan-ethnic associations (Nakano 2013). This community-building and decentering of White standpoints means a newly centered vantage point on the world, race, and journalism. For the participants in this study, their racial activation occurred because of a combination of a recognition of and resistance to White racial hegemony and affirmative heterogeneous, Asian American-centered relationships and meanings.

Indirect and direct experiences of anti-Asian racism produce an awareness of structural inequality that can lead to collective identification because "having experiences of discrimination motivates Asian Americans to question and ultimately reject institutional racism, which strengthen their racial identification" (Tran and Curtin 2017, 505). When they are rejected for being Asian American, an immutable visible identity, they experience what Cheryan and Monin (2005, 717) refer to as "identity denials" that can further strengthen identification as Asian American. As Hannah said, "I think being Asian American, I think it's really important to me because it's, it's not something I can hide." Because of race's visibility and the salience of it as a marker of difference and hierarchy in the United States, it leads to marginalization that reminds Asian Americans that they do not fully belong. Amy said, "I do think that there is an element of, you know, when you grew up in a predominantly White school, I was bullied a lot for looking different." Although she points to direct harms during childhood, it is important to recall that Amy discussed not being racially activated until she was an adult working in White-dominated newsrooms. As such, this means that it is quite likely that, despite early experiences with racism, she has internalized harms, which will cause continued psychological damage until she can reflexively deconstruct those harms while articulating more self-affirming meanings as an Asian American woman. As Oyserman and Sakamoto (1997) note, Asian Americans frequently blame themselves when they experience racial discrimination, even when it is plainly evident that the cause of discrimination is racism and not some personal failing.

Dana points out that undoing these harms is emotionally difficult labor. "I really felt this is kind of identity stuff that I'm unpacking now as an adult . . . I really felt like I just needed to assimilate into the dominant culture. I did not ever think like, oh, my culture is as worthy as the White people." That perceived need to assimilate, however, takes a psychological toll when realizing that White normativity means that White lives are valued as they are while hers is treated as undesirable. She said, "Um, because [White people's] sort of status was always assumed and mine had to be earned, right? Because I didn't naturally fit in, so I had to sort of fit in with them, so there's real, I think there's real, um, a real price to pay for that, you know, kind of having to be ashamed of who you are." Because articulation is a process of identification, it also means the deconstruction of dominant discourses about Asian Americans and assertions of a more affirmative self is a continuing project.

For this reason, challenging racism continues well into the participants' adult lives. Clara points out that after her move to a new city, she has been made to feel like she is a foreigner, an enduring stereotype of Asian Americans as an alien other (Lee 1999). "It was very White when I got here and, uh, and then it seemed like a few times a year I would get somebody who would treat me like I had, I was visiting from another country. Like Asian Americans are born here, too." Asian Americans frequently voice their frustration that although they believe themselves to be fully U.S. American, they recognize that other U.S. Americans often do not see them as part of the imagined community[3] of the nation (Cheryan and Monin 2005). For Clara, the racialization of the pandemic has motivated her to talk back and to claim her place in the nation.

> So, recently, I started getting out of the habit of now, of shrugging off when people make remarks like you speak English really well, or "ni hao," bow their heads. And I've decided from now on, I'm not gonna shrug it off. I'm gonna tell them. And I have done this a couple of times, like to a guy at a gas station, like, you know, Asian Americans, Asian people are born here, too. Just because you see somebody Asian, you shouldn't assume that they don't speak English. . . . I was like, yeah, I'm done. I think it's time to not shrug it off. To kind of educate people, even if it means I have snapped up a little bit.

For Dana, it means accepting that assimilation is not possible because of the limited acceptance Asian Americans can gain and that choosing to accept and assert herself as Asian American is how she can gain agency.

The more I understand about certain neuroscience and the more I understand about sort of ourselves and our biases, the more I have come to accept that people are going to make these quick judgments about us, whether that's inside our newsroom or the people in our audience. And, so for me, it seems more whole and, um, integrated just to acknowledge, like, I am who I am. I cannot take away from my name; I cannot take my appearance away from my skin, like my face, and so I will come at you as I am, and, um, try and be as fair as possible.

In a White racial hegemony, Clara's and Dana's corrections and self-assertions are positions of defiance built through a reflexive experience of racial activation that resists the ways in which Asian Americans are constructed as a foreign presence.

As the research on ethnic identity formation indicates, awareness of racism can catalyze an exploration of ethnic belonging, but as that same literature indicates, ethnic belonging is imperfect because Asian Americans' U.S. cultural habitus means that they do not fully feel a part of their ethnic communities and that they are made to feel apart from dominant culture in the United States. (Tse 1999; Phinney 1989). Mark expressed this tension most clearly.

You know, you get caught up between, you know, the predominant white majority identity and then always constantly feeling that you're not of that even though you may want to be, and, you know, when I was growing up, my, my dad lived and still lives [abroad], and so I'd go there in the summers, and then, so, when you go there, you, you also don't feel real belonging because you don't, my [language ability] is terrible, and I'm not really fluent in it at all, and so, it just felt like, oh, my God, you're just, you're never belonging, whether you're here in California or you're [there].

Like many Asian Americans, Mark feels culturally and linguistically out of place in his parents' homeland, alluding to a unique, second-generation identification (Park 2008; Tuan 1999). Like Mark, Kate pointed to multiple exclusions, a.k.a., not fitting in. She said, "I just feel like I've been kind of, you know, floating like I don't really fit in with Asians who have, who speak the language and practice Chinese traditions and whatnot. But I don't necessarily totally fit in with people who, you know, aren't Asian but culturally identify with me more." One exclusion is because of culturally different knowledge and habitus with her ethnic heritage culture, but another is because of racialized exclusions despite shared culture in the United States.

Affirmative racial identifications cannot just be constructed out of a rejection of Asian American exclusions. They must be formed from available discourses, but because the discourses of dominant culture and the discourses of

ethnic heritage culture do not provide the materials to create new racial identifications, this comes from experiences within Asian American communities
and Asian American-specific discourses and representations. One of the participants pointed to her U.S.-born father, who has a well-developed racialized
identification. Amy said, "My dad coming at things from the angle of being an
Asian American, who was here in like the '70s and '80s and experienced a lot
of racism against Asians as he grew up here, and so he kind of passed that along.
And, I think that he had kind of a hyper-vigilance about racism and not seeing
his children exposed to the same racism that he was." Among all of the participants, Amy was the only one who mentioned a parent as a socializing presence
for Asian American racial activation. For most other participants who
have first-generation Asian American parents, the resources they provided
were largely ethnic, not racial.

Where several participants say they were racially activated was in college.
This is often a site at which Asian American identification begins to happen
(Chong 2017). Although some of the participants grew up in communities with
a critical mass of Asian Americans in their schools, their conversations about
their friends focused primarily on community and similarity, but they did not
point to their friends as a source of racial activation. Instead, the friendships
appear to have provided ethnic and pan-ethnic comfort and community. Ethan
said, "I grew up in a . . . heavy, heavily Asian community, um, so I think those
issues never really were something that I recognized until I went to college."
Without shared racial activation from family or childhood friends, it was often
experiences at college that were an early, salient site of racial identification.

Most obviously, some participants activated their racial identifications
through their Asian American studies coursework. The critical pedagogy of
some Asian American studies provided a framework for Ivan to understand systemic inequalities. He said, "Yeah, I think it's a big part just because I think
the reason that it is a big part, and I'm a little bit more conscious of it is 'cause
I did study Asian American studies in college, which is also very heavily rooted
in critical race theory, and the foundation is found in that type of studies, so I
think I had the language and the pillars of, like, let's say logic to try to put things,
view things in that situation, right?" Using metaphors of buildings—
foundations and pillars—Ivan suggests that Asian American studies is a
mental framework that has provided new, or at least, fortified structures that
provide a sturdy worldview. This language clarifies that his view of critical racial
perspectives is not about superficial, decorative mental structures but a meaningful edifice that provides the shape for social knowledge. For Hannah and
Clara, learning about Asian American history revealed the erasures in the pedagogy of dominant culture. Clara said, "And then, um, and then I think, like,
it's sort of it evolved, and in college I took some Asian American studies courses,
and that sort of brought in my mind like, hey, why am I studying one side of

history in my whole life when there are other sides?" Hannah pointed out that this erasure was not only experienced as a loss but as a violation.

> Yeah, I do think that, like, when I finally started paying attention to the history of Asian Americans in the U.S., I felt really robbed of that experience growing up just because there were race riots, and no one told me about the Chinese Exclusion Act, and no one told me about how many people died, like, building railroads and, like, ways for people to get around in the country, and no one told me about all these wealth of things; so when I finally found out about it, it was just like, oh my God, like I have been complicit in so many ways like to the suffering of the people, like the people I care the most about, and that's why history, and that ties into history in journalism.

Hannah relies on two metaphors—theft of a valued resource and discovery. Together, they point to a sense of re-acquiring what was taken rather than acquiring something new. Thus, it shifts blame to an unnamed historical thief, which can be understood as White racial hegemony. Asian American history, then, is constructed as an especially valued resource to which Asian Americans are entitled but are denied.

Participants who attended a university with a sizeable Asian American student population also pointed to the diversity of Asian Americans on campus, an ordinary feature of the campus but not of society, particularly for those whose childhoods were in predominantly White neighborhoods. For Rose, seeing Asian American classmates whose family histories extended multiple generations in the United States legitimated the idea that Asian Americans are also fully U.S. American, and seeing working-class, mixed-race, and undocumented peers revealed a range of the Asian American experience that she had not previously experienced.

> Going to college in a predominantly Asian setting and . . . because the people, the types of Asian people who were there were different from the ones that I'd grown up with . . . but in California, a lot of those, a lot of the Asian families there have been there for a long time. And then, I also met, you know, like Asians who were Latin American and Asians who were undocumented, Asians who were first-generation college students who came from, like, low-income backgrounds. So that kind of really expanded my understanding of like what it means to be Asian American; it's not just East Asian child of successful immigrants, hardworking, you know, came here for school. It's all, it's, it really encompasses the entire spectrum of what you could be as an American, but you happen to be Asian.

Her quote points to how experiencing diversity in Asian American communities allowed for a stronger claim to U.S. Americanness because she had new discursive resources to cast off the restrictions she had felt, whether externally imposed or internalized, as she described the narrow understanding of what Asian American had meant.

This was also true for Hannah, who felt liberated after seeing Asian American diversity of interests because it allowed her to engage with her own interests while being freed from a sense that these interests were in opposition to being Asian American.

> I think it's, like, just in terms of interests and, and the way that, like, people were brought up, whether they were Christian or not Christian, or if they were second generation, third generation, fourth generation, if they were from, grew up their whole life in L.A., or if they were from the East Coast. I think it was just like, you had the hipsters, you had the preppy people, you had the goth Asians, and you had all these people like, it's like, kind of, what's the word. Sorry, brain still waking up. Presenting all these different interests and skills, and you had people in the business major, you have people in, yes, in the engineering and the med school-like route and all of that, but you had creatives, you had musicians, and it was just all these different experiences.

This desire for an individual path and freed experiences points to a U.S. American identification that values individualism. As such, seeing this diversity allowed an integration of the U.S. American valorization of individualism with a shared racial identification. This might appear paradoxical, but it illuminates the hybrid, unique construction of Asian Americanness.

Conclusion

Like the rest of Asian America, the reporters reflect heterogeneity in their identification practices, yet these articulations are not solely individual but are, rather, formed within discourse. They all self-identify as Asian American, but by drawing on different discourses of what this means, whether those meanings are valued, and which different social contexts make articulation meaningful, they enact agency to construct identifications that are contextually valued. Some are largely disinterested in identifying as Asian American on a day-to-day basis; some identify in ways that conflate ethnicity and race, producing an ethnic-centered racial identification; others identify in multiple, parallel ways that value ethnic and racial identifications; and others articulate a racial identification that is freer from ethnically specific expectations. Though it is ontologically useful to understand the ways in which identity positions cluster, it is also important to recognize that these identity positions are neither fixed nor discrete. As we argued before, identifications are a process of becoming rather than a state of being (Hall 1996a). We also want to emphasize that we do not make normative evaluations about which is a preferred identity position. This is not to ignore the psychologically beneficial results of having either an ethnic or racial identification (Kiang, Witkow, and Champagne 2013), but it is to recognize the strategic and contingent nature of identifications for different people with different lived experiences.

In closing, we want to emphasize that the purpose of the book was not to explore identifications, per se, but, rather, to understand how identifications and news work intersect. To that end, the purpose of this chapter has been to simply provide context for understanding the participants' racial identifications. Of course, because of confidentiality norms, we have trodden a fine line between providing detail for the sake of vividness and credibility while maintaining privacy. Yet, hopefully, the chapter allows the reader to understand how the journalists' racial identifications interact with the norms of their profession. As we will argue in later chapters, it is primarily a binary difference. Those who are racially activated are generally critical of the objectivity paradigm, see a need to diversify sources to include everyday Asian Americans, pitch stories about Asian American communities, and find dissatisfaction with the White normativity of the newsroom.

3

White Normativity in the Newsroom

• •

A persistent fact of U.S. American newsrooms is that they are stubbornly White spaces. Efforts to improve newsroom diversity are largely half-measures, and even these half-measures are resisted by White editors and reporters (Newkirk 2000). The commitment to diversify newsrooms following the Kerner Commission has fallen infamously short of ASNE's pledge to have newsroom diversity match the local community by 2000 (Byerly and Wilson 2009). As the *Columbia Journalism Review* notes, U.S. Americans of color are 40 percent of the population but less than 17 percent of the newsroom staff and only about 13 percent of newsroom leadership (Arana 2018). When newsrooms failed to meet ASNE's lowered 2020 targets, ASNE "paused" the gathering of diversity data, creating suspicion that these diversity targets were being abandoned altogether (Scire 2020). As such, journalists of color are required to navigate predominantly White institutions if they hope to advance in their careers.

While the fact of the White newsroom has been well documented, there is little research on how journalists of color navigate these spaces and how they make sense of White newsrooms. Thus, the purpose of this chapter is to explore how Asian American reporters' racial identifications mediate the meanings they produce around White newsrooms. Do they internalize the White norms of the newsroom? How does racial activation matter? The chapter addresses why Asian American journalists claim that newsrooms are White spaces and what they understand as the harmful consequences of White newsrooms to journalistic practice. Drawing on the previous chapter, we also explore how their racial activation situates the reporters within identity positions from which their responses emerge.

White Normativity

Although Asian American journalists' racial activation situates their identity locations differently, resulting in heterogenous views of news values and practice, one area of agreement is that newsrooms are White spaces not only in their demographic representation but also in the newsroom cultures. Speaking about her own newsroom, Sophia said, "It's not diverse. And I think right now in our news department, we have me and a photo editor [who are Asian]." Although she believes there are structural reasons that her newsroom would not attract journalists of color, her concerns are consistent with the prevailing discursive, but not structural, support for racial diversification since the Kerner Commission report. Speaking more broadly about newsrooms across the nation, Hannah said, "If you just look at how newsrooms are made up, the numbers don't lie, and the interpretation of those numbers, some people can be like, oh, well, at least we have one Black reporter. That's unacceptable." By claiming its unacceptability, she suggests a moral argument about underrepresentation—that it is a moral failure of the industry to congratulate itself for token inclusion and not take more seriously its commitments to diversify. Although Sophia and Hannah are racially activated, it does not take racial self-consciousness to notice the simple numbers. Even Paul and Kate, who do not have racially salient identifications, understand newsrooms as predominantly White spaces. The difference is that they do not make an evaluative judgment about newsrooms that are not diverse.

Only one reporter, who has an ethnic but not racially salient identification, defended the lack of diversity within newsrooms. Brian claimed that Asian Americans are reluctant to enter the profession because of the relatively low salaries compared to medicine or finance, and he claimed that the lack of diversity reflects a lack of talented journalists of color. He said, "This is purely my own opinion with no backing or research or any sort of thing in it whatsoever, but I think that a lot of Asian Americans feel a need to pursue a more financially lucrative career. I think it's like there's a lot of pressure for you to be like a doctor or to be like working in finance, you know." Both the idea of opting out because of more lucrative opportunities and the belief in newsroom meritocracy are based in two White racial myths—the model minority myth and the myth of meritocracy. It is the argument that Asian Americans are upwardly mobile to the extent that journalism is an unattractive field, and the underrepresentation of other communities of color in the field means that Black and Latinx journalists are not qualified. Although some other reporters pointed tenuously to a lack of Asian Americans in the profession, they did not use this as a defense of a lack of diversity, and they understand it as coterminous with structural racism in the industry, which has devalued Asian American reporters, particularly men in broadcast news. Brian's argument, instead, ignores structural racism in the newsroom that would produce unequal hiring outcomes and puts the responsibility on Asian Americans themselves. The argument assumes Asian Americans are especially driven by material concerns, which might be favorably read as a response to the material disadvantages of racism or unfavorably as a moral judgment about Asian Americans' greed.

Either way, to the extent that Brian's own racial group is harmed by unfair hiring and retention practices, he cannot believe that Asian Americans themselves are incapable or else it would lead to an internalization of racial inferiority; thus, the only way to reconcile Asian American underrepresentation is to believe that Asian Americans themselves are opting out of the journalistic labor market. This follows dominant racial beliefs in post-racism and a partial endorsement of the model minority myth. Post-racism, or more frequently referred to as post-racialism or new racism, is the belief that racism no longer meaningfully structures life opportunities for people of color (Prashad 2001; Bonilla-Silva 2010b; Bhopal 2018). This denial of racism blames people of color for their economically and culturally impoverished status in society (Holling, Moon, and Nevis 2014; Eng and Han 2018).

Writing about Indian Americans, but applicable to other upwardly mobile Asian Americans, Pande and Drzewiecka (2017) note, "Instead of aligning themselves with people of color in terms of common oppression, they aligned themselves in terms of the discourse of race denial." This is because the model minority stereotype is used as ammunition to argue that racism does not exist (Bhatt 2003; Wu 2002) and to substantiate the myth of the "American Dream" (Min 2003; Paek and Shah 2003). The model minority flatters Asian Americans, but at the same time presents Asian Americans as not fully human and not fully U.S. American (Eng and Han 2018). Asian Americans-as-model-minority are useful insofar as they benefit White racial hegemony as labor and as a denial of structural racism and Black American claims for redress (Wu 2002). It is generally through Asian Americans' experience of and inability to deny racism that the ideological work of the model minority myth is rejected (Tran and Curtin 2017). For the majority of the interviewees, however, there has been sufficient exposure to racism in their lives or newsrooms that they at least mildly criticize Whiteness in the newsroom and its impacts on news coverage. Brian, Paul, and Kate are the only participants who do not link White numerical domination and domination in leadership with problematic consequences.

Across all identity positions, Asian Americans noted that White newsrooms are about access and about whose values predominate once in the newsroom.

That is, Whiteness as a standpoint, and Whiteness as a structuring logic are taken for granted as normative. Although as Heider (2000) argues, White news managers and workers do not intentionally construct White spaces; these spaces are, nonetheless, created. Even when there is sensitization to problematic racial coverage and when journalists become reflexive about the extent to which they have internalized denials of racism, it only has led to temporary improvements and openness to the perspectives and criticisms of their colleagues of color in the newsroom (Drew 2011). Critical Whiteness scholars point out that White people often treat Whiteness as an object that can be possessed and that provides social, legal, economic, and cultural benefits (Lipsitz 1998; Eng and Han 2018). As Sullivan (2006) has argued, this sense of possession extends to spaces that become raced and policed as spaces for White people through implicit boundaries. As such, White journalists may conceive of their newsrooms in neutral ways, but they may engage subconscious habits of boundary formation and exclusion that they become blind to seeing. After all, most White people willfully do not acknowledge racism nor consider Whiteness as a racial identity, and they frequently deny "seeing" race as a strategic move to maintain their status quo position of dominance (Omi and Winant 1994; Bonilla-Silva 2010b; Jackson 1999; Nakayama and Krizek 1995). It is, however, visible to most of the Asian American reporters in this study.

Larry, whose ethnic and racial identifications are not salient and are situationally activated, pointed out that stories that appeal to the imagined White reader are understood as obvious and obligatory to cover. Pointing to a human-interest camp story that is covered every summer regardless of its lack of newsworthiness but appeal to White readers, he argued that it is relatively more difficult to pitch an Asian American story. He said, "Yeah, I wouldn't say necessarily if I pitched one, it would be shot down. But it's, kind of, let's make sure we do those stories kind of thing. It's not like you know every year, it's like we got to do the camp story. You know, if we didn't do the camp story, you know, why aren't we doing the camp stories? So, one thing is obligatory, and the other thing is optional." Notably, he frames the normativity of Whiteness not as discrimination or loss but, rather, as a position of privilege and taken-for-granted assumptions about newsworthiness and news necessity. This is likely aligned with his sense that he has not endured racism in the newsroom. That is, since experiences of racism are often the trigger to developing racial consciousness and racial identity, the lack of perceived racist harms will lead to a perspective in which he believes that White perspectives are advantaged but not necessarily that the perspectives of people of color are disadvantaged; rather, they are merely not similarly advantaged. That said, because of his racial difference, he is able to see Whiteness, which as a default norm is often invisible to White people and denied with various strategically discursive moves when it is pointed out (Nakayama and Krizek 1995). The invisibility of Whiteness gives White racial hegemony power because status quo norms of coverage are unquestioned and followed; whereas, the invisibility of Asian America symbolically annihilates communities of color, to use Gaye Tuchman's (1978) terminology, because it is in a position of marginalization.

Likely because racism is not salient for those like Larry, he was the only participant who articulated concerns, even muted as his are, about White normativity in the newsroom. Almost all of the other responses are from reporters whose racial identifications are persistent in their activation. Referring to newsrooms, Dana, for instance, said:

> It has a White dominant culture, like the way that it behaves. Um, the defensiveness, the sort of decision by committee, a lot of, maybe some passive aggressiveness. I think a lot of those aspects are actually part of what some scholars have noted, right? As a White dominant culture, irrespective of the number of White people in charge, but there are also a lot of White people in charge. There's a, there is the sense that the way that things were done that are normal are kind of come from the people and the culture that established the organization, which was largely White.

Her quote articulates a clarity about seeing the newsroom culture like Larry has, but the difference is she does not understand White normativity in the newsroom as benign indifference but, rather, as the habits of White space.

White Newsrooms as White Spaces

Writing about White spaces, Sullivan (2006) argues that they are raced and that White people unconsciously police the boundaries of those spaces. In her larger thesis about the performed habits of Whiteness that constitute White privilege, she claims, "It is white people who are particularly prone to complicity with racism because they tend not to acknowledge the asymmetrical racial constitution of space and place" (Sullivan 2006, 158). Although she is not writing specifically about newsrooms but about White-dominant spaces more generally, there is no reason to expect newsrooms to function differently. This runs somewhat counter to Heider's (2000) argument about "incognizant racism" because in his formulation, problematic coverage is caused by unintentional choices as constrained by structures. As a psychoanalytically informed philosopher, Sullivan (2006, 144) also argues about unconscious processes, but she attributes intention to the unconscious habits that create embodied Whiteness and the "ontological expansiveness" into racialized White spaces. As she points out, the protection of White space is not simply unconscious as challenges to it are met with defensiveness, passive aggression, denials, and other discursive moves. These strategies are common in Whiteness and are a way to deny the existence and benefits of Whiteness while maintaining them (Nakayama and Krizek 1995; Bonilla-Silva 2010a; DiAngelo 2011). Indeed, Amy shared a story of explicit White denial: "I had offered to have a workshop with our newsroom about how we could cover topics in more culturally competent ways, and they shut it down. They said no. They didn't want to talk about it anymore. They felt like it was upsetting everybody too much, and so they just kind of buried it." Thus, when incognizant racism is punctured, it does not produce racial awareness; rather, it produces further cognizant denials. Dana said, "There are people who, when there are issues or complaints about lack of representation that surface newsroom-wide, who have quietly said to others like, I don't understand what the diversity problem is here in this company. So, there's a lot of just ignorance about it." As Robin DiAngelo (2011) points out, most White people respond with outrage and denial even when people of color *gently* point out that White people view the world through their own particular racialized standpoints and advantage, which produces discomfort and emotional distress. The choice of the newsroom, in this case, was to soothe White reporters' egos and to protect White colleagues' emotions.

The consequence is that maintenance of these racialized norms of newsrooms reproduces news that expresses a White perspective. This can be manifest in White colleagues' centering stories of White people at the expense of people of color. Nina provided an example of White reporters' desire to amplify a White celebrity during the BLM protests:

> I remember there was a discussion, and one of our channels, there are just so many stories that were coming out of it, and Taylor Swift had said something about it, the singer, and, there were some people who thought that we should do a story just about her and like what she had to say about the protests, and then there were other people, including people of color, who said I don't know if we need to do a story just about her, like, there's so many other people who are saying things. She's a White woman. Why does her voice, you know, why should she be centered in the coverage about this, right? Because the whole point of the protest was to talk about the unique struggle that the Black people have faced in this country. And I remember there's a disagreement about that, and it got resolved by, like, I think people, someone wrote, like, here's all the celebrities, you know, a bunch of celebrities saying, giving statements about the Black Lives Matter and not just Taylor Swift herself. But I remember thinking like, oh, that was, you know, that's it. That is something that may not have been obvious to people who were White, right?

Her example demonstrates newsroom's centering of Whiteness in both the newsroom and in the coverage. That is, as she demonstrates, her colleagues are unaware of the ways in which making a White woman celebrity's support the focal point is problematic. Likely, it would be argued that the story is newsworthy because it meets requirements of newsworthiness, such as unusualness given Swift's apolitical history and country music background as well as prominence because of the scale of her celebrity, but it also is based in a White desire to demonstrate that there are "good" White people. A common representation to deny the existence of White racism is to present the stories of White heroes who defend people of color from "bad" White people (Wayne 2014). In particular, the elevation of White women as moral figures—the protectors and caretakers of people of color—is a common, colonial-era trope (Coloma 2012; Syed and Ali 2011). Even with the criticism from colleagues of color in Nina's newsroom, the compromise did not center Black celebrity voices but leaned into a universalist, post-racist tendency of dominant culture (Herakova et al. 2011; Gilroy 2012).

Even when White colleagues are interpersonally warm, this does not necessarily mean that they are receptive to hearing the perspectives of reporters of color because they are self-assured in their goodness and in their "unbiased" understanding of news. Jennifer said, "There were times when I worked at [a newsroom], when it was led by a very old-school, White older gentleman who was incredibly nice, incredibly kind, but he was a White man who was pretty well off... and I would remember, I remember like pitching stories about race or stories about poverty, and it would, it would just go nowhere." So long as racism is understood only as overt bigotry and as cartoonish villainy, then it is possible, even likely, for White colleagues to believe that their actions are not motivated by race or racism. Yet, the belief that White viewpoints are most correct has been noted in even the earliest colonialist discourse, where European scholars and colonizers believed that the colonized were unreliable narrators of their own experience and that White colonizers had the clarity of perspective and the right to speak for the colonized (Said 1978). This is not to claim that White colleagues are actively, overtly oppressive but, rather, that centuries-old historical discourses do not simply vanish with time but remain as remnants. In Sobande's (2019, 2730) article about "woke" advertising, she says, "The subject position of the 'White saviour' foregrounds the perspective of a white person who is conventionally framed as selflessly and authoritatively aiding allegedly disempowered Black people and/or non-Black people of colour. This subject position connotes hierarchical colonial relations, without challenging associated issues to do with racism, colonialism and white supremacy." The overreliance on White experts in news coverage about communities of color or the Global South is a manifestation of this White subject position (Owens 2008; Domke et al. 2003). In coverage of Nigeria, for instance, the Western press uses Western, White sources and erases Nigerian experts, reflecting a colonial view of the nation (Malaolu 2014). This is true even for people who are "incredibly nice." Racism, or at least White normativity, is not predicated on meanness but, rather, racism can be banal in its expression (Mueller 2017; Gandy 1998). Indeed, it can be bourgeois in form.

Just as Jennifer noted the socioeconomic class of the editor, which made him out of touch with the struggles of ordinary U.S. Americans, Olivia claimed that class and other intersecting forms of power exist in newsrooms—classed, college-educated, able-bodied, masculinist, heterosexist, White supremacist. She said that "the newsroom is overwhelmingly White and, moreover, I think, is, you know, newsrooms as a whole, have a problem with not just being White, but they also have a problem with being kind of homogenous in other ways too, right?" Because of the resources required to take unpaid internships and the low starting wages in many newsrooms coupled with the economic malaise that has hit the print news industry, it produces a classed and raced perspective in news. The point is that Whiteness does not only replicate racial advantage but also is intersectionally connected to various hegemonies. Olivia made this point the most clearly by explaining the different treatment of Black and White sources:

> A good example of that is, if something happens to a Black person, I shouldn't say our policies, but what I've experienced is that if something happens to a Black person that I want to write about, they'll want to have a background check done on that person to make sure there's nothing in their past. But if the same thing happened to an Asian person, they wouldn't do that. They wouldn't do a background check on them, or a White person, or anyone that isn't Black, basically. And those aren't things that are, it's not like it's written down, like, check the background of every Black person, but that's how it works in practice, right?

Just as critical race scholars argue that even when laws are written neutrally, their application can produce de facto racism, Olivia demonstrates that even though there are no explicit policies on treating sources with skepticism, more skepticism is reserved for Black people, reflecting an anti-Black and classed subject position. It is only White Americans and Asian Americans, who are viewed as either benign model minorities or as adjacent to Whiteness, who escape skepticism and background checks.

As such, White perspectives are trusted as more credible and judged as more newsworthy. To explain the persistence of White normativity in newsrooms, racially activated journalists presented various arguments, including White newsroom leadership and the hierarchal structure of newsrooms, a White status quo in journalism training and practice, and the dominant White society in which newsrooms and news practices are located. Mark, who is also the only male reporter to discuss the causes of White normativity, mentioned that the heads of news organizations are predominantly White. He said, "Let's look at the mastheads of all the, of all the prestige papers, *The New York Times*, *The Washington Post*, *The Los Angeles Times*, and see how many of them are non-White and, like, you know, surprise, surprise, very few of them were people of color." Hannah added, "I think specifically, in terms of management, it's incredibly White as well, not just like the editor level, but, like, above them as well." Similarly, Gwyneth argued that decision-making reflects a White perspective, saying, "I do think that, I mean, speaking generally, you know, the, the lack of diversity in newsrooms. The lack of just diversity at the decision-making table as far as, like, story selection and also who you interview, you know, are they all White?" As such, the White normativity of the newsroom is understood to be driven by the power at the top of the organizations. Although there are few scholarly findings about White leadership in newsrooms as a detriment to diverse coverage, feminist studies of newsrooms have noted that many women reporters, particularly those who leave the profession, believe newsrooms reflect male leadership (Elmore 2009). Those arguments, it appears, can be extrapolated to Asian American reporters and their views of White management and also the implicit hope that diversifying the top of the newsroom can lead to progressive, downstream changes.

This power is understood as problematic within the specific structure and culture of newsrooms, which are believed to be vertically organized and authoritarian. Dana said:

> I would say that it's kind of command and control in the hierarchy in the way that it's run, in the way decisions were made and the people at the top, unless they're really iconoclastic and trying to change things the way they've always done. Then even when there's new people coming in at the top and there's churn there, they're also preserving the way things have always been done, and that is to the detriment of new ideas. . . . That's to the detriment of new, young people. That's to the detriment of any sort of like voices that are more, less traditionally at the center, right? And, so, without leadership that goes out of its way to say, "Hey, you know, we aren't, we shouldn't be the ones who are always speaking up, and there need to be more voices at the table," I don't think things change. Things haven't generally changed in my newsroom where I've been for almost a decade.

Dana's argument hints at structural obstacles not only in the practices of White newsrooms but also in the hiring practices of news editors and senior executives. As her point about iconoclasm indicates, change at the top can only come about when there is a substantial exercise in managerial agency. That also reveals some of the pessimistic findings from feminist journalism scholars, who point out that women leaders in the newsroom produce remarkably similar news as men (Steiner 2009). This is because any attempts at change run into a newsroom culture that is a White, masculinist space with the attendant habits and power of White racial hegemony. Structurally, then, news organizations reinforce and reproduce the status quo even with different managers. This is especially trenchant in news because of the prevailing views of objectivity that hide racism and sexism. Making changes would mean risking the alienation of White reporters, the majority, in the newsroom, as well as cause accusations of journalistic malfeasance, and even "reverse racism." Pushing for change is perceived as that much riskier for journalists of color that are not in management. Amy said, "I feel a level of being the least senior person and the least experienced reporter on staff, so I feel a lot more concerned speaking up about these things because I don't want them to have a certain image of me as being just like someone who's a squeaky wheel or something like that." This socializes journalists of color either to stay silent or to assimilate into White newsroom norms. By the time they have reached management, to the extent the option is available or desired, it also means that journalists will have practiced everyday habits of not challenging White newsroom norms directly. Because newsrooms have been resistant to diversify, it would take decades to reach the critical mass necessary to change newsroom cultures. To the extent that White norms are internalized or socialized to avoid upsetting White colleagues, this will further decrease the pace of change.

All of these moves reinforce a White status quo, which a few racially activated participants attributed to the persistence of White newsrooms—their demographics and norms. A couple of journalists pointed to the slow pace of change.

I don't know. I think change is incredibly slow.—Hannah

I know they're trying to make a push for more Black reporters and journalists of color, but that's a slow, tidal change. It's not happening immediately, so.—Rose

Both Hannah and Rose use metaphors of speed to refer to progressive change, pointing to the lack of change. However, embedded in the cynicism is also optimism about the direction of the change, oriented toward a newsroom that decenters White normativity and replaces it with heterogeneous perspectives. They do not point to the reason for this change, but Dana argued that it is because newsrooms are oriented toward the status quo:

Like what the alternate universe would look like? Um, you know, I don't know. Just because I can't imagine the counterfactual, you know. But I do think we're conservative. I do think we're conservative in our coverage. I think we haven't been as willing as we could have been earlier in the Trump administration calling out some of the more blatant racism out of the officials, the policies, and the man himself. But this isn't just true of [our newsroom]. This is true of the traditional legacy media, in general, just because there are social norms that govern journalism and how we practice journalism.

Because of the White normative standpoint of the newsroom, it means that obvious explanations of racism and White supremacy are averted for more unlikely, timid, or universalizing explanations. As mentioned earlier, White racial hegemony engages in common discursive strategies to obscure White ideological and material domination.

According to Amy, journalism schools, particularly the elite schools, are places that have propagated White norms that socialize journalists even before they enter the newsroom, leading to academic and, later, professional socialization that act as racially conservatizing forces.

> I think that looking back on my time in journalism school, I do think that my experience and the journalism student experience is very much colored by the faculty there, and I will note that, I mean, I went to a well-regarded journalism school, and very few of the faculty were Asian American journalists. In fact, I don't think many of my primary professors there were, and so I think that you come out of journalism school as an Asian American with a very White-focused way of being a journalist.

Although her quote might run the risk of racial essentialism, assuming that Asian American professors would encourage different approaches to journalism and that White professors necessarily reinforce White norms of the profession, the general point is that White professors are more likely to be invested in not seeing how their racial identities matter and are privileged within journalism. Thus, White racial hegemony is interlocking with multiple institutions, including most obviously newsrooms and journalism schools. To disentangle White newsrooms would mean change would have to occur across institutions.

Even if the socialization is understood and challenged, being in a majority White society where White people hold most positions of influence means that White perspectives dominate the pages and airwaves. Sophia said, "I mean, it's just a lot of work to, you know, and it's not second nature to a lot of people. I don't think it's second nature to me really. I think it's just more like we fall into old habits, like, we have a deadline, and we need to call a certain amount of people. So, it's so easy just to fall into the old Rolodex." Her use of filler words and repetition suggest that for a moment she had to produce uncomfortable or unfamiliar ideas, acknowledging the limitations that news routines have on racialized coverage (Heider 2000; Gandy 1998). As Meyers and Gayle (2015) point out, it requires intentional agency and increased labor to avoid the rut of source representation and story perspectives that news routines generate.

Racial Limitations and Harms of White News Norms

Participants believe that this is not just about who is given opportunities but also about the quality of the coverage. It is interesting to note that while most of the quotes in this chapter are from racially activated journalists, there are a few who do not have salient racial identifications who claim that news coverage would be improved with a more diverse newsroom. What is important to differentiate is that this is primarily a "value-added" framing. In other words, it does not criticize White newsrooms, per se. Larry, who does not have salient racial or ethnic identifications, said, "I think there's just a greater sensitivity that a person of color has that a White person just doesn't notice." Because he did not expound on this point, it is unclear whether he means that he believes White people have a lack of sensitivity to the perspectives and issues that people of color face or that White people are, generally, less sensitive to the world in which they live.

Ethan, who has a salient ethnic identification, provided an example of the former—that White people lack sensitivity within a specific domain—racial knowledge.

> I think the most prominent example in the newsroom that I can think of is that we have a sister paper . . . who had a daily case count of the coronavirus in its community and a photo that the newspaper put in for one of the stories was a photo of an Asian food truck. You know, handing out the food to the community. I think if there was an Asian representation in the newsroom, he could, he or she could catch that and say to the editor, "Hey, this, this may not look right." I understand where you're coming from, and I know we are all working very fast, and it's more of a file folder than anything else. We're just looking for any photo to put in the story because our policy is that we put in a photo for every story because it gets better social media use and everything else. But if we had an Asian representation in that newsroom, somebody could have pointed out, and avoid, you know, harming the community, avoiding, you know, perpetuating the stereotype and also avoiding social media pushback that the story got because of the photo.

Ethan also presents a value-added argument, but he also mildly criticizes the lack of awareness of what would be quite clear to an Asian American reporter, whose lived experience has sensitized him to racial stereotyping. His argument is essentially that diversity is beneficial because it avoids trouble rather than diversity is important for its own moral imperatives in spite of the "trouble" that might be caused to achieve it. Thus, he is not challenging but, rather, arguing for diversity to protect the news institution.

Like Ethan, Quinn is also ethnically activated, and he argues that diverse newsrooms are beneficial because it means there are reporters whom sources can trust and because it takes away some of the burdens of representation since Asian American reporters are heterogeneous in their outlooks.

> How do I feel about being the only Asian in the newsroom? [Long pause.] Do I wish there was more diversity? Yes. It's not something I always think about every day, like every hour, and like, oh, why is my editor not hiring more Asian people? But, considering, especially considering what's going on these days, I think it's important to have diversity in the newsroom. . . . I'm not saying, let's say there's 25 percent Asian in my city; I don't think it necessarily means that there has to be 25 percent Asian in the newsroom . . . and, you know, and not every Black person or Asian person feels, is going to feel one way, even amongst themselves are going to have different views. So, I think, it's just the more diverse it is, I think it's healthier for the newsroom.

There are two interesting points in Quinn's quote. First is his qualification of his concern, and the second is his somewhat ambivalent views of diverse representation in the newsroom. His qualification demonstrates that newsroom diversity is not a salient concern. This disavowal of concern works rhetorically to show that his views are temperate, making them more acceptable. This is only necessary in a discursive environment in which discussing problems of underrepresentation is considered inappropriate. This conforms to the racial logics of "colorblindness," which requires disavowing the recognition of race and racism (Bonilla-Silva 2010b). This is, as mentioned before, a strategy of Whiteness. Thus, his quote reflects an uneasiness with criticism of White racial hegemony. Second, his quote demonstrates ambivalence as he disavows the necessity of the ASNE stand to have newsroom diversity match community diversity while also claiming that some diversity is important. Indeed, by his last sentence, he argues that more diversity is preferred because it means that there are more opportunities for heterogeneity among Asian American reporters and other reporters of color. This ambivalence perhaps is reflective of an identity position that has not yet exercised frequent practices of racial reflexivity.

Of the participants who made arguments for the benefits of diversity, Rose is the only one who has a racially activated identification. Instead, several argued for the reverse, claiming that a lack of diversity produces harms. Amy said, "You can't be covering the country when you're not represented by the country." Similarly, Clara said, "Yeah, because I mean, yeah, you need a broad range of perspectives in newsroom. That's just the way it is." Both quotes replicate the arguments made by the Kerner Commission that a predominantly White newsroom will fail to understand the perspectives of people of color and will not only perpetuate a White perspective of society but also White othering of people of color (Delaney 2018). It reflects a rejection of the idea that journalism is or can be objective and free from the worldviews of its workers. Their statements, then, are an indictment on White newsrooms for the production of White news. As Clara indicates, not being diverse means that journalism is not covering its communities accurately or fairly. For racially activated participants, their view is not only that racial diversity will improve coverage but that a lack of racial diversity works against the journalistic credo of being truth seekers. Nina said, "I think there's like a moral imperative for journalism to reflect a lot of different viewpoints and staffing, and, you know, it [non-diverse newsrooms] can circulate the very White, extremely White, extremely male-dominated industry." By believing myths of the objective White male reporter, Amy notes that this can create a lack of reflexivity that prevents White people from seeing their own racial standpoint and that reproduces White racial hegemony. Amy said, "They are naturally more inclined to feel comfortable speaking with people who look like them, and they feel inclined to tell the stories of people who look like them, which I think understandable, and I think if we can all accept that as journalists, we can accept our internal biases." In Amy's view, accepting biases and acknowledging standpoints becomes a necessary condition to produce more truthful coverage. Indeed, she does not particularly fault White colleagues but, rather, calls for all journalists to be self-reflective, using universalist racial logics. This tempers a systemic criticism of White racial hegemony, which appears to be a way to navigate racial criticism while surviving within predominantly White newsroom cultures.

Most of the racially activated journalists point out that White newsrooms are not just an issue of employment fairness or even representational equity. Rather, the concern for White newsrooms is the production of White racism in coverage. To illustrate this point, Amy shared an example of the newsroom's coverage of a plant that was named after Japan and the station's decision to use racial puns and stereotyped sounds that conflated Asia as a racially monolithic formation in ways that she interpreted as mocking. She said:

> I think there was like one catalyst, in particular, at my old station that
> happened . . . where somebody published an article that was kind of, I don't
> know what the word is but "minstrelizing" Asian people. It was, like, it was
> a food article. It was about something that just had the name Japanese
> whatever . . . they went all out on covering this plant . . . all the stereotypes
> about Asian people they put into this piece just because they felt like it would
> be cute . . . to make this entire piece, like, Asia-themed, which is like pan-Asia,

not specifically Japanese either. Offensive on a lot of levels, and I brought it up with the newsroom . . . they basically did a yellow peril story about a weed, but they were confused because they thought it was a fun puff piece. I don't think they were trying to make an argument for its journalistic integrity or anything, but I think they were just like, "Why don't you think it's funny? It's supposed to be a funny story."

Amy also pointed out that her former newsroom was particularly resistant to hearing challenges to racially problematic coverage. Her description of this coverage as minstrelsy is provocative as it might be argued that minstrelsy was a very specific articulation of virulent anti-Black racism; however, her point in drawing the association is to make clear that the coverage was spectacular in its purposes of bigoted racist mockery. Minstrelsy presents the other as unusual and harmful in order to justify the imagined superiority and benevolence of White people and, in this case, even their plants. The point is that the newsroom does not simply make mistakes because of racial blind spots but that they welcomed an opportunity to engage in racist mockery in ways that would be considered safe—journalistically safe because it is merely a puff piece and socially safe because it is manifestly mocking the plant while carrying obvious connotations about Asian people.

Similarly, Gwyneth recalled that "the opinion page had this very controversial headline. . . . But in this case, I think it was a bad judgment, a case of judgment on the part of an editor on the opinion page." What she describes as a controversial headline was one that included the racist label "Chinaman." Although the word may read to non-Asian people as an innocent discursive construction such as Englishman or Frenchman, it is understood as racist because of the connotations it carried and the ways that it was leveraged against Chinese immigrants in the nineteenth century. Indeed, "John Chinaman" was a character in minstrel shows who displayed degeneracy and slothful excess (Lee 1999). Chinaman became associated with the marginalized ways in which White people viewed Asians. Arguably, Chinaman mocks Chinese immigrants' use of English as the construction clearly differs from Englishman or Frenchman. To clarify, it is different because it is Chinaman rather than Chineseman; indeed, the English and French are also not referred to as Englandman or Franceman. For the English and French, their countries of origin are used as adjectives rather than as nouns. Although Gwyneth maintained that opinion pages should have more editorial leeway, she noted that this headline was galling for its use of an anachronistic racist slur.

Another example that a participant shared was the description of Asian foods as bizarre and disgusting. Describing coverage about boba tea, or bubble tea, a popular drink that includes tapioca balls, usually with a sweet, decadent, and creamy tea, Clara shared that the headline "was something like those gross little blob, black blobs." She continued, "Asian American Twitter was not happy [laughs], and then I, I couldn't believe it, and I looked at the byline. It was, like, it was obviously like a White [laughs] or a European last name." Here, she expresses alignment with an Asian American standpoint, siding with the viewpoints expressed by Asian Americans online. She implicitly references an understanding of racial stereotyping about Asian American food as disgusting and bizarre. As Edwards, Occhipenti, and Ryan (2000) note, tropes of indigestion around Asian foods are metaphors of disgust about Asian people entering the White body politic. This indigestion trope produces a "distinction between raced-abject-Other-bodies, and clean white eaters" (Han 2007, 361).

This trope of disgust around Asian foods also extends to the Asian body. Indeed, a common stereotype of Asian Americans has been as carriers of disease (Mallapragada 2021; Le et al. 2020a; Oh 2020). The persistence of this stereotype was made clear especially during the early days of the COVID-19 pandemic when anti-Asian hate crimes surged as Asian Americans were attacked, regardless of heritage background or generations in the United States. The disease had become racialized, and a few participants pointed to what they perceived as microaggressions that reified this racist association between Asian Americans and contagion. For instance, Hannah said, "It's like those aggression, microaggressions like that. There are other stories here besides, oh, Chinese people have coronavirus, like, there are other important stories here. . . . It's like this weird caricature of your community where no one speaks English. No one's doing anything good for the community, and it's just full of viruses and, like, people eating bats and shit." Her point demonstrates that in a time of racialized crisis, news operated from a White vantage point of ethnocentric hysteria, ignoring stories of Asian Americans that constitute them as fully U.S. Americans who actively contribute to society. Instead, the stories lean into stereotypes of being Asian Americans as perpetual foreigners (Lee 1999), as outsiders who harm White America through their unusual and disgusting cultural practices and diets.

Similarly, Gwyneth pointed to the use of images that may not have been motivated by malicious intent but, rather, ignorance of harms when representing a disease as people. Referring to the early coverage of COVID-19, she said:

Masks. Every single story that was done on coronavirus or the flu, especially when it hadn't yet really broken out here but remained in China, there were a lot of photos, for instance, that would show people in masks, and, there needed to be some consciousness-raising that, in Asia, there are people who also wear masks when it didn't have anything to do with the pandemic. . . . You're just grabbing the first photo on this Getty server or whatever that had to do with coronavirus, but because there was such a prevalence of photos of Asian people in masks, you just had to raise the issue that, hey, when there's a story that has nothing to do with China, let's not do a photo of an Asian person with a mask because, basically, it's reinforcing the image of an Asian person having COVID-19 or being associated with COVID-19. It's just a subtle image that sticks into your mind.

To make this point demonstrates a sensitivity drawn from an affective, lived experience with racial stereotyping. In her case, Gwyneth does not assign blame, not even microaggressive blame, but rather situates her argument in a lack of awareness, i.e., a need for consciousness-raising. Her position, interestingly, implies a structural cause for the unintentional choices, yet it suggests individual agency to resolve it. Although unclear, the only explanation for why Gwyneth might differ from Hannah in providing the benefit of the doubt to her colleagues is that her racial identification is primarily ethnic in meaning. That is, if racial identification is activated through an acknowledgement of racism, then it produces a different response than if racial identification is mostly constructed through cultural and heritage ties to an ethnic identification, such as Thai or Filipinx.

Ivan has a salient racial identification and was bothered by the dangers of referring to the virus by its place of origin, noting that the use of Wuhan was not limited to its originating site but that it also used verbal imagery that others China.

I tend to think that the less obvious, in this case, a little less obvious use of that word Wuhan even started to be called Wuhan coronavirus and the type of coverage that we did around that, such as like the heavy coverage around the meat markets, the wet markets. I think that those could be a little bit more insidious, because it is a little bit less obvious, and it buys into I think some of the rhetoric that was around in the late eighteen, my Asian American history is leaving me like, the 1882 Chinese Exclusion Act. But even before that, we were calling Chinese women lewd and lascivious women. I think Asian American women, Chinese women specifically, are labeled as that. So, I thought that it bought into that a little bit. So, I tried to look at how journalists can be hypocrites.

As he shares his concerns, it is noteworthy that there is a movement from discussing stereotyped coverage of China to discussing harms to Asian Americans. As Palombu-Liu (1999) notes in his construction of "Asian/American," U.S. Americans do not make meaningful differentiations between Asians in Asia and Asian Americans. Thus, he recognizes that alarmist rhetoric about China and the images of it as a place of bodily threat (through disease in this case) also produce harms for Asian Americans. This is a sensitivity and perspective that his colleagues, who are not Asian Americans, will likely not share or, to the extent that they do, share less strongly. Where his point about hypocrisy fits in is that his coworkers argue that they are unbiased in their coverage while drawing upon a White, Orientalist imagination of China that acts as the frame within which news is placed, affecting the news agenda and the news frame. Therefore, from the perspective of racially activated journalists, White newsrooms reproduce White racial perspectives that can marginalize, stereotype, and construct racist associations for Asian American communities.

Conclusion

It is important to emphasize that this chapter reflects the perception of White newsrooms, their causes, and their harms to Asian American coverage. It is beyond the scope of the study to investigate the precision of the reporters' claims, although the existing literature would suggest that there is merit in their arguments. Given the hiring patterns, the evidence of racially problematic news coverage, and various scholarly and professional accounts of journalists of color, the Whiteness of newsrooms is not likely limited to the demographics of newsrooms but also their culture, values, and perspective. That said, our purpose is to understand who is making which claims about White newsrooms. Largely, what we have discovered is that Asian American reporters across all of the different identity positions that we interviewed claim that newsrooms are White spaces. This is largely agreed upon as factual. Whether this matters and how it matters is where opinions diverge. For participants whose racial and ethnic identifications are situationally activated and are not a persistent feature of their identities, there is largely silence about whether this matters.

For those who are racially activated with either parallel ethnic and racial identifications or with a primarily racial identification, their arguments are situated in systemic racism, although it is quite rare for them to use this term directly. For instance, they see White newsrooms as not racially neutral or meritocratic but as specifically and stubbornly White spaces. They point to structural causes such as a lack of Asian American editors and news managers, socialization into White norms in journalism school and their newsrooms, and economic barriers that filter out Asian Americans and other people of color from starting careers in journalism. However, most of the solutions that are offered are not structural but, rather, acts of individual agency. This suggests a baseline faith in the industry to believe that enough micro-level decisions and raised awareness are sufficient to produce equitable newsrooms and more truthful, inclusive news. This might be linked to their investments in the dominant news industry to not imagine more transformative, structural change, or it might be because dominant racial ideologies in and outside the newsroom encourage individual agency rather than collective action for structural change. In the next chapter, we elucidate how Asian American reporters have been harmed themselves and how they resist the professional and psychic damage of White news.

4

Navigating White
Newsrooms

● ●

The bamboo ceiling refers to the invisible barriers that prevent Asian Americans from moving into senior ranks of an organization (Varma 2004; Omatsu 2007). Stereotyped qualities that make Asian Americans desirable entry-level candidates—hardworking, polite—hurt opportunities for advancement as they are not seen as having leadership material (Varma 2004). In the tech industry, Asian Americans are the racial group least likely to be promoted to managerial and executive ranks (Gee and Peck 2018), and the same patterns are found in other industrial sectors. Even when Asian Americans advance, they are paid less than U.S. American peers with similar levels of education (Fong 2008). However, there is little attention paid to Asian Americans because the model minority stereotype obscures systemic racism and Asian Americans' limited opportunities for advancement. Asian Americans also receive little sympathy from other people of color because of the prevalence of the model minority stereotype discourse and the punitive ways that discourse is used to discipline Black Americans (Fong 2008).

We begin this chapter with a brief description of the bamboo ceiling to point to the systemic racism Asian Americans experience in their professional lives, one that values them as technical workers but not as creative workers, popular figures, or leaders. The point is that Asian Americans' unique experience of racialization means that they are allowed access but limited advancement in the workplace. This differs from Black and Latinx Americans, who have more difficulty gaining access but, relative to Asian Americans, more access to positions of leadership. This is because of the overdetermining function of the model minority stereotype as a particular kind of racial discourse that configures Asian Americans as useful to White America for their role in racial politics and for their labor meant to directly benefit, not challenge or threaten, White racial hegemony and privilege (Kim 1999a; Eng and Han 2018; Fong 2008; DeCook and Yoon 2021). The purpose of this chapter, then, is to understand what kinds of racialized marginalization Asian American journalists say they experience, how racial activation matters in their perception of harms, how they navigate White newsrooms, and how they resist their marginalization to empower and challenge.

The Asian American reporters in this study argue that they have experienced career limitations and devaluing just as their co-racial peers in other professions. This can take various forms, including trivialization of their racialized concerns, disciplining and silencing, and interpersonal racism from colleagues, sources, and readers/viewers. Like other discussions of racism in this book, these claims are more salient for racially activated participants. What differs across identity positions is their interpretation of these harms—who harms and the nature of the harm. Similarly, there is a salient difference in terms of responses to harms. Racially activated Asian American reporters emphasize efforts to mentor and support, to participate in affinity groups, and to speak up in the newsroom.

White Marginalization of Asian American Colleagues

Most Asian American reporters with activated racial identifications clarify numerous ways in which they are marginalized in newsrooms. This includes issues related to employment, including hiring and promotion; silencing; alienation; burden of explanation; racist microaggressions; essentialization; marginalization; and dehumanization. They also deal with racism on the job with hate mail and mistreatment from White sources. As such, White newsrooms can be fraught. Although Asian American journalists may share camaraderie through their work and struggles with their White colleagues, the White normativity of the spaces can lead to direct harms that alienate and marginalize. Yet, it must be pointed out that not all of the reporters feel this way. Participants who do not have salient racial identifications generally do not perceive newsrooms to have any racist harms, and, overwhelmingly, men do not point to racist harms in the newsroom. After discussing the possibilities for these patterns, we turn to the harms reporters have identified.

Regarding racial identification, there is a clear correlation between racial activation and discussions of racist treatment participants have endured. As correlation is not causation, however, we are uncertain whether it is the accumulation of mistreatment in the newsroom that transforms the space into an activating site for racial identifications or whether racial activation is fairly persistent because of previous exposure to racism. Although we cannot provide a conclusive answer, we believe that the cause is not mutually exclusive. In chapter 2, we point out that those who are racially activated have socializing influences like parents, school, friends, and training in ethnic studies that produce ongoing racial sensitivities that existed prior to entering newsrooms. However, the newsroom itself also acts as a space to reinforce their racial consciousness and identification because of the persistence of racist treatment.[1] This is to say that rather than being mutually exclusive, we believe it is more likely that outside socialization and newsroom socialization to racism is mutually constitutive. For those who have chosen to not seriously consider anti-Asian racism, it is only rare moments in which a racial identification is contextually or opportunistically activated.

As scholars point out, Asian Americans frequently blame themselves even when the more obvious, likely, and substantiated reason to explain their mistreatment is racism (Oyserman and Sakamoto 1997; Osajima 2007; Yoo and Lee 2005). They might attribute blame to their own personalities or believe that Asian Americans are responsible for mitigating and accommodating racist abuse (Sun and Starosta 2006). This is, in part, because Asian Americans' claims of racism are rarely believed and often dismissed (Sue et al. 2007). It is also because most Asian Americans believe that the racism they experience is not as severe as other people of color, so, therefore, they understand their complaints of anti-Asian racism as racially self-centered (Kuo 1995). In other cases, it is because Asian Americans have internalized racism, believing that they deserve their mistreatment (Trieu and Lee 2018; Osajima 2007). Instead, Asian Americans are made to feel the burden of fitting into White racial spaces rather than demanding or expecting an accommodation of multiracial difference (Sue et al. 2007). One way they do this is to use distancing strategies to dissociate with other Asian Americans (Pyke 2010), closing themselves off from support systems and community.

In this study, there is an overwhelming correlation between gender and the awareness of and dissatisfaction with anti-Asian racism. This could be because of the intersecting nature of racism and sexism for Asian American women, who are hyperfeminized and devalued in a patriarchal White racial hegemony. Although some Asian American men claim that Asian American women are advantaged relative to Asian American men (Mak 2021), whatever "advantages" of racialized exoticism in the dating market that may accrue do not extend to patriarchal workforces, including newsrooms, which are particularly masculinist spaces (Elmore 2009; Löfgren Nilsson 2010). Asian American women, who have intersectional marginalized identities, must navigate the harms of White patriarchy, which, in the workforce, devalues them as having an excess of femininity (Espiritu 2004). As such, women Asian American reporters may have activated racial identifications because of the intersecting marginalization they experience. Clara said:

I don't know if it's more because I'm Asian or because I'm a woman. I'm, I'm certain there are, I had moments I would categorize as somebody talking over me or assuming things about me, or I'll do the cleanup or the little secretarial tasks. I'd be the one to do that. Yeah, when I feel that kind of moment come up, I push back. So, I think, I think that's part of it. Bias against females, maybe not so much Asians. But I'm sure there's always that fear that someone's going to treat me like the quiet little wallflower because I'm Asian.

We would suggest that her gendered treatment as a colleague who is not worthy of equal respect is not separate from her colleagues' reading of her racial identification. That is, her gendered treatment is also her racialized mistreatment as these are inseparable, intersectional identifications. This likely means that Asian American women deal with more microaggressions in the newsroom, microaggressions that are simultaneously raced and gendered.

Another possibility is that Asian American men and women have different coping styles to anti-Asian racism. In the few studies that have examined these differences, psychologists find that Asian American men are more likely to practice avoidance strategies than women. Because of dominant culture's feminizing of Asianness and assumptions of "Asian cultural values," Asian American men are generally uncomfortable expressing their feelings openly, particularly with other men (Liu 2002). This leads to an exaggeration of masculine performance, which demands toughness and a lack of emotional sensitivity. This also corresponds with masculine values that are privileged in newsrooms, socializing men to deny racist abuse. As such, Asian American women are more likely to seek professional help than men (Yeh and Wang 2000). Perhaps because of direct engagement with harmful emotion, Asian American women are more likely to use problem-solving strategies than men, who are more likely to use "emotion-focused" strategies such as ignoring or trivializing the harms or believing themselves to be superior to racist abusers (Kuo 1995). For Asian American men, this leads primarily to two coping strategies—avoidance or peer support. We believe that Asian American women reporters were more open to thinking about the racism they experienced because of *both* the intersectional racism they experience and more problem-solving coping strategies that directly address racist harms. Whatever the exact reason, it is clear that Asian American women with racialized identifications were much more likely to describe their experiences with racist marginalization in newsrooms than men participants.

Employment Marginalization

One way in which racially activated Asian Americans discussed harms was to talk about direct barriers to employment. This includes under-hiring Asian American journalists, being unfairly compensated, and being prevented from equal opportunities for promotion. Hannah shared a story of her firsthand experience of working on a diversity residency program at a newsroom whose White leaders made false promises about retaining her. Hannah said, "I think maybe even less than a month at the end of my residency, they were like, oh, well, we can't bring you on, and I was just like, what are you talking about? You just pulled the rug out from under me." This anecdote points to the resiliency of White racial hegemony in newsrooms that take advantage of funded diversity programs that provide fairly cheap labor from journalists of color. Newsrooms can also cynically boost diversity numbers to appear more racially progressive and aligned with ASNE goals. Referring to her peers of color, not just Asian Americans who were also hired in the newsroom through similar programs, Hannah continued:

> They bring in talented, young people of color to cover these communities who bust their ass to not only cover things that they're interested in but also every assignment that's asked of them. They are forced to be flexible, regardless of whatever obstacles might be in their way, because that's the expectation. And then, at the very end, they're told, despite doing absolutely nothing wrong, getting front page articles every single week, that they are not going to be hired, which is bogus. It's just absolutely ridiculous.

This points to the limits of diversity programs when there is little serious interest in inclusion and racial equity in newsrooms. Although it is unclear how many newsrooms operate in this manner, that some do is a concern for proponents of racial equity in news and the use of philanthropic means to achieve it. In the end, Hannah took a demotion to join the newsroom because of personal circumstances that prevented moving for a job, and, months later, the newsroom used Hannah as an example of its commitments to diversity, a discourse that Hannah viewed as egregiously hypocritical. She said, "They ended up using me as an example of keeping on people of color, which is not the case, incredibly infuriating as you can imagine." Her use of the word "using" is particularly informative because it implies her diminished agency and the White newsroom's self-serving treatment of reporters that takes advantage of their labor but without respecting them as colleagues.

Dana challenged the idea of reverse racism and affirmative action hiring. She said, "There is this assumption that because a person, that a person of color who was hired is less than, so there's people who make comments like that's a diversity hire." When White people in the newsroom hold this view, it reveals White reporters' implicit belief in the inadequate ability of people of color, either because they think hiring is unfairly driven by diversity initiatives or because they believe in the inherent flaws of journalists of color. Another way of phrasing this is to say that there is a naturalized belief in the superiority of White reporters. Challenging this view, she points out that the opposite is actually true. There is less hiring of people of color than is deserved because of tokenism. Dana described that at least in broadcast news, there is discomfort with giving two Asian Americans announcer positions, so it means that this artificially caps the number of Asian Americans a newsroom will tolerate hiring. In what might be described as divide-and-conquer strategies of White racial hegemony, she said, "Other Asians in the newsroom would like psychologically psych ourselves out into thinking we're in competition with one another for these very limited spots because it's, culturally, you get the feeling that that is the way it is, that there's only a few spots." As such, tokenizing not only produces underrepresentation in the newsroom but also an internalization of racist systems that views co-racial colleagues as threats rather than as resources and support.

Hiring decisions also reflect a narrow band of acceptable peers—White, middle- or upper-middle class, elite education, and city or suburban life experience. Hannah noted that despite stated commitments to diversity, hiring runs counter to those commitments. "The people that they do end up hiring on are White, and it's, it's just like so apparent, and in a newsroom, especially watching, like, all these important stories in a community that you care about being not covered because they don't have the time or don't care about things is really frustrating." Her point disrupts myths of affirmative action hiring and "reverse racism" (Lipsitz 1998; Gabriel 1998), and it points to one cause of White overrepresentation in newsrooms—the hiring managers and their racially subjective evaluations of talent and potential. From Nina's perspective, these hiring patterns are marked by the intersection of race and class.

> Most people cannot do like unpaid internships for a summer, right? Or, work for the college newspaper for free because, you know, it's just, they have bills to pay, they don't have a deep support system that would allow them to just work for several months without, with very little or no money, anyway, so and that, that continues to complicate the entry of minorities into journalism, right? And, so, I think that that just shouldn't be the case. I think that newsrooms should take it as seriously as, it should be like a, like a top priority for newsrooms in the twenty-first century.

Implicit in her criticism is that many qualified, potential journalists of color are falling through the cracks before they are even able to seriously begin a career in journalism because of the economic capital required to join the profession. Her response can be read as a rejection of pipeline justifications that suggest talented people of color do not exist to hire but, rather, that the systemic racism and classism of journalism filters out potentially talented, hard-working colleagues of color. This challenges the idea that White journalists are simply the most qualified within a meritocratic system but, rather, shows that White journalists become the most qualified because the societal deck is stacked against people of color, who have less wealth because of legacies of racism and continued, contemporary structural disadvantage. By criticizing such practices, Nina articulates a position that rejects post-racism and colorblind meritocracy.

Despite the gains that have been made in spite of these obstacles, the internet's threat to the economic model of for-profit news has meant that many of those gains have been reversed and worsened because of downsizing. Olivia said:

> I actually used to work in the same newsroom way back in, like, 2000, and back then, I mean, we could never have imagined where we would be now, but back then, the newsroom was more than double the size. There were significantly more journalists of color, just numerically, but also percentage-wise even back then twenty years ago. News organizations were really conscious of their lack of diversity, representation, and were working really hard to do something about it, and the numbers were going up and up and up every year right and then, the recession and the internet and everything, and it's gone, it's actually gone the other direction like so it's actually gotten worse over time.

Because journalists of color often have less seniority in their newsrooms, they are the most vulnerable in times of economic precarity. This is a pattern across most industries in which women and people of color are disproportionately harmed by downsizing and economic hardship (Carpenter 2019).

For those who survive these structural dangers, some reporters point to the devaluing of their labor. Paying people less suggests they matter less in the newsroom and is a way of establishing newsroom hierarchy that is coded not only by merit, experience, or commercial appeal but also by race. Jennifer said:

> Now this is about ten years ago when I found out that they [newsroom management] paid these two White men more than me; I was kind of like okay, that's interesting. That's cool. Like these are good people, like they do good work. I'm good with that. One of the White men was like, I can't believe you don't get paid as much as me because you're the editor of the website and you do a lot more. And, so, he was more outraged for me than I was, and so it's just not really in my personality to be angry about those things, but now at ten years later, I'm like, oh yeah, that was probably not cool, you know, or like that was, I should have been compensated more.

There are multiple points to unpack. First, the devaluing of Jennifer as an Asian American woman reads as both a sexist devaluing of women's labor and a racist devaluing of Asian American labor. It is, of course, widely known that there are gender pay gaps (Barroso and Brown 2021). What may be less well understood because of the model minority myth is that there are racial pay gaps for Asian Americans (Varma 2004). Not only do they lag behind White Americans with similar educational attainment, they lag behind White Americans with lower levels of education (Varma 2004). Discourses that equate Asian Americans with capable technical work but deficient leadership, creativity, and humanity have a historical precursor in the stereotype of the "coolie," which imagined Chinese Americans as low-skill, low-wage workers whose lack of full humanity justified exploitation and exclusion from artisan classes (Lee 1999; Chang 2003). Although it would be an exaggeration to claim that coolie discourses circulate in the newsroom, the point is that the historical legacies of these discourses have remained as traces in dominant culture and are manifest in the devaluing of Asian American labor. Second, Jennifer's initial silence and acceptance of her lower pay might be viewed as passivity, but we believe that it can also reasonably be understood as a tactic of survival, understanding that in her devalued condition, standing up for herself as an Asian American woman is an economically dangerous act, particularly in the context of the previous evidence of tokenism and of the devaluing of Asian American labor.

For others, their marginalization has been the bamboo ceiling's limits on opportunities to achieve their potential. Dana pointed out that when leadership changed at her news organization, replacing managers of color with all White newsroom leaders, her career trajectory was adversely affected.

> I think my career really stalled at [my organization]. I think the leader, the leadership became all White, and I didn't have anybody that I trusted. So, I lost sort of my sense of allyship, a sense of just being, just having anybody in the upper ranks to go to, to be really honest and transparent. And that is really alienating when our jobs as journalists is sort of to speak truth to power.

The most obvious point here is the White normativity that is reproduced when leadership does not reflect the identities of reporters of color in their newsroom. What is less obvious is that Dana's sense of allyship did not come from having Asian American news managers specifically, but managers of color more broadly. This suggests that the reason for harms to Asian American careers is not racial difference as might be argued from a universalist, post-racist discourse that concludes that everyone treats their own race with more affinity (Alcoff 1998; Gilroy 2012) but, rather, that the cause is specifically White racial hegemony. For many White people, their subconscious investments in Whiteness and the ontological expansion of White space limit their ability to understand the experiences of people of color (Karmaker and Sarkar 2021; Sullivan 2006). Indeed, as Dana said, "There wasn't, there isn't a sense, and I'll say that for today, right now, there isn't a sense that the folks in power are people that you can go and talk to and, like, get honest and have a really honest conversation because they just get their backs up and get defensive." As DiAngelo (2011) has famously argued, most White people are sensitive to any racial discomfort, regardless of how slight, because it is so unfamiliar to their habitus of racial privilege, resulting in multiple defensive moves. This is a feature of Whiteness to deny the existence of White racial hegemony (Nakayama and Krizek 1995; Jackson 1999). This discomfort and discursive moves also socialize and discipline people of color to not discuss racism because of the threat of consequences for creating White discomfort and for disrupting myths of colorblindness that reveal White racial hegemony. Because Asian American reporters have to navigate these spaces, knowledgeable of White racial hegemony but unable to acknowledge it openly, at least with White colleagues, it requires psychological armor to defend from harms but few means of conquering the harms, including the journalist's usual weapon of truth-telling and accountability.

Mark's experience was not a lack of promotion opportunities, but, early in his career, it was the limited, stereotyped vision through which his peers viewed him that stunted his growth. Instead of ladders of support, Asian American reporters must climb rugged terrain with few footholds. Mark said, "For people to make these, like, you know, racist assumptions. Like, oh, you're good at math or, you know, or, or whatever, that you kind of put it in the box. You're kind of seeing that there are limits on your potential, you know, that are ascribed to you when they just kind of look at you, you know, something that, you know, a White male would not get." Although Mark has described not being interested in being an editor, his quote has echoes of the bamboo ceiling such that Asian Americans do not have the same opportunity to rise in their respective organizations (Gee and Peck 2018). In his case, the limitations were primarily about who he can be as a reporter and how he has been perceived, particularly early in his career. This is a kind of pigeonholing that is less discussed in the scholarly literature. That is, he is less concerned about being pigeonholed for telling stories about race and more concerned about being pigeonholed into less valued roles because of his visible racial difference. Because of his own direct experiences of newsroom racism, his sensitivities are mobilized to be more engaged with the community he covers.

> I think that perspective really, it feeds a lot into my, I guess, identity as a journalist because I understand at its root nature when the system is kinda unfair to you, and, so, when there's an unfairness that happens whether it be, you know, when there's a racist letter to the editor saying that we really should have, we really should intern Japanese Americans or it would be good to lock up certain groups of people today, you know, I will respond to that, and just in terms of my own sense of reporting in this pandemic and other things.

Notably, Mark is one of the few to openly use the language of "racism" when referring to the kinds of microaggressions, stereotyping, and other constraints on his professional potential. Naming racism directly challenges dominant racial conventions that only claim racism in cases of overt, interpersonal racist bigotry (Oh 2022; Cisneros and Nakayama 2015) by understanding racism as everyday systems. To return to the question of whether it is the newsroom or outside experiences of racism that activate racial identifications, it is, in these cases at least, both.

Emotional Burdens and Marginalization

Because of Asian Americans' underrepresentation in newsrooms, it produces a burden to explain and to be the spokesperson for all of Asia and Asian America. Rose said that this expectation is alienating.

> I will say it's still isolating because even though they don't treat me as the expert, I'm still the only one in the newsroom covering the community. Like, I don't have any, there are no editors who have covered it before. There's only one editor of color and so sometimes it's isolating because I, there's no one I can turn to for like generational or institutional knowledge, like I'm it. If I have questions, I have no one to turn to in the newsroom; I have to go to someone in the community and ask them. So, that is, that is kind of isolating.

Although Rose does not feel tokenized in the newsroom because of the support she receives, the lack of Asian American co-workers and, especially, editors creates a burden of representation. In predominantly White institutions, people of color are often required to be spokespeople for their entire community, which causes stress for the individual and renders Asian American monolithic when one person is understood to be sufficient to express its diversity. As Rose indicates, it produces a psychological feeling of isolation. Although the counter-argument may be that colleagues' questions suggest that she is important to the group, the questions reinforce a sense that there are no other people like her in the newsroom and, perhaps, that she does not quite belong. Even though the intentions of the newsroom to hire an Asian American reporter and to rely on her as a resource may be well-intended, the lack of diversity itself can produce psychic harms. Thus, the structural problems of representation produce individual-level stresses and alienation. Sadly, alienation is a common condition for Asian Americans (Tuan 1998).

For other Asian American journalists, the response to these questions or demands is resentment and frustration that White colleagues expect their colleagues of color to educate them in conversations that are often emotionally fraught (see DiAngelo 2011). Dana said, "You know, I've had one of my white foreign correspondent colleagues call me and ask me to school him about the diversity problem. . . . Like it's my responsibility. I was like, excuse me. And, so there's a real, there's stuff like that." As Calafell (2010) argues, it is exhausting for people of color to have to teach and expose vulnerabilities to White people, including White liberals. When women of color express frustration or educate in a way that is seen as unacceptable to standards of polite White, middle-class femininity, women of color are often disciplined harshly (Calafell 2010). The accumulated demands or requests for explanation can be microaggressive acts as people of color understand the emotional work as well as the time and energy needed to have these conversations.

For this reason, Hannah is ambivalent about requests to educate because she understands the toll that explanations exact while also recognizing her ability to help her colleagues gain a new perspective or knowledge.

> People will come to me asking me if something is like racially insensitive or whatever, and I do want them to ask because I would rather them ask than to make a fool of themselves, but it's a huge burden to take on when someone is, like, you're in the middle of something, and someone is like, oh, can I consult you on this thing? Then you have to stop everything that you're doing to help them. . . . I do find myself defending things a little bit more if I find it offensive where other people don't, so, I think that, like, I don't know, in addition to just being the Asian reporter on staff, just like, on a day-to-day, there is the burden of feeling like you're representative for all, and then when people come to me with questions about Korean things or Japanese things, I'm like, honestly, I like, I can't help you. Like, I don't know Korean, not Korean, don't know Japanese.

There is a bit to unpack in her quote as she points to several problems with these requests: (1) time and interruption to workflow, (2) resistance to offensive perspectives or reporting, (3) burden of representation, and (4) expectation of knowledge about the largest and arguably the most heterogeneous continent. Her point alludes to the unrecognized labor that she has to carry as an Asian American in the newsroom. As we describe momentarily, this additional knowledge does not carry benefits. Newsrooms might argue that diversity is a strength, but it is not rewarded.

Instead, diversity means extra burdens. As Gwyneth argues, these burdens should not be solely the responsibility of people of color: "It shouldn't be the person of color, and the burden shouldn't be on the person of color to bring up these things. These should already be part of the conversation from the top down. Any leader of a team should already be having these conversations. This shouldn't be new stuff, so it does speak to a newsroom if these conversations are brand new." Gwyneth clearly makes a systemic critique about institutional power, and she is also shifting the lens such that the burdens are not placed on rank-and-file journalists of color but on White newsroom leaders. It is a challenge that turns responsibility onto White people such that the role of the journalist of color is not to assist White colleagues but to demand that they share these burdens. As mentioned in the previous chapter, however, White normativity is an ideological driving force of the newsroom, so it is unlikely that this will happen without extraordinary effort and a willingness to deal with resistance from White managers and rank-and-file White reporters and staff. The fact that newsrooms have been historically reluctant to place people of color in the highest positions of the newsroom also makes this leadership less likely, placing burdens on reporters of color. Amy shared an anecdote in which she had to carry this burden. She said, "We have a reporter who definitely said to us, he didn't think the Proud Boys were actually racist because he saw a Latino person holding a Proud Boys sign or something like that. It was like, okay, let's explain way back about why that Latino person may specifically be doing that and why that doesn't make them not racist." As such, Asian American journalists and journalists of color like Amy are placed in uncomfortable positions where they feel a burden to remediate their White colleagues' dominant racial thinking. Doing so, however, places Asian American reporters in a position of greater precarity when they stand up to White colleagues, who constitute the majority of the newsroom and whose perspectives dominate its culture. Dana said:

> I think it's had certain effects on my career trajectory for sure, one, but then, in terms of how I work, I had to, I've had to, like, not speak up as much, I think. I think I'm far more outspoken, and I'm far more emotionally reactive than I have shown myself to be at work just because [the newsroom] is one of those, you know that 1980 Robert Redford, is it Robert Redford, uh, *Ordinary People*, where there's a death in the family, and everybody just like sits around the table? It's very White. It takes place in Connecticut. Everybody just, like, sits around the table and doesn't acknowledge the death in the family, you know? I feel like that, that sort of repression and being pent up in the newsroom a lot.

Her anecdote interestingly flips this notion of repressed emotion, which is often stereotypically (and sometimes therapeutically) attributed to East Asian cultures (Eng and Han 2018), to White people. In her case, the repression she deals with is anathema to her usual personality, but as stated in this context, it is a survival mechanism to avoid upsetting White taboos in the newsroom, such as pointing out systemic racism in the newsroom that devalues Asian Americans. The damage of repressing herself is not only harmful to her career, it also causes emotional harms as it means a denial of one's self.

When anti-Asian racism is brought up, it is often not believed. This is not surprising given the usual deflections that the model minority myth permits.

Amy said, "I still think that it's not being taken seriously enough. I still think that, okay, so people can acknowledge the words 'Asian Americans experience racism,' and that's something that, sadly, maybe a lot of people weren't able to acknowledge before." Many White people deny the reality of racism for Asian Americans, usually by claiming that it is a compliment to claim that Asian Americans have achieved parity with White people, but this is an erasure that denies Asian Americans' understanding of being racially harmed (Sue et al. 2007). Instead, as Amy explained in a different example about the risks of covering Trump rallies, concerns about anti-Asian racism are only believed when a White ally validates them. She said, "Whereas here, I feel I had a White ally, or a newsroom ally, who kind of just opened the door for this conversation to happen, and then I felt safe with him having laid the groundwork for me to say yes, for me, as an Asian American, I don't feel safe at these protests, so I think we need to think of another way that we cover these." When making this point, she stated it optimistically—that there are White allies in the newsroom. Although it is important to recognize this as a hopeful sign, it is also an indictment of the White racial hegemonic culture of the newsroom in which a White man's support is validated but her concerns as an Asian American woman are dismissed. Her White colleague's support is helpful in this moment, but it is a remedy that also furthers a problem in which journalists of color must rely on White patronage. The motivations to believe or deny may be different, but it still imbues White men with authority to substantiate or deny Asian American colleagues' claims.

For Amy, because some newsrooms may not have White allies and because she cannot be certain of their support, it silences her dissent because to be alone would leave her vulnerable. She said, "Yeah. Overwhelmingly, I think Asians are still just like worried that if we speak up, we're going to lose our jobs, or if we speak up, people are going to think of us in a certain way, I don't know. I don't know what laid the groundwork for that, and I really don't want people to think of Asian American journalists as being disposable, but sometimes I guess maybe we're worried that people think of us like that, and that's why we don't speak up more." It is important to also clarify the causes of silence. Thought pieces in the popular press often argue that Asian American silence is because of supposed "Asian values," a criticism that both exotifies and flattens the diversity of Asian societies. In a word, it racializes. What Amy makes clear is that, contrary to a deficit in Asian American families and cultures, it is a survival response to the dominant cultural view of Asian disposability, a view that is replicated in discourses of "yellow peril" hordes during war and visible in U.S. films. It is this view that justified the use of the atomic bomb and the imperiled labor conditions of Chinese laborers on U.S. railroads. In other words, there is a historical, inter-generational understanding that White society views Asian Americans as plentiful, interchangeable, and disposable parts; this is still manifest in Asian American invisibility, marginalization, and discipline to even mild resistance. This likely takes an emotional toll as Asian American reporters are expected to navigate their anxieties of speaking up and their anxieties of endangering themselves. For Clara, it means being resigned to not trying: "Um, I just feel like there are some things that people in the newsroom just won't get; they'll be, like, oh, you know, they'll probably give me the requisite sympathy and then just say, well, if you ever feel unsafe, just leave, you know, but that's about it. I just, I just think they just don't have the same understanding. So why bother?" Her point is that while White colleagues may express sympathy, their advice is trite and betrays a lack of understanding about possible harms and the expectations of their work. This is a silence of a different sort—a resignation to indifference that maintains the status quo of the White newsroom that allows White colleagues to imagine themselves as sympathetic non-racists. This means that for Asian American reporters, newsrooms are not "safe spaces" but are fraught as places that discipline silence and that dehumanize.

To return to an earlier point about being devalued, Hannah shared that her multicultural identity and bilingual fluency are considered assets for the newsroom but that Hannah herself is not valued for possessing them. Hannah's skill set is a tool for White editors to take advantage of but not to reward. During COVID-19's early months, there was an acute need for a Mandarin speaker, so they pulled Hannah from her own desk and temporarily reassigned her. She said, "I think it was like, a Thursday morning, I had a whole day of interviews for my actual beat. . . . I walked in, my editor told me to cancel everything, that Metro needed me, and I ended up spending the whole day doing interviews in Mandarin, and talking to the Chinese community about how they felt about coronavirus." Hannah perceived this as unfair because this was exceptional treatment.

> No one else is being asked to, like, cover multiple beats and being asked to move their schedule around because of this. We had another reporter that was tapped for coronavirus coverage; he wrote zero coronavirus stories. Absolutely none, and it's like, okay, so you're choosing me because apparently I can do this and no other people can, but when it's all said and done, you're not gonna give me a raise and you're not going to hire me onto a role that you clearly still need someone for because you're just putting me in for emergency purposes, and that's, that's messed up.

Hannah claimed that she felt she was put on the "back burner" in case the newsroom needed her. What she wanted was the newsroom to recognize her unique contribution and its need for a Mandarin speaker on its Metro desk, which is where she wanted to work and which she viewed as having more cultural capital in the newsroom. Instead, as indicated earlier, she was dismissed at the end of the diversity program only to have personal circumstances dictate returning in a lesser role. This example reveals the fallaciousness of post-racist rhetoric, which claims that only individual merit matters (Bonilla-Silva 2010b), and instead points to the persistence of White racial hegemony in the newsroom when it invests in and supports White colleagues who may be equally talented as reporters but who have fewer multicultural tools in their journalistic repertoire. Multicultural, multilingual knowledge is seen as a resource for White reporters and the White newsroom but not a skill that is rewarded. Doing so would distinguish the Asian American reporter (and other journalists of color) as preferable to monocultural White colleagues.

Perhaps, a reason that Asian Americans' unique skillset is devalued is because the model minority myth would have people believe that Asian Americans are submissive and will not resist the distribution of newsroom resources and capital to White peers. Jennifer said, "I think this, this is, this is something that I've experienced again and again every, every job that I've had is people assume that you're just a quiet, you know, I don't like the word submissive, but you're just kind of a quiet, docile, like, go-with-the-flow kind of person just, just because you're Asian so that's, that's their initial like okay, that's Jennifer." These assumptions about Asian Americans cause them to be valued as subordinates but not as leaders. It points to an expectation of subordination regardless of Asian Americans' own desires or values. As Dana mentioned earlier, not conforming risks disciplining, a common response particularly from White people when Asian Americans do not support their perspectives or point to White racism because this is interpreted as a betrayal of the adjacency to Whiteness that the model minority is understood to have been granted (Jo 2004; Fong 2008). In this formulation, Asian Americans' humanity is rendered invisible, and with repeated experiences, some Asian Americans internalize this racial disciplining, denying their own experiences of racism and conforming to White expectations (Son 2014; Lin 2020). Jennifer continued: "I think that's also part of the part of the thing about being Asian, right? We don't make noise. We don't complain. We just kind of keep our, that's the stereotype, and I think a lot in some ways I've internalized that over time. And so that's probably why I'm like, it's fine. You know, but maybe it's not." This moment of self-reflexivity was incisive, recognizing the ways that patterned accommodation can lead to self-harm that was not previously known to the individual herself. As Yamato (2004) has claimed, invisibility, including self-denials, carries psychic harms.

Another manifestation of the dehumanizing ways in which Asian Americans are not seen is White colleagues' confusion with their Asian American colleagues. Several Asian American women reporters noted this as a regular, dehumanizing experience. Jennifer said, "Sometimes, I've been called, there's another Asian girl at another magazine that I used to work with, work for, and people used to call me by her name all the time, and they would just get us mixed up, which is not, you know, they're not intending to be racist, but we don't look anything alike." For Jennifer, this means she has been rendered unnoticed and unrecognizable through an expectation that she would not use her voice and through confusion with other Asian Americans in the newsroom. This contributes to a sense that Asian American individuality does not matter. What is interesting to note is her willingness to re-interpret these racist acts as innocently performed. This is, as mentioned previously, a tendency of Asian Americans to not attribute racism and to give White people the benefit of the doubt.

Even when there is obvious visible difference, White colleagues still mix up their Asian American coworkers, people whom they would see frequently. Hannah said, "Yeah, I mean, people are getting me mixed up with Emily [pseudonym] all the time, even though there's like a twenty-year age gap." Nina tells a similar story of being mixed up.

> There were two other young Asian reporters, who are women, and we all started, I think within a year of each other, and we worked on different desks, and we did not look anything alike. And yet, it became this running joke where not infrequently other people, White employees would refer one of us by the other person's name. I'll just make up some, two other names like Sarah and Jennifer and me, Nina, and they'd be like, oh, hey, Sarah, or like hey, Jennifer, or they'd say like whatever; they'd just mix us up, and we really looked nothing, well not nothing but like we don't look alike, and I found that really frustrating. I mean that's, that feels so minor compared to, like, I think I've heard so many horror stories from other newsrooms, but that, that does stick with me. It was like, okay, there's really not that many of us. We don't look alike; I forget why you can't just remember our names. I would say all in all, I don't feel like I've experienced too much discrimination or maybe, maybe I'm not aware of it, but I don't, I don't feel like I've been like singled out.

Like Jennifer, Nina excuses the behavior as unimportant and even discounts the reason that these experiences might "stick" with her. As Sophia argued: "Sometimes that's why microaggressions are so dangerous because they're so subtle, and they're so, but they add up over time, and then we work, we try to work through 'em, work our way out of it and not really address the underlying issue. And so, yeah, I think, I think that is where I think, you know, for me, where it's harmful is like, it's like, it's not so much coronavirus specifically." As such, despite the accumulated harms and frequent experiences of deindividuation, they are treated as inconsequential. Indeed, Asian Americans often feel uncomfortable claiming that racist transgressions against them are racist because it feels, relative to the violent harms of anti-Black racism, for example, inconsequential (Son 2014; Lin 2020). Yet, this denial of their own feelings also means that harms cannot be addressed adequately. Of the reporters who pointed to this harm, Dana was the only one who named why it is harmful. She said, "We are, I don't know, eight years apart in age. We don't look alike. To this day, we still get each other's emails and accolades, and when I show up, they'll ask me where my dog is . . . so there is a sense that we are interchangeable." Here, she is recognizing not only that microaggressions are common and cumulative but that the nature of this particular microaggression is to suggest that individual Asian Americans do not matter. Interchangeability means a lack of uniqueness and disposability, common themes that have emerged in the experiences of racism by Asian American reporters.

Another microaggression experienced by the participants is stereotyping. Arguably, the most common stereotype in this specific sociohistorical moment is the model minority. As Fong (2008) makes clear, this stereotype is inflected with both seemingly attractive but also repulsive qualities. Kawai (2005) astutely demonstrates that the stereotype is part of a dialectic with the "yellow peril." Thus, the qualities that might make Mark a desirable colleague—smart and hardworking—also are what dehumanize him as a threat. Mark said, "You know, some people will say, 'Oh, you're friendlier than I imagine you would be after I saw you'; I'm like, you know that's really strange. Really, like, what did I do to make it seem like that I was kind of like I had a stick up my butt? That seems to be the impression that some people had with me." Asian Americans are often thought to be socially distant and less emotionally connected. Consider, for instance, the "tiger mom" stereotype in which the Chinese/Asian mother trains her children to be smart and high-achieving through harsh disciplining and a withdrawal of parental love (Lee 2016). Interestingly, this was the only experience of stereotyping described by a male participant, and it clearly carries gendered inflection—Asian American man as threat, Asian American woman as docile/invisible/interchangeable.

Asian American Empowerment

In the face of newsroom marginalization, some racially activated Asian American reporters work to strengthen support within the newsroom and to challenge racism, particularly in news representation. They mobilize agency in order to create networks that build group solidarity and strength so that emerging reporters are better prepared for the challenges they will face and so that they can recognize that their struggles are not their own, which acts as a deterrent to the kinds of harmful internalization of racism that have been discussed above. Notably, it is only those who have salient racial activations who engage in these pan-ethnic movements within newsrooms and across the profession. This points to an identification that is constructed at least in part in resistive ways to White racial hegemony and its harmful impacts. Recounting her second-generation father's experience and interpretation of racism, Amy said, "I've always had my dad's kind of comments in my, in the back of my mind, how he pointed these things out, and I guess I just came to a point, maybe in my adult life where I was just somewhat frustrated. . . . It seemed that things hadn't advanced since my dad was a teenager in this country, and I just didn't want to sit back and let it happen or continue to happen again." Her comment demonstrates that racial activation is dependent upon a fertilization of ideas that may not activate at the moment that the ideas are learned but that the fertilization of ideas provides the discursive resources for later activation and reflexive racialization.

For several participants, the clearest step to ameliorate the harms of White normative newsrooms is to mentor. Mark actively volunteers so that interns of color, Asian American or otherwise, have a role model who reflects their experience as a racial minority in a White profession.

> For people [interns] who are trying to find their way in this very kind of delicate time, for them to be able to see other people that look like them or you can relate with. I mean, some, some of the people that we brought into the program aren't Asian American, and, you know, for them to see someone who's not like, you know, old White guy and who they can't relate to but someone who is, who they can relate to and see that they can be successful, and they can, they can do a hard-hitting investigative story. Like, that means a lot to them, and so, you know, I have been lucky in being able to get to the degree of influence and prestige that I've been able to achieve, and I want to make sure that I can try to provide that kind of support for other people who can make it because not everyone is gonna make it. So, it's so important that people can see in themselves that they, if they really wanted to, they can see a path that they can get to there.

Mark recognizes the importance of representation to visualize belonging, and despite the additional burden that mentoring work requires, he demonstrates a sense of duty to cultivate future journalists of color as a means of social equity. His work creates stronger candidates in the job pipeline and helps ensure that more make it through the filtering structures that leave people of color out. This reflects Calafell's (2007, 425) description of mentoring as a critical practice that offers embodied "homeplace" that would otherwise not be found within the hegemonic structures of institutions. It is a practice of a politics of love that recharges lost emotional reserves that are spent surviving in predominantly White institutions and systems. Hannah is similarly motivated to exercise personal agency to address structural obstacles and harms. She said, "As an Asian American and a person of color who has been in the newsroom for a long time, it's very important for me to always reach out to, like, the younger people of color to offer mentorship or even just like professional guidance and anything like that so that they don't get taken advantage in the same way because I do really feel like there is a huge disinvestment." Recalling her own struggles as an up-and-coming reporter and the ways in which her labor and talents were overlooked and exploited, she actively seeks to help other journalists of color, including Asian Americans, to avoid similar harms. It is important to note that both Mark and Hannah not only form pan-ethnic racial networks of support but also pan-racial networks. That is, by activating an Asian American racial identification, it also produces a racial consciousness that understands harms as a result of White racial hegemony and as producing interlocking, shared fates with other journalists of color.

Indeed, while some Asian Americans talked about the importance of pan-ethnic community and reflexive racialization, they *all* also talked about the importance of pan-racial community. Indeed, some talked about the latter and not the former. Regarding pan-ethnic community, Nina, Mark, and Clara all discussed the importance of Asian American colleagues and support structures, particularly the Asian American Journalists Association (AAJA).

> I'm very passionate about improving, like, minority representation in journalism. I belong to the Asian American Journalists Association. I'm not, like, an extremely active member, but, you know, I have belonged for several years and, and very supportive of the mission. So yeah, it does matter.—Nina

> I mean, I suppose I guess my community is, a lot of it is family and then also the Asian American Journalists Association, where I would be in the local chapter.—Mark

> I didn't really talk to anybody about it [racial harms] in my newsroom. I just, I guess I did, I did talk to a few Asian American friends. I guess just because I felt like they could really empathize more. So, I mean, I'm sure I would've got sympathy from co-workers, but, but yeah, I don't really talk to, I don't talk to my colleagues that much about these kinds of things that bother me, you know? But with this, I just felt like Asian American friends would understand more.—Clara

As the comments indicate, Asian American support structures are important to several of the reporters in the study. Indeed, research on Asian American coping points to the importance of social networks for Asian Americans as they experience racist harms, particularly as Asian Americans are less likely to utilize professional counseling and, instead, rely on co-racial social networks as a means to cope (Liang et al. 2007). As these quotes indicate, Asian American networks are important for a sense of belonging and for a space to engage in reflexive racialization, a sharing of everyday harms that legitimates experiences of racism as not trivial nor their own faults (Parker and Song 2006).

Although pan-ethnic racial peer networks help, many more participants discussed pan-racial community with journalists of color. Indeed, even in Nina's quote about belonging to AAJA, she claims its importance is to improve "minority representation," not Asian American representation, specifically. It points to an outward-directed affinity that rejects expectations of the model minority in which Asian Americans will demonstrate White adjacency and gratitude. Indeed, the goal is the opposite—the active community-building of pan-racial networks. It seeks coalitional partnership rather than opportunistic, but marginalized, access. Although it is unclear from this data, it is arguable that Asian Americans who do not have salient racial identifications are more likely to opportunistically choose White adjacency because of its availability and more immediate, tangible benefits. It requires racial consciousness and anti-racist intention to choose coalition-building.

For the participants who have found pan-racial community, they point primarily to feeling understood by colleagues of color. Clara said, "I may, like, grouse about this kind of stuff because I feel like people there will get it, and they'll have thoughtful responses, so I have that little cushion, which is helpful." This point of "getting it" is an expression of being fully understood because of shared experience. Equally as important, they emphasize they are able to provide the emotional support and advice necessary to navigate difficult experiences and to cope with harms. Similarly, Gwyneth said the connections and relationships come more easily: "I think it's very easy to, um, to talk. Like, the person who sat next to me, a leader, she's African American, and so we can always talk about stuff, so it's very open; you could, you could easily talk about, I don't feel hindered in raising issues like this." This also implies that it is difficult to talk to White colleagues openly, perhaps because of the defensiveness and dismissiveness that was discussed previously. It points to the possibility of Black-Asian affinities that are so often represented in dominant culture as unlikely or in opposition despite long histories of shared struggle and connection (Prashad 2001).

This idea of shared oppression is made clear by Dana, who said, "I think there's a lot of commiserating among the factions, among the other people of color." This sense of reflexive racialization does not always mean weighty conversations, however. It means being able to unload and feel the warmth of human connection and understanding that is a salve, albeit incomplete, for racial harms. Hannah said, "It just means, I think it means exactly how you think it means. It's just like, when you go through so much garbage from your employer, you, it kinda goes back to the not needing to explain anything because everyone's been through that experience [laughs]. It's just very much that; it's just complaining, crying together, drinking together [laughs], like, just, just sharing and, like, unloading our experiences on people that have been through the same thing, or are still going through the same thing and feeling, like, a sense of closeness because of that [laughs]." This reflects early Asian American activism that promoted pan-ethnic and pan-racial coalition-building to achieve anti-racist goals, which might improve conditions for journalists of color and address some of the structural obstacles to promotion and hiring. Making the point more forcefully, Hannah referred to the reason for their social connection as "trauma bonding": "Yeah, it's funny. It's not necessarily like a super structured or professional thing; we just end up being friends because we like trauma bond essentially, and, yeah, no, we talk about [it] all the time. We are all very aware that we work for a very exploitive company, and almost all, if not most of the people, are on their way out or looking for a way out." The expression "trauma bond" is evocative as it conjures metaphors of tragedy and loss. It expresses emphatically that White newsrooms are psychically harmful for journalists of color and that being in them creates emotional wounds and scars. Frequently, coalitions are built when there is a common cause and drift apart when there is not. In Hannah's workplace, at least, she describes that common, unifying bond as their shared, racialized hardships that smooth over their different interests, backgrounds, and worldviews.

The pan-racial affinities are experienced as affirming, particularly as different groups rally together when one group is harmed. During the time of the interviews, because of the anti-Asian hostilities, Clara felt particularly affirmed as other journalists of color who are not Asian Americans expressed support: "They've been good about starting [an] email thread or Slack channel about, you know, if anybody needs help or feels overwhelmed and then also ways to help the Asian American community, keep highlighting xenophobia and the racist incidents. So, yeah, that's, that's been good like that. That's probably where yeah, I feel I think the sense of community there has gotten a little bit tighter, a little bit stronger." Thus, the overwhelming Whiteness of news appears to bring together journalists of color since Asian American reporters do not feel there is refuge or a "safe space" with White colleagues, who might amplify or reinforce the sense of harm Asian American journalists are feeling because of anti-Asian harms in society. Even during times that are not crisis moments and even when the group is cynical about the possibility of effecting change in the newsroom, Olivia feels hopeful and affirmed simply because the community exists and she has a place to belong. She said, "I think having that group of people is very validating, and it's also very, it helps create the momentum that's needed to make change, I think, so I'm very grateful for that." Having that sense of identification also likely means that racial consciousness and salience are emotionally rewarded and legitimated, leading to a stronger sense of racial and pan-racial commitments. These shared commitments produce a desire for racial equity that extends beyond the interests of their own racial group for broader newsroom inclusion. Olivia continued, "I think like in terms of minority representation in newsrooms like Asian Americans, like Latinos, African Americans, like indigenous people, etc. I think Asians are more closely represented in a lot of newsrooms, like proportional to the population of the U.S. as a whole, and I think, I would like to see, I mean, I would like to see more Asians, yes, like in charge of stuff, absolutely. Um, I also think we need more like Latino and Black leadership as well." Thus, pan-racial affiliation produces a desire for broad coalition and equity. To primarily advocate for Asian Americans would suggest own-group self-interest rather than a broader equity mission.

In addition to pan-racial affinity and desires for employment equity, Asian American reporters who are racially activated and who identify with broader pan-racial coalitions also desire improved cross representation in news coverage in addition to improved coverage for Asian Americans (as discussed in chapter 6). For Clara, it was a point of pride when a reader, who was tweeting from a Black standpoint, indicated her appreciation for the mainstream coverage of an issue important to Black Americans.

> I think one of the best compliments I had was a couple of years ago or last year, I wrote a story about the issue of colorism, but mostly focused like Black communities, but how, like in pop entertainment and, see, the darker you are, the less exposure you're given, or in the entertainment industry. . . . Then when the article came out, somebody like tweeted about it and said, I can't believe the [news institution] of all things is talking about this issue, and I was like, oh, oh good, that's good. So, yeah, that made me happy. If I can do more of that kind of thing where people don't expect us to address, you know, certain issues because they're just, because they're only important to one community.

Being responsive and covering an issue that has historically been argued to be too niche to be newsworthy was especially gratifying and affirming. It produced pride that Clara went outside the usual strictures of White news to legitimate an issue important to Black Americans.

Mark also expressed a similar sentiment, especially when he recognized the disparate impacts of COVID-19 on Black and Latinx communities. Instead of sidelining the story, he used his own experiences with inequality to provide a vantage point and raise awareness of the harms felt because of structural racism and poverty.

> Being the son of immigrants speaks to how I approach my work all the time, so, you know, in covering the virus, there was a lot, you know, this issue of Latinos and Black Americans being disproportionately hit hard by the pandemic is like a really big part of the story . . . but in, in my own reporting, because I'm very aware of being a non-White person in the U.S. that raising that to the issue,

where it is part of the primary news story, that is something that is, is important to me, and I think me being an Asian American or just being a non-White person helps me make sure to elevate that to the point where it's like you have to talk about it, it is an essential part of the story. It's not just a sidebar. It's the story.

For Mark, having an activated racial identification and being reflexive about social inequality means recognizing shared struggle born out of a collective understanding of racial marginalization that aligns with class and immigration. His goal of shaping the news agenda so that racial disparity is at the heart of the COVID-19 story points to the powerful ways in which news is always subjective—questions of what to cover and how to cover it introduce into any story a perspective even if the presentation of the story is molded to fit into standards of objectivity. In this case, it is his subjective experience as an Asian American from an immigrant household and his journalistic value to speak for the powerless that shape the agenda and perspective he has on news.

Mark is somewhat exceptional as other participants do not express as strongly their desire to center racial inequality but, rather, to provide a voice for people of color who would otherwise be left without representation. Olivia and Sophia feel a burden to represent not only Asian Americans but all people of color because in their newsrooms, there are fewer Black, Latinx, and Indigenous reporters that bring the stories. Olivia said, "I feel like my role is to really be that POC person who's, like, but how does this affect Native people, you know, or let's make sure we don't forget these folks just because they're not sitting here at the table. . . . I'm more just trying to make sure that we are representative of the community and, and that, particularly folks that have trusted, trusted me to try to put their stories forward, have the honor of, are honored by having the ideas voiced." Implicit in her quote is the expectation that White colleagues will not pitch stories about people of color, and when they do, it is considered exceptional and laudable. For them, however, it is an expectation they have for themselves that may be accompanied by skepticism rather than gratitude. While she talks about this work as an honor, it is also undergirded by connotations of duty and responsibility, which can be a source of pride but also of stress. Sophia is positioned as the person to know and to report on people of color in her community, less because of duty but because of a default expectation.

> Because we don't have a Latinx person, it's really easy for me to fall into that "people of color" role. I'm the person of color, and I should be, you know, I should be, so I kind of in a sense have to embrace that role of being the diversity person, you know, and so I, oftentimes, that's why I'm saying as a person, I think I've used my asset as being a person of color almost by necessity, and also,

because of the assimilation route; well, you know, I'm part of the two percent, so I, like, might as well just go along with it kinda, I guess.

Again, it is important to note that she could abdicate this responsibility as many of her White peers have done, but because of her racial identification, it is morally less tenable, meaning that she has to not only carry the burden of representation but the additional labor burden as she has to not only know her own beat but also multiple communities of color. This is invisible labor that Asian American reporters take on if racial identification is salient and meaningful as structures push against it, i.e., it requires more knowledge of communities of color, additional labor to uncover news stories beyond her own beat, and likely pushback as stories she pitches may be argued to not be "newsworthy" or lack cultural capital as the stories are understood to be less important. Ironically, then, covering stories about communities of color produces more equity in the pages of the newspaper but produces more inequity in newsroom labor.

Conclusion

Our research demonstrates that White normativity is not only manifest in coverage but is manifest in the treatment of Asian American journalists. It is important to understand the structural nature of racism in the newsroom that may be "incognizant" as Heider (2000) argued, but it is also manifest through the decisions and the agency of White peers, editors, and managers. Newsrooms are not just spaces with incognizant racism but spaces that are subconsciously and consciously constructed as White normative spaces. As the participants in our study demonstrated, their marginalization includes their under-hiring that is based around de-valuing assets that Asian American reporters bring that would differentiate them as more capable in some arenas than their White colleagues, namely multicultural knowledge and multilingual ability. Not valuing these skills means that it is easier to justify not hiring Asian American reporters, and it means exploiting their particular skills when needed for the benefit of White peers, treating Asian Americans as helpers rather than as fully subjectified peers. Not valuing these skills while viewing Asian Americans through the dehumanizing stereotype of the model minority means devaluing Asian American reporters after they are employed, and it also justifies paying Asian American reporters less than their White peers even when they are in similar positions with similar experience. Indeed, in some cases, it means being paid less than peers who are in positions with lower rank. The reasons could be because of barriers to entry into the employment pipeline, White leadership that subconsciously (or consciously) values White reporters more than reporters of color, and the reproduction of the dominant culture status quo in the newsroom.

Asian American reporters deal with multiple stresses because of the White normativity of news and the overrepresentation of White colleagues and underrepresentation of Asian American colleagues. Asian American reporters, particularly women reporters, describe being confused with other Asian American colleagues in the newsroom despite not looking alike or even being born in different generational cohorts. They also describe being treated as subservient, treated as model minorities who are supposed to do their jobs while being silent and invisible in the newsroom, and having their claims of anti-Asian racism in their jobs trivialized or not believed. Because they are underrepresented, they also are expected to represent not only Asian America but also Asian nations and ethnic groups abroad. In addition, White peers, at times, demand or expect that their Asian American peers explain racism to them, which can create anxiety and frustration. Although shrinking from these harms is a possible tactic, many of the participants describe being proactive, such as actively seeking to mentor early-career and student journalists of color and creating pan-racial affinity groups to advocate for the shared concerns of journalists of color, not only for Asian American reporters. The understanding is that the cause of their marginalized status is not merely preference for own-group status that might be argued in universalist theories such as social identity theory, but that the cause is specifically White racial hegemony.

To reach this particular conclusion, however, means that Asian American reporters must be racially activated such that being Asian American is understood as being a racialized minority in the United States. Even though participants across all identity positions note that newsrooms are predominantly White spaces, it is only racially activated participants who understand this discrepancy as produced and maintained through structures that benefit White racial hegemony. In other words, it requires racial consciousness to interpret marginalization as racially informed. As mentioned previously, Asian Americans are likely to attribute their marginalization to their own personalities or to seek other explanations, even when they are less likely, perhaps because of the adjacency to Whiteness that the model minority provides or because of socialization in predominantly White suburbs, where most Asian Americans are raised. That is, not all of the participants in this study believe that newsrooms reproduce White normativity or interpret harms, but nearly all of those with racially salient identifications do. This points to the diversity of Asian American experience and interpretation, and the importance of identification to the interpretation of objective experience. Although we do not make normative suggestions for how individual Asian Americans should identify as we understand identification as meaningful acts of agency by individual reporters, we simultaneously acknowledge that, as critical scholars, the White normativity of newsrooms is unlikely to change without racially activated journalists challenging structures. We also point to the conclusion of cultural psychologists who indicate that internalizing harms as the fault of Asian Americans themselves can create psychic harm. As Atkin and Tran (2020) note, developing strong ethnic and racial identifications is protective against mental health harms of racism. In the following chapter, we discuss the ways Asian American reporters understand and challenge objectivity for its work in furthering White racial hegemony in news.

5

What Counts as News

· ·

News Norms and Racial
Identifications

In the summer of 2020, during the height of the Black Lives Matter (BLM) movement, *The Pittsburgh Post-Gazette* barred a Black American reporter from covering police and racial justice issues because of White American editors' concerns about "bias." This caused an uproar in the newsroom from rank-and-file reporters, and it was followed by an intense debate in journalism circles about the role of reporters' racial identities in news coverage, about whose identities are scrutinized, and which stories are raced (Folkenflik 2020). Around the same time, *The Philadelphia Inquirer*'s newsroom was in turmoil after running a story headlined "Buildings Matter, Too" about damages to the city's buildings and infrastructure during BLM protests. Journalists at *The Inquirer* pushed back, saying the story and headline equated property damage to human life; this led to the resignation of a top editor at the paper (Tracy 2020). Both cases point to assumptions of White universality and Black particularity as well as White neutrality and Black bias. Though BLM is marked as a "Black story," it is not only Black Americans who have investments in it or who are impacted by it. As such, a White editor's racial standpoint on BLM is not understood as biased, whereas a Black reporter's racial standpoint is. These cases demonstrate that objectivity, a key norm sustaining mainstream journalism, is constructed from a White perspective.

Though meta-news stories for Asian American journalists have not received the same visibility, Asian American reporters also have to contend with questions about "bias" when they cover local Asian American communities and issues related to "Asia." This is because dogged journalistic norms such as objectivity and detachment have reigned as ideals of good journalism since the market-based conventions of the Associated Press and the penny press (Schudson 2003). Despite strong criticisms, those norms persisted like "the God who won't die" (Hackett and Zhao 1998, 82). Practicing journalists, especially those in mainstream, general-interest media organizations, tend to be judged by these norms, whether they like it or not. The Asian American journalists studied in this book also operate under these norms, and because they are situated in different identity positions, they articulate a range of different attitudes, including endorsement, uncertainty, and rejection of such norms. Many see mainstream news norms as being constructed from a dominant White standpoint in journalism, so they re-examine and re-frame the norms to become more "color conscious."

The purpose of this chapter is to probe the Asian American journalists' skepticism, ambivalence, and endorsement of news norms, especially objectivity. We discuss how their experiences in White newsrooms interact with their racial identifications to shape their understanding of the news norms and the stories they try to tell. Overall, we argue that those who identify as Asian American and are racially reflexive tend to conceptualize objectivity as a de facto White news value and tend to argue for multiple paths to truth-seeking in journalism. Partly because of this difference in journalistic philosophy, they more actively cover Asian American stories and the perspectives of racially marginalized U.S. Americans. It is important to note, however, that these arguably resistive efforts do not subvert journalistic norms in a totalizing fashion but specifically challenge objectivity by drawing upon other discourses about good journalism, such as muckraking and the Fourth Estate.

Truth, Objectivity, and Racial (In)activation

What does it mean to practice good journalism? What are journalism's enduring norms and values, if any, and how are they applied to Asian American journalists? Participants' ideas of what constitutes good journalism largely come from socialization in the field—education, newsroom structure, and culture. This socialization then interacts with journalists' own reflexivity about their own identifications. Considering the individual journalists' racial identification as well as the transforming journalistic landscape, this section discusses how journalists relate to news norms. We begin by discussing the dominant paradigm of news in the modern era.

For much of the history of modern journalism, especially in the United States, fact-based, informational reporting has been the hallmark of good journalism. In a widely quoted phrase, seasoned journalist-scholars Kovach and Rosenstiel (2001, 17) claim, "The purpose of journalism is to provide people with the information they need to be free and self-governing." Kovach and Rosenstiel (2001) address other important functions of journalism such as serving as a place of public conversation and offering voices to the voiceless, but what's emphasized in the quote is the importance of journalism in providing accurate and reliable information to citizens.[1] For many, that is the very basic value of journalism—serving as the chronicler of society and providing information to citizens so that they can make informed decisions in their lives.

This mode of journalism, which is the most dominant understanding of what journalism should be, is also known as the trustee or informational model because journalists' key function is to work as a trustee of a busy public and to provide them with important daily facts and information. In doing so, journalists engage in truth-seeking that will enlighten the public. A natural extension of this informational model is the idea of the monitorial press, or watchdog, which claims that the press should bring critical information about any dysfunction of the state and the market to the public's attention. The trustee-informational model of journalism is in line with modern liberal democracy's core tenet that considers popular representation as the utmost value. In liberal democracy, political representatives make decisions on their constituents' behalf since the public does not have the time or resources to do so—what the public needs to care the most about is voting. Likewise, journalists in trustee journalism become citizens' representatives, monitoring the powers-that-be and providing information and facts to citizens (Min 2018).

Trustee-informational journalism, however, is just one model of journalism, a product of a particular historical and cultural context. Chalaby (1996) argues that the rise of journalism as "fact-centered discursive practices" and its normative values are uniquely an Anglo-American invention, as the press in the United States and Britain developed in a market-based capitalist economy and also independently from the literary field in the nineteenth century. Such emphasis on fact-based reporting practices did not exist in other countries where facts and opinions were often mixed in journalism (Chalaby 1996). In other words, the trustee-informational model began as a modern invention specifically tied to the economic, political, and cultural conditions of the United States, and to a lesser degree, Britain, at the time. These specific Anglo-Saxon conditions are also the products of the Enlightenment. As Schudson (2018, 28–29) argues:

> Journalism, as we have come to think of it and as we have come to value it over the past two centuries, partakes of and has been shaped by the spirit of the Enlightenment. The Enlightenment held a heady and overconfident view that

permanent solutions to all problems of knowledge could be achieved through objective methods and rational procedures. . . . I think it is fair to say that journalism—as a particular practice aimed at contributing truths to public discourse, and discussion and criticism in relation to governments—still generally holds to the liberating optimism of Enlightenment aspirations.

The Enlightenment in the West in the eighteenth century argued for individual autonomy and rationality and adopted the scientific method as the source of knowledge production. Modern journalism also adopted a similar framework, and its ideal of fact-based, objective reporting to maintain public discourse in society is tied to the ideology of the Enlightenment and liberal democracy.

Consistent with the ideals of modern trustee-informational journalism, several reporters in the study named "truth-seeking" as the essence of journalistic practice. While the concern for truth is nearly universally shared among the participants, it is a contested concept. Some believe that truth exists to be discovered while others problematize positivistic, singular truth and argue for multiple truths. Given the criticisms of White news discussed in chapter 3, those who do not recognize news to be raced as White have less reason to scrutinize its norms, and, as such, reporters who do not have activated, salient racial identifications adopt a positivist notion of truth.

> When we do our job well, we are only reporting the facts, and that's not to say that we don't make mistakes and that's not to say that we don't editorialize from time to time. But, you know, when it comes down to it, we are trying to report the truth, and I think that for me growing up, being truthful and being honest and being factually focused on facts was very important to me as a person.—Brian

> I just think we're supposed to gather as much information as we can and let the viewers make an informed decision. I think that sometimes we go too much into the advocacy side, and I think a lot of times, we just need to let facts speak for themselves. So, if someone did X, Y, and Z actions, and you know that were correct or that were corrupt, or whatever, then we can just say this is what they did X, Y, and Z and let the readers decide what they think about that person in this situation. Just let the facts speak for themselves and let the readers decide from there.—Kate

Brian's use of the definite article "the" before truth indicates that he believes truth is singular. Equally as important, he equates truth to fact; thus, the straightforward reporting of facts is an articulation of truth and, thus, the moral obligation of a good journalist. Kate, likewise, suggests that truth is self-revelatory even if she only implicitly references truth. For both, facts and truth are presented as essentially interchangeable. In both cases, there is also little recognition of the role of storytelling, framing, gatekeeping, and the "news net" that shape which facts are mentioned and the interpretation of those facts (Tuchman 1978). Brian's and Kate's understanding of truth-seeking in journalism through facts is in line with mainstream journalism, which considers facts and information as its foremost value.

The trustee-informational model of journalism is associated with a positivist worldview and scientific thinking. In positivism, it is assumed that truth is "out there" and that it can be discovered by scientific methods—the heart of which is objectivity. To obtain objective truth, journalists' prescribed form of communication is "detachment," or a civil and reasoned communication devoid of emotions (Ferree et al. 2002). This "objectivity paradigm" in journalism has become the dominant model that guides journalistic tasks (Reese 1990). Key features of the objectivity paradigm are separating facts from opinions, presenting an emotionally detached view of the news, and striving for fairness and balance (Dennis and Merrill 1984). Most journalism textbooks and training in the United States adopt this objectivity paradigm. Mindich (2000), for example, finds that journalism textbooks break down objectivity into five major components: detachment, with a focus on the facts over a reporter's preconception; nonpartisanship, where reporters provide both sides of a story; inverted pyramid, where the most important facts come at the top of a story; naive empiricism, which reflects a reliance on facts in reporting the truth accurately; and balance, a goal that leads to fair reporting.

Beyond the philosophy of positivist science, the objectivity paradigm arose for a variety of other reasons. Scholars suggest that objectivity in U.S. journalism began between the mid-nineteenth and early twentieth centuries through the professionalization of the journalistic occupation (Schudson 1978), newspapers' attempts to become non-partisan to reach heterogenous audiences to maximize profits (Baldasty 1992), and the wire technology that promoted a terse and "objective" style of news writing (Carey 1989). Following the free press's enshrinement in the Bill of Rights, this model of journalism has also been regarded as the best ideal for modern liberal democracy due to its maintenance of critical distance from authorities and its elevation of facts and balance needed for democratic discourse (Kaplan 2009).

Despite becoming journalistic "commonsense," however, there are numerous well-known criticisms of the objectivity paradigm. They include the critique that (1) objective journalism is morally irresponsible because it hides and legitimates immorality by presenting it as an equally valid perspective (Glasser 1992); (2) objectivity itself is a form of bias that is oriented toward event, official, and "negative" news, which is less attentive to the voices and life-worlds of the working class and people of color (Gitlin 1980); and (3) philosophically, the separation of facts from values is not possible nor desirable (Anderson, Dardenne, and Killenberg 1994). In addition to these criticisms, we argue that the objectivity paradigm is also *raced*. As suggested above, journalistic objectivity has been a specifically Anglo-Saxon ideal tied to White masculine rationality. This is a critique that is only made implicitly by previous scholarship. For example, Gitlin (1980) argues that objectivity reflects the experiences of news executives and elite sources, who frame news to be compatible with the main institutional arrangements of society. As Omi and Winant (1994) argue with their theory of racial formations, U.S. society has been historically structured with race as not a peripheral organizing feature but, rather, as its primary organizing feature. Thus, news that relies on elite sources will necessarily reflect the legacy of racial formations and White racial hegemony. Thus, race is structured into policy and social practice.

If this is the case, then it is necessary to understand how White racial hegemony functions. Since the Civil Rights era, it generally has not used overt ideologies of White biological and cultural superiority that mandate a natural order and God-given right to dominate people of color. This view has become mostly socially unacceptable (Bonilla-Silva 2010b). However, White supremacy's legacies are still intact, albeit in more complicated and ambivalent forms, operating through colorblind racism and Whiteness. Scholars note that Whiteness operates by remaining "unmarked," or invisible (Dyer 1997; Nakayama and Krizek 1995; Oh 2012; Jackson 1999; Oh 2022). Dyer (1988) writes that Whiteness is paradoxically represented as nothing and everything. Whiteness is unmarked, and its unmarked quality allows it to be anything. For instance, there are few racial stereotypes of *all* White people, regardless of nation, region, class, special interest, etc., that are widely known like there are for people of color. This invisibility allows White people to be anything, particularly in representation, including samurais, Native Americans, and yogis. When it comes to news, it means that White news workers can cover any story or interview any source without their White racial identifications being scrutinized as a potential source of bias. For instance, White reporters cover White politicians, European nations, White business leaders, and predominantly White suburbs without editorial or audience concern that they cannot cover the stories fairly. Claiming neutrality and a detached, invisible position in reporting is akin to how Whiteness maintains an invisible yet privileged position in society (Dolan 2011).

This critique of the objectivity norm being steeped in White normativity, and fact-based, informational reporting being inadequate to pursue truth was mentioned by roughly half of the participants. Cross-referencing their critique with their understandings of Asian American identification (see chapter 2), it is those whose racial identifications run parallel to, and not conflated with, their ethnic identities who problematize the journalistic commonsense of the objectivity paradigm of news. Thus, criticisms of objectivity primarily emerged from racial standpoints. Having a distinct, meaningful racial identification is situated in racial reflexivity, which, arguably, produces a discursive position through which objectivity is recognized as de facto advancing White racial perspectives in news and White practices in the newsroom. In other words, racial identification is the cognitive scaffolding required to see "neutral" news processes as formed within and structured by White racial hegemony. In fact, there was only one exception—with Felix, who identifies racially as Asian American but for whom racial identification is not persistent and salient. He said, "You know, now that I think a lot of newsrooms are facing this sort of reckoning over what is considered by us . . . reporters of color bring significantly different perspectives to the picture than others." Even then, he does not advance his own critique of objectivity directly but only implies his support for this belief.

Journalists whose primary identifications are *ethnic* rather than racial mostly desire to conceive objectivity differently. Drawing upon available discourses within the journalism profession, they cite norms of "fairness" and "impartiality" as more important than objectivity. For example, Tara said, "What does objectivity mean? I mean, I think it means being fair, and when telling a story, getting different sides to a story and trying to stay impartial, and whether or not you agree or disagree with the topic, telling it fairly regardless." As such, Tara reframes objectivity to focus on fairness. The goal, then, for journalists to discover truth is not to eliminate their own subjectivity but, rather, to provide fairness in representation. This view recognizes that avoiding subjectivities and biases is not possible or maybe even desirable in reporting, and it could even have a social justice component if fairness is tied to the idea of empowering the voices and subjectivities of the powerless. That being said, Tara's idea of fairness, conceptualized as presenting different sides in a balanced manner, still largely operates adjacent to the powerful objectivity paradigm. Discourses about journalistic norms over the years have evolved from a narrow conceptualization of objectivity and neutrality toward a foregrounding of "accuracy," "balance," and "fairness." But these concepts still involve a separation of reporters' perspectives from the events covered, a "separation that is so rigid that it is the equivalent of erasure, the eradication of the reporter's position from the reporting" (Durham 1998, 119).

Journalists who have salient, activated *racial* identifications challenge objectivity, because their newsroom experiences affirm that objectivity is unable to provide fair and truthful coverage of Asian Americans and other communities of color. Instead of merely looking at objectivity differently, they actively challenge objectivity, either to redefine it or, in some cases, to subvert it. For racially activated journalists, their responses varied from race-neutral, postmodern questions about objectivity to overt claims that it is a practice that reifies White racial hegemony in the news. Jennifer, Nina, and Ivan were particularly insistent that objectivity is an impossibility because it is not consistent with how people interact with and make sense of the world. Jennifer said,

> I think that's where I say that objectivity, I don't know what that means. I don't even, like, no, we humans are not objective. We just are not and so how can you even pretend you're like a robot? I mean, that concept is hard for me to understand. And, I think that's the idea that was used over decades and decades to ignore the stories of a lot of people, and, so, I think that's harmful.

Jennifer's argument not only questions a practice that denies human emotion and perspective, but she claims that this practice of objectivity has been used as a way to hide the perspectives, emotional lives, and experiences of marginalized communities. As such, objectivity is understood as a hypocritical practice—a guise of neutrality in order to not be neutral. Ivan presented a similar view: "We just gotta realize that neutrality in itself has been used by power with power to say, 'Oh, this is the way that journalism should be.' The way journalism should be is that it should empower people without power." This does not mean that Ivan ignores elite, powerful sources but that he incorporates into his practice the search for many different perspectives in order to provide a collage of truths of an event. It is not a counter-hegemonic, oppositional practice to write against, but it is mildly resistive because it writes alongside. It does not decenter Whiteness but it expands the horizons of whose voices matter. Similarly, Nina said, "There is a point of view because I'm a human writing something, like, there is no such thing as a completely objective story. But the point of view should be informed by a lot of research. You talk to experts, you read, you try to consider points of view that are not your own." Thus, for some racially activated Asian American journalists, objectivity is a fiction that maintains status quo power relationships, and it is best countered with multiple perspectives and attempts to be well-informed.

Jennifer and Ivan additionally question the practice because it requires a loss of humanity. Ivan said, "The most important part about being a journalist is being human." As Jennifer clarifies, this argument is not merely stating an obvious truth, but it is a dismantling of the idea of being dispassionate or, as she said earlier, being "a robot." Her following quotes are instructive.

> You know, for example, there's been many interviews, especially after COVID but even before that, many stories that I've done, where an interview subject that I talked to would start crying, experiencing some really profound and sad moment, and I would, if I sit there, and I'm like, I'm like, emotionless and unable to sympathize or empathize with that person, then as a human being, I've already failed. . . . And, so, I think for me, it's, it's about being a human being first and then telling the story from that perspective, and so, you know,

I don't have a problem crying with my source. I don't have a problem sympa-
thizing with my source, and I don't, I've never been accused of not being
objective, and I don't like that word objective, anyway.

Jennifer's comments together reflect a subjective position that understands the
experience of the marginalized and the harms caused when institutions of
power, including journalism, objectify the people they cover and serve.
Although the quotes above do not specifically mention specific powerful
groups, she signals this with her discussion of who advances objectivity. Jennifer
continued: "What you're told by White reporters in journalism school is all
keep your emotions out of it, keep your personal feelings out of it, but I think
sometimes, that makes for better, when you're able to, like, feel something and
experience something together with somebody that you're telling the story
about. I think that makes the storytelling more powerful." In addition to her
direct criticism of journalism schools as places that advance the racialized training of White instructors, she implies that there is a shared White racial subjectivity that benefits from objectivity. It hides White racial hegemony, which
makes it more attractive, even if implicitly so to White reporters and editors.
Where Jennifer makes this criticism implicit, others address it directly.

> Then it becomes a question of like, well, who came up with the idea that if
> you're from the community, it actually undermines your credibility, rather than
> enhancing how you understand it. Generally, it is White reporters who came
> up with it because journalism historically has been a very White institution in
> this country.—Rose

> Yeah, there's a problem with that because that's a very White male perspective,
> because they're kind of the arbiters of what is objective and, then, you get into
> these weird, horrible situations where they're like, you know, if you take that to
> a certain extreme, then you can be like, what's going on in Pittsburgh, like, 'Oh,
> you're Black, you can't cover you.' But no one, would ever say, 'Oh, you're a
> taxpayer, you shouldn't be able to write about Congress raising taxes.' Like, no.
> It's just ridiculous.—Mark

Pointing to their own experiences of being marginalized as unprofessional and
the conversations about Black American reporters covering Black Lives Matter,
including the infamous *Pittsburgh Post-Gazette* case mentioned earlier in this
chapter, they all point to a similar conclusion—White managers mark the race
of journalists of color as sources of possible bias while hiding that White journalists' racial identifications also substantiate a racial standpoint. Instead of
arguing for White identities to be similarly marked, they point to the absurdi-
ties and arbitrary double standards of the objectivity paradigm in practices that

favor White interests. As Robinson and Culver (2019, 78) argue, "Objectivity and other hegemonic practices have reified a system of White supremacy for a White community that traditional Western reporters are not only a part of, but reporting for and within."

Likewise, Sophia agrees with the idea that White-normative objectivity in newsrooms is a taken-for-granted assumption. In the context of the *Pittsburgh Post-Gazette* case, she said that the same objectivity standard does not apply to White reporters: "I don't think a White person was ever asked, 'Oh, hey, can you cover one of those open up rallies? You know, one of those rallies about protesting stay-at-home orders or coronavirus restrictions.' You wouldn't tell a White reporter, 'Oh, hey, can you cover that fairly when most of the people who attend these are White people?' It's the same thing, right? It's White people covering White people. Like no one ever says that about White people. Like no one says, 'Hey, can you cover X event where everything, everyone is predominantly White?'" As she argues, neither the news event nor the White reporter is racially marked. Implicitly, an opposition is constructed in which news that involves people of color is racialized but news that involves White people is not so that anyone, including White reporters, can cover the latter without accusations of bias. Thus, the questions of who is biased, what is biased, or how objectivity is practiced are argued to emerge from a White racial standpoint.

Hannah is particularly forceful in her criticism, saying that "objectivity is a myth because objectivity is the lens that White supremacy uses to beat other people's perspectives down." The use of the word "myth" is particularly informative. As a racialized *myth* rather than a mere fiction, it functions to reify White racial hegemony by smoothing over contradictions (Campbell 1995). Butterworth (2007), for instance, claims that racial mythologies construct heroic White figures and villainous people of color. Though that claim does not find direct parallel in this case as it is not simply the White reporter and the reporter of color who are positioned in these roles, the function of the myth constructs the "good" journalist as the person who is guided by the (White) objectivity paradigm. Rhetorically, Hannah challenges this mythological configuration directly by casting the Whiteness of objectivity into the antagonist's role.

A huge pet peeve of mine is when people are, like, journalism is objective. No, it's not, like stop. Just stop. It is not. The only reason that we say that is because, like in every career path, whether it's journalism or not, White supremacy has made the standard. Objectivity just means the White perspective, and that's why, you see, these issues with food publications and journalism publications, where it's like, you have these White people writing recipes that they have no idea about.

Thus, Hannah changes the equation from detachment equals good, objective journalism, to detachment equals bad, uninformed journalism. From this perspective, the trustee-informational model of journalism is inadequate to pursue truth because of its racialized blinders. Instead, a subjectivity in which journalists draw from a deep well of knowledge about a community is seen as producing more nuanced and truthful news. Having a lack of personal knowledge is seen as not leading to truth but distorting it with ignorance and misinformation. Thus, objectivity becomes a barrier rather than a vehicle to truth.

Moving away from the more abstract White perspective to White journalists themselves, Jennifer positions White journalists as incompetent when they cover communities of color because of their lack of understanding, and she positions detachment as detrimental because it produces flawed coverage.

When you see that White people, White journalists are continuously failing at covering issues that have anything to do with people of color, you realize like something's missing there. You know, this idea of objectivity is actually detrimental, because they are such foreigners to what people of color experience. They come in, and they're like, 'Oh, I am an objective person because I don't have any personal experience about this.' You come in and you make all sorts of assumptions. You don't know the questions to ask.

In her argument, White reporters are practicing news from a White subjective racial standpoint but fail to understand this, thus truth is hidden. The objectivity paradigm's normative Whiteness hides White racial interests and obscures, trivializes, and marginalizes communities of color while escaping criticism. This is evident in the practice of seeking predominantly White elite sources and official government documents that they believe to be tied to legitimate fact, reason, and objectivity; this sustains Whiteness and relegates the experiences and perspectives of people of color to the margins (Dolan 2011).

Questioning Objectivity

If not objectivity, then other norms are necessary for the professionalization of journalism and to evaluate quality. Toward this purpose, journalism scholars and practitioners have identified other important norms such as transparency, interactivity, and fairness. "Transparency," in which journalists truthfully disclose news processes, before, during, or after, so that the audience can see how the story came to be and why it was presented as it was, has recently become an important part of journalistic value sets (Singer 2007; Vos and Craft 2017). With the assumption that truth is multiple and layered, "interactivity" constitutes another important journalistic norm because truth can emerge through interactions between journalists and the public. Interactivity allows news stories to be rearranged and challenged, and a greater variety of voices and different competing descriptions of events can be heard (Karlsson 2011). "Fairness," as briefly discussed in the previous section, is not a very well-developed concept, but it generally refers to the idea that journalists must minimize biases in reporting by being balanced and providing multiple perspectives of a story (Weber 2016).

In this study, we found that journalists who have an activated racialized standpoint are especially geared toward the position that truth is multiple and layered and that journalistic objectivity is not capable of obtaining truth. On the contrary, journalists without a salient racial standpoint tend to be more comfortable with the objectivity norm. For example, Larry takes a moderated view of race—familiar with and generally comfortable in White American spaces while recognizing the existence of structural racism. With his relative lack of a critical racial standpoint, he takes an "old school" position in his commitments to objectivity. He said:

> I've known political reporters that refuse to vote in general elections because if you let it, it taints their objectivity. It might be a generational thing, but that is very much an old-fashioned way of thinking but one that, kind of, has that sort of simplistic appeal to a lot of people. . . . In general, it's kind of a long, almost second nature now. You know, I voted in the [presidential] election, but I won't vote in the primary. I won't give money to a candidate or put a yard sign in my yard. I don't generally tweet anything that can be viewed as political.

Larry simultaneously distances and claims objectivity. He references political reporters' choice to not vote in order to maintain fidelity to objectivity as simplistic and antiquated, but he also points to his own comfort with objectivity, albeit in a negotiated, less rigid form, i.e., his compromise on voting. Larry's mild support of objectivity reflects his decades of socialization in traditional newsroom spaces that valorize the objectivity paradigm with his interaction with increasingly diverse, upcoming journalists, who are more willing to challenge the journalistic status quo.

Many of the racially activated journalists in our study question the valorized legacy of journalistic objectivity and attempt to reframe it. They drew upon available discourses in the journalistic tradition in order to forge new norms for "good" journalism. For instance, they turned to ideas of professionalism such as accuracy, investigative reporting, storytelling, and the Fourth Estate's role of empowering the powerless and holding the powerful accountable. The point is that reporters are not engaging subversive tactics to overturn the journalistic status quo but are working *within* existing journalistic discursive formations to re-center desirable journalistic practice by emphasizing existing values. In this sense, the goal is a shift rather than a rupture.

Rose's case illustrates the above point. In her story about Japanese internment camps during the Second World War, Rose tried to avoid using the official term, "internment," because the term is euphemistic. It does not represent the horrific experiences of the Japanese Americans who were incarcerated. For Rose, simply accepting the official version and terminology is not truth-seeking. Truth, instead, is discovered by examining different worldviews and how they are tied to the existing social order and power. As a reporter with a critical racial consciousness, she recognizes that word choices and language are loaded with ideological meaning. Resisting elite framing for what she understands as a more truthful, accurate description is both a means of enacting racial awareness and of reporting more truthfully. Such an idea was espoused by other journalists, as well. Gwyneth says she strives for truth in her work, but it cannot be obtained by objective, fair, and balanced reporting: "I've been thinking about these things because in this particular era that we're in, when there's so much misinformation and outright lies, fair and balanced doesn't cut it, whereas truth offers so much clarity. . . . If you get the side of the White supremacist, do you give that person equal time? When it comes to racism, is there the other side?" Thus, for Gwyneth, pursuing objectivity obscures, rather than discovers, truth. She referenced President Trump's words, which were said just ten days after George Floyd's death on May 25, 2020. Trump said, "Hopefully George is looking down right now and saying this is a great thing that's happening for our country. It's a great day for him. It's a great day for everybody."[2] Gwyneth said that inserting such a quote "doesn't jibe with the truth." Instead, she says she believes that "the truth is, he [Trump] is a White supremacist." As such, Gwyneth contends that journalists should use their judgment and interpretation to reveal truth.

Hannah used a similar example of denying voice to White supremacists, but her response differs for two reasons. First, she points to the reason for denying the platform as specifically rooted in a history of racist harm, and, second, she clarifies that her role is not only to deny but to affirmatively include. Providing a hypothetical, she said:

> If you wanted, you could write a story about race and interview someone from the KKK and give them the same exact voice as someone else, and I find that incredibly irresponsible. They're a hate group. Like, don't give them a voice. They're actively contributing to pain, suffering, violence, and all this brokenness that's happening in the community. Don't interview them, but someone who would argue for objectivity would say, like, oh, but they're the other side. No, that's not the other side. That is a voice that you don't need to amplify, and you should choose not to do that. I think that's just very important, like being fair is being fair to your readers, being fair to your community, being fair to where the direction of society is going, being fair in the choices you're making, the decisions that you're making every day covering a story and covering your topic, whatever beat that you're doing, and also being fair to,

like, the history of the country, and the struggles of people that have been marginalized.

Like Gwyneth, Hannah argues that it is not newsworthy to include clearly racist points of view, but she emphasizes and adapts the question of what counts as fair. Gwyneth views fairness from the perspective of what an appropriate oppositional point of view is, while Hannah views it from the perspective of historical marginalization and harm. As such, her view of fairness moves closer to equity. Indeed, elsewhere in the interview, she said, "I think being fair is really important, and I think being right is not only, like, evaluating who you're talking to, but how you're approaching a topic. I think there is this lie in journalism that you have to get both sides, but I think that as a journalist, you make a choice whose voices to uplift and which voices to amplify and you make those choices every single day for every single story." As such, she does not consider questions of fairness from the perspective of dispassionate impartiality but, rather, from an awareness of the community and how news can be inclusive and provide "fair" representation. Similarly, Sophia said, "Just because you have a story where you cover both sides doesn't necessarily mean that it was accurate or fair. It means that you checked the boxes for that story, and so I think that's where I think it's played out for me more, because it's just like realizing those voices have been underrepresented historically." Having an activated racial identification, Sophia challenges the status quo idea that fairness is inclusion of "both sides." Her point seems to take into consideration arguments about false equivalence, pointing to the limitations of objectivity as a technical practice of fairness rather than an ethical one (Glasser 1992). As such, Hannah, Sophia, and Gwyneth redefine what counts as fair and argue for the affirmative inclusion of marginalized communities. This understanding of fairness operates under a logic of equity rather than neutrality. For racially activated reporters like Hannah, Sophia, and Gwyneth, fairness is not just simple impartiality and the inclusion of multiple perspectives.

Moving further from the objectivity paradigm, several reporters sought to include marginalized members of the community in order to create social change. This desire to highlight the struggles of marginalized U.S. Americans draws upon muckraking and the Fourth Estate as esteemed journalistic traditions in order to humanize and uplift. Although they did not name these traditions specifically, the resonances with their comments are clear. Ivan, for instance, said succinctly that "journalism is a way to power, empower people who are powerless." Hannah extended this argument further:

> I do think that a big part of journalism is keeping society, powers that be accountable. And there's always been a social justice component to journalism, whether it's investigating fraud in the government, or whether it's writing

about a recipe by a West African grandmother, whether it is writing about the environment and climate change and talking to experts, whether it is covering schools and what it means to give children an education and what the right and wrong ways of doing . . . If that is our mission and goal as journalists to not only provide a record but to create change, I think those are good motives.

By referencing "social justice" specifically, she discursively resists conservative vilification of social justice, and, in particular the mocking moniker of the "social justice warrior" (see Massanari and Chess 2018). Instead, she links to activism that seeks feminist, anti-racist, queer, and class inclusion. In the tension between objectivity and the inherent subjectivity of the watchdog as working on behalf of the powerless, she chooses the watchdog, which might be argued to be a journalistic tradition that allows for the possibility of anti-racist standpoints and affirmative Asian American reporting.

For some scholars, equity-inflected journalism might be understood as "advocacy journalism." According to Charles (2019), it is a more active approach to journalism that is focused on leading the public toward solutions to societal problems. In a quest for a social change, advocacy journalists often rebuff the principles of objectivity and impartiality in favor of sincerity and other values. Although advocacy journalism is demonized for being like propaganda, contemporary scholars argue that the binary opposition of objectivity and advocacy is a false dichotomy (Bachmann 2019). Fisher (2016), for instance, claims that advocacy exists in all journalism because decision-making and news routines lead to the inclusion of some news items at the exclusion of others. Framing scholars have long pointed out that the angle of a story can also shape meaning, often to the detriment of marginalized groups and less powerful nations (Correa 2010; Douai and Lauricella 2014; Entman and Rojecki 1993; Gandy 1994; Kumar 2010; Liebler, Schwartz, and Harper 2009).

That said, it should be emphasized that only a handful of journalists in this study even consider an advocacy framework. Most of the reporters strongly rejected the suggestion that this practice could be understood as advocacy, and this points to a site of discursive struggle to define. One of the primary reasons for this dissociation is because advocacy is understood to be about taking positions on issues. For several journalists, their objective is to tell their stories and report on issues that matter to these communities but not to take sides on those issues. Instead, the goal is to report with complexity and truthfulness. In other words, moving beyond the gatekeeping and agenda-setting function is the line by which many reporters believe their work would cross into undesirable advocacy.

I mean, the basics of journalism is to do no harm and benefit the community that you serve, and the Asian American community is part of the community that our paper serves. It's the case for many newsrooms, and I think what I do is, it's promoting that basic tenet of journalism ethics. I don't know if I see that necessarily as advocacy.—Ethan

I don't see it as advocacy journalism because I'm not trying to advocate for any specific cause. Also, because I think advocacy journalism leaves out room for critical journalism, which is also important in covering any community, especially the Asian community.—Rose

For Ethan, then, colorblindness is not the goal because it leads to inequality. Rather, race consciousness that promotes equitable coverage is considered ethical and fair. Rose also clarifies that inclusion does not equate to uncritical, glowing coverage. As she defines critical journalism, it is an investigative practice that can point to injustices and harms, including those caused by members of marginalized communities themselves. Therefore, the rejection of advocacy is not merely a question of semantics but also a cultural question about what is normatively acceptable as Asian American reporters negotiate multiple tensions—equitable coverage, truth-seeking, and watchdog roles for accountability.

I think I would not agree with the characterization of what I do as advocacy in a sense that, yeah, I'm always pushing for more coverage of the [Asian American] communities and, and fair coverage of its communities, but I don't see myself as advocating for, you know, specific policy or specific benefits to the community. I do, however, try to get as close to the ground as possible and tell stories pertaining to Asian Americans as their reality. You know, like telling the story of, like, Asian American immigrants; that's something actually happening that American media has ignored for many centuries.—Jennifer

I'm not beating people over the head or something, like, I'm not part of something, you know, part of an advocacy group or whatever. Yeah, it's a little bit of a sticky area at times.—Clara

Despite some similarity with advocacy defined by scholars as part of a continuum of journalistic practice, the broad rejection of this label is likely because advocacy implies that the journalist's primary goal is to provide solutions rather than to seek truth. The journalists interviewed believe it is up to others to decide what to do with the truths that are reported. Indeed, the concern seems to be that advocacy might even obscure truth to present a group more favorably.

Advocacy also produces negative connotations in the profession, especially in mainstream media where objective-informational reporting is still the norm. Journalists of color are already scrutinized for potential bias, so reporting in ways that management and editors interpret as advocacy would be professionally fraught, and identifying as such would be even more so (Nishikawa et al. 2009). Indeed, even though a handful of the journalists in our study specialize in community and race reporting, they do not think of themselves as advocacy journalists. Instead, they navigate an in-between space between objectivity and advocacy. As Waisbord (2009, 375) observed, "More than impartial reporters of reality or passionate political advocates, journalists often perform balancing acts between personal politics and newsroom Realpolitik, clutching to professional principles and observing editorial expectations." The balance for journalists whose racial identifications are activated is limited to standpoint—what news is seen as valuable and what news can be gathered—but not to framing and the investigation of "truth."

Even when journalists accept the label, it is partial and the practice of it is similar to that of Jennifer and Rose. Amy, for instance, said:

> For me, I see my role kind of almost as an advocacy role a lot of times. I think that Asian Americans are not often elevated in media, and the issues that we face as Asian Americans are not often covered because there are not a lot of us. And so I often see my role as just being a community connector and elevating those stories and so I took it upon myself to really diversify the voices, to really like dig to find people who looked like me, both for my own sense of community and also because I think that it's important that [the news] has a diversity of voices on the air.

More than the reporters above, Amy explicitly connects her news work to her own racial identity, but it is important to emphasize that although she is more willing to make a claim to advocacy, what she asks for is similar to other reporters in the study, who believe that finding stories in Asian American communities and giving voice to everyday Asian Americans is important in reconciling their racial identification with their work as journalists. In this way, the advocacy is restricted to news gathering. It is important to note that these journalists do not view their work to mean being advocates for Asian Americans but to tell stories about Asian Americans truthfully and completely while avoiding racist tropes and stereotypes. Sometimes, these stories challenge dominant narratives of U.S. Americanness and, sometimes, they present the ugliness and abuses within Asian American communities.

Among those with salient racial identifications, Olivia has perhaps the most cynical view of objectivity and offers a counter viewpoint to avoid objectivity's pitfalls while practicing good journalism. That is, instead of trying to eradicate biases, she attempts to acknowledge and incorporate her subjectivities into the structure of the journalistic process. This resonates with what Durham (1998) calls "standpoint epistemology" in which journalists use their social locations and identities to openly acknowledge their role in story construction rather than present the illusion of a transparent communication of reality. Olivia said, "I think I get to see things differently from my colleagues. I can, you know, I could be looking at the same phenomenon happening with a White colleague or Black colleague and what we think of it and what we come out of it could be different, just because of our cultural background, our environmental background, and our family upbringings. I'm not saying that I see it better or more holistically than others. I just have a different viewpoint because of my identity." Challenging the notion that facts produce truth, Olivia suggests that different standpoints produce different understandings of the same facts, producing multiple truths. Her clear intersectional identification as an Asian American woman generates an implied need for diverse voices in the newsroom in order for the mosaic of truths to be represented as fully as possible. This also places the objectivity paradigm in direct challenge as it is presented as obscuring truths by presenting them as singular.

Simply acknowledging and expressing biases in news stories may beget epistemic relativism, however. Thus, what is important in standpoint epistemology, as Durham (1998, 134) suggests, is journalists' "reflexivity," or an "examination of social relationships between the knowers and the known, that is, between the journalist, journalistic institutions, the person who would experience marginalization in the context of the news story, and the knowledge claims at stake." Journalists are asked to step out of the privileged positions of investigation and engage with a story from the viewpoints of those most disenfranchised by events. Again, Olivia's case illustrates this point. She said:

> I have a lot of unearned privilege in a lot of ways that a lot of White folks have unearned privilege. I have class privilege, academic privilege, English-speaking, generational, able-bodiedness, and that's not true for all Asian Americans because a lot of Asian Americans are very marginalized in different ways, right? And that's not been my life, and so I feel like, for every one of those privileges comes responsibility, comes an obligation to be honest about those privileges and honest about the ways in which I've had access to things that other people have not. So, I guess the same ways that we challenge White folks to not, you know, center themselves, I think I try to challenge myself, to not center myself in that way, too, because in a lot of ways, like, I have marginalized identities.

Olivia reflects upon her various intersecting social identities and how they shape her approach to news stories. She triangulates her own social positionality with the standpoint of marginalized communities and White racial hegemony. Hers is a reflexive practice that considers social justice and the discursive power of the press.

Conclusion

This chapter looked at how Asian American journalists recognize their racial identities and how they navigate newsrooms largely perpetuated by White perspectives and norms. The analysis of the journalists' views demonstrates their complex, heterogeneous understanding of news as shaped by their different backgrounds, racial reflexivity, and the cultural and socialization processes within their respective newsrooms. Overall, we found that the journalists' racial identifications shaped their support for or resistance to the dominant objectivity paradigm and their interpretation and reframing of mainstream news norms. This goes against the conventional wisdom that such factors as individual journalists' race, gender, and class are insufficient to affect news coverage or newsroom culture, because "structural forces have far more bearing on the nature of the news images than the racial identifications of the personnel" (Entman and Rojecki 2000, 84).

Our analysis found that journalists have agency, albeit limited, in challenging and re-constructing news coverage and norms. It was the reporters who had salient, activated racial identifications who engaged in the reflexivity necessary to recognize and challenge White dominant newsroom culture. On the other hand, those with non-salient or situational racial activation largely followed the objectivity paradigm. Yet, even for those racially reflexive reporters, their oppositional tactics were constrained by existing journalistic discourse and practice (e.g., providing more Asian American sources and correcting stereotypes) rather than radically subverting the news paradigm. Indeed, almost all of the reporters rejected understanding their work as advocacy, although they were passionate about Asian American visibility. This is in line with Meyers and Gayle's (2015) findings about African American women journalists' "resistance tactics" against the dominant journalistic construction of race and gender. They found that Black American women journalists primarily engaged in tactics such as including more Black American sources and role models, challenging and removing Black American stereotypes, encouraging Black American news sources to be camera ready, and educating co-workers and management about racial issues. These are attempts to better "balance" and resist the hegemony of White male perspectives and norms that dominate daily newsroom operations (Rivas-Rodriguez et al. 2004).

Though journalists in mainstream news organizations operate within the boundaries of the hegemonic newsroom system based on profits and professionalized routines that structure their news work and behaviors (Gitlin 1980), we believe it is important to note that counter-hegemonic agency is possible with racial reflexivity and more active resistance among contemporary journalists of color. The hegemonic boundaries still exist but have become a little more porous, here and there.

6

Covering Asian America

• •

Coverage of racial minorities in U.S. media has long been criticized as both inadequate and biased. Historically, representations of minorities are rarer compared to White Americans, and existing representations have often been unfair and demeaning, such as Black American men being more likely to be portrayed as "thugs" and criminals and Asian American men as nerds, foreigners, and sexually emasculated. This has been the case not just for fictional movies and television shows. News media also tend to favor coverage of White people, while perpetuating negative stereotypes of minorities (Dixon and Linz 2000; Min and Feaster 2010). As such, presenting more nuanced and humanizing stories of people of color is important to achieve a more equitable and just news. Thus, the purpose of this chapter is to understand who choose to tell stories of Asian American communities, their goals for telling the stories, and the ways they get these stories in news.

Almost all of the journalists in this study recognized the need for more and better coverage of racial minorities in the United States. They stated the importance of elevating the voices of Asian Americans, who often have been marginalized in mainstream news media. This was true even for reporters whose racial identifications are not salient and who support the objectivity paradigm. The extent to which they were motivated and the kinds of actions they would take differed, but a general consensus was that there is a need to cover more Asian American issues, humanize Asian American communities, and demonstrate that Asian American stories are stories of the United States. The majority of the journalists we interviewed argued that their cultural and racial identities are assets that enable more nuanced, deeper coverage of issues, although they do not go so far as advocating for Asian American communities and promoting Asian American interests. So, instead of eschewing their identities, they leveraged and used them as a lens through which issues and events are understood. The purpose of this chapter, then, is to understand how their racial identifications mattered in their interests in telling Asian American stories and the kinds of stories that they hope to tell.

Racial Identification and Coverage of Asian American Communities

The previous chapter showed how journalists' racial identifications are connected to their re-conceptualization of journalistic norms. Similarly, racial identifications shape their efforts to cover Asian America such that racial activation matters in terms of how they feel about the need to cover Asian American communities. While this is largely true, we observe a more complex dynamic in this case. We find at least some interest among almost all of the participants to cover Asian American issues and communities, but the form that interest takes varies largely by identity position.

First, journalists who do not have salient racial identifications are generally ambivalent about covering Asian American stories. If, like any other story, it conforms to usual standards of newsworthiness, then they would not *mind* covering the stories. Their interest in covering Asian American stories is passive, meaning that they do not seek out stories or leverage their knowledge of Asian American communities to produce enterprising stories. However, this is not true for all reporters who identify in this way. For instance, Felix draws upon his lived experience and knowledge, even though he generally supports the objectivity paradigm and generally does not think about racial identification in everyday life. He said:

> I cannot ignore the fact that I am an Asian American reporter, but first and foremost, I am a reporter. But I do try to, I mean, bring some of my own perspective to the coverage. So, for example, I think there's just some things that you get as a person of color, a person of any given affinity group, that you might not otherwise know in a story. So, for instance, for me, writing about the coronavirus xenophobia, a lot of the histories, it's stuff that I've picked up over the years through American Studies and also just being an Asian American, so backgrounding, you know, when a politician references Vincent Chin, that's easier for me to write than it would be for someone who didn't know about that, or when a politician talks about, you know, the model minority myth, that's something that I don't have to deliver a whole lot of background on or do a ton of research on.

Thus, what matters is the activation. For instance, although Felix does not think about his racial identification as salient in everyday life, there may be specific contexts, such as covering an Asian American-specific news story, when it becomes activated. Even though racial identification is not persistent, it does not mean it is not present. Identifications are, of course, activated in context-specific ways (Hall 1996a).

Similarly, Quinn wrote a profile about an international student athlete whom he was able to humanize and empathize with because of his own childhood experiences as an immigrant to the United States. In this case, he did not necessarily seek out the story in order to include Asian Americans, but he recognizes how his subjectivity improved the story.

> I know what [the athlete] is referring to. And I can carry a genuine feeling. I feel like it was one of the more intimate conversations and interviews I had with a subject, just because I think I could understand [the athlete]. I remember after the story came out, I talked to [the athlete] for a bit. And [the athlete] was like, "oh, I thank you for writing the story. I'm glad it was you who wrote it." It was because of that connection that we can make.

Although Quinn did not share the same ethnic heritage as the athlete, he was able to form pan-Asian connections because of their shared experience of racial difference in the United States, activating racial identification in that moment. It also could be because it was a feel-good, human-interest story that Quinn felt freer from the usual constraints of objectivity.

For Asian American reporters whose identifications are primarily ethnic, there is not a clear pattern. Brian, for instance, was ambivalent about covering Asian American stories. This is because, historically, roles for journalists of color in major newsrooms have been narrowly defined. In what is known as "pigeonholing," journalists of color are asked to focus on the coverage of minority issues and events, and in what is known as "tokenism," newsrooms hire a limited number of journalists of color to demonstrate their liberal, humanistic credentials without engaging in structural change. These practices have been considered major constraints for journalists of color (Shafer 1993). This is tied to the idea of newsroom economics: Consistent with economic theories of news making (Hamilton 2004), journalists of color are not incentivized to cover racialized issues and tend to conform to mainstream patterns of coverage designed to appeal to majority White audiences (Sui et al. 2018). Without a sufficient profit base and without enough sustained pressure from activists for fair coverage, newsrooms may be less interested in communities of color (Byerly and Wilson 2009). Brian said:

> We don't want to get kind of shoehorned into becoming the Asian story guy, you know, like it's something that I think about a lot, and I don't want to only

cover stories in Asia. Hey, you know, I think that my skills are broad. I can cover any story, and I think they would all be within my wheelhouse, you know. So, these are stories I'm passionate about, but they're not the only thing that I want to do within my career, and I think that's something that a lot of people who work in news think about, too. I don't pitch as much as I do because I don't want to become known as the Asian guy, the guy who only covers Asian stories, and then I think there are some people within my company, or in my show, who are okay with that, who want us to cover only those types of stories. But for me, I have higher aspirations than just covering race.

Brian's comments demonstrate the tensions many Asian American journalists experience in newsrooms. Although Brian strongly identifies with his ethnic heritage, he demonstrates the internalized newsroom valorization of racelessness. In other words, the logic of the newsroom is that covering an ethnic or racial community is narrow and devalued while being "raceless" is broad and valued. This, too, obscures the Whiteness of colorblind ideologies in the newsroom such that covering powerful White institutions and elites is understood as providing cultural capital in the newsroom. As demonstrated in chapter 3, colorblindness is ideological cover that reifies White racial hegemony in the newsroom. This is problematic because it means that Brian has to deny not only his personal interests but his own racial identification in order to be valued by his peers, who operate under the White cultural logics of the newsroom.

What else is interesting about the quote is that Brian switches pronouns from "we" to "I." It appears that his use of "we" in the first sentence might signal an imagined desire to draw other Asian American reporters into association with him as a way of gaining strength for his position. This suggests that he subconsciously believes that the argument needs rhetorical reinforcement, perhaps because of an implicit understanding that his viewpoint might be challenged. Another interesting point is that Brian is the only reporter to elide Asian American with Asian. The reason for this is unclear, but one possibility is that because Brian's identifications are primarily ethnic, his views of Asian Americans are largely through a Chinese lens. Another possibility is that if he used the same construction of not wanting to be the "Asian American guy" rather than the "Asian guy," then this would be a more obvious denial of his own embodied identification, a claim that would seem more problematic.

While Brian understands other Asian American reporters as operating from the same space of ambivalence, this was not true for other reporters, at least in this study, not even for those who primarily identify ethnically. For instance, Ethan volunteers when there are Asian American stories to write, despite it being apart from his ordinary beat. It may be, indeed, that it is precisely because Asian Americans are not part of his usual beat that he is provided more freedom to cover these stories without the concerns of pigeonholing that Brian has shared. Ethan said, "I enjoy it. I think it is what I came to journalism for. It is to tell the stories of people whose stories have not been told that much from the point of mainstream media. It's just that I have a mindset. If I'm not the one telling those stories, who will? Because there are not many people who are thinking about these issues in our newsroom, I try to do the best I can to bring that voice into our coverage." As he mentioned elsewhere in the interview, covering Asian American stories is a source of pleasure because he has more confidence that he can cover Asian American communities more accurately and fairly than his White colleagues. He continued, "And, those stories may not get told at all, get told by people from, you know, other communities, you know, the White people who don't have the background, don't have the expertise, don't have the knowledge of the community like you do, and their coverage can be detrimental to the community itself." However, it should be noted that Ethan's volunteering for coverage of Asian American issues still takes place in the confines of the traditional White newsroom, and that he conforms to the norms and culture of it. Ethan offered a defense of his newsroom's inadequate coverage of Asian American communities, saying,

> It is I think most of the times, what the newsroom does in terms of covering the [Asian/minority] community is that it's not intentionally trying to ignore those communities. It's not intentionally trying to harm those communities, but a lot of it comes in an unintentional way because they didn't have the voice and that representation in the newsroom that, you know, is putting a stop to some of the mistakes that the newsroom, um, makes.

This explanation bears similarity to Heider's (2000) account of incognizant racism. Heider argued that White reporters and news managers practice unconscious racial negligence because of a lack of understanding and involvement in communities of color, which leads to problematic coverage. Ethan, who has a salient everyday ethnic but not racial identification, shares this perspective. Racial inactivation matters because it produces a standpoint upon which racist coverage is excused as an unfortunate consequence of personal biases that lack racist intention.

Ethan also navigates his interest in Asian American stories by claiming that it is aligned with his commitment to objectivity, saying that "I disagree with the characterization that, you know, covering your own communities, is something that's not objective." His rejection of the claim that covering his own racial group is not objective appears to be his way of resolving this tension, particularly as his primarily ethnic identification does not make salient the practices of structural racism. Because Asian American reporters with racially activated identifications have largely rejected objectivity as a White news practice, it seems that Ethan's concerns about objectivity are limited to those who do not have salient, everyday racial identifications.

As suggested so far, either ethnic or racial activation can generate an interest and responsibility to tell Asian American stories. However, for the racially activated reporters, their desire and interest to do so are more urgent. For them, reporting on Asian Americans is a chance to humanize and elevate the voices and experiences of members of the Asian American community, a group that they say is largely overlooked or misrepresented, so the social good of their reporting outweighs the possible harms. Ivan, for example, said he doesn't feel tokenized or pigeonholed when he covers Asian American issues. Instead, he said, "One of the things that I have noticed is that I subconsciously or consciously, I think I embrace identity politics a little bit more when it came to news coverage, especially during a time when I was hearing about Asian American businesses and business owners or individuals being discriminated on." Ivan's use of the term "identity politics" signals that he feels solidarity with Asian American communities and desires to empower marginalized Asian American communities through his reporting. It is also important to note his use of an expression that is oftentimes disparaged, thus demonstrating a reclamation of the term; his racial identification and reflexivity generate a desire to uplift Asian American stories. Ivan also provided poignant examples to demonstrate the racist harms in coverage that spur Asian American stories. Referencing the pandemic moment, Ivan said,

> Reporters themselves called it the Wuhan Virus, if my memory serves me correct. Yeah, that was before President Trump's obvious attempt at racializing that virus. I tend to think that the less obvious, in this case, a little less obvious use of that word Wuhan even started to be called Wuhan coronavirus and the type of coverage that we did around that, such as like the heavy coverage around the meat markets, the wet markets.

Particularly as then President Trump's rhetoric has been frequently cited as racializing and politicizing COVID-19 as a foreign, Chinese threat, Ivan turns his critical gaze back on reporters, who contributed to this discursive formation. Scholars and commentators have frequently pointed to former President Trump's White ethnonationalism and racism (Kelly 2020; Sanchez 2018), and, in this context, Ivan's argument suggests that the press, although not as blatantly, also contributes to this discourse. Unlike Ethan, Ivan does not qualify his argument in the language of innocence, i.e., lack of intention.

Similarly, Amy claimed that racist associations are discursively common, referencing *The New York Times*'s coverage of the Asian giant hornet, or what they called, "murder hornet," during the vilification of Asian Americans as carriers of COVID-19. She said, "I still think that it's not being taken seriously enough . . . I think *The New York Times* positioning that specific story, the Asian hornet, without any forethought or thought about how it might make other Asian Americans feel or the fallout of what might happen in the comments section." For Amy, this has to do with her perceptions of Asian American invisibility, particularly the invisibility of anti-Asian racism. Because of this, she claims that newsrooms are not sensitized to nor care about the harms it causes Asian Americans. Referencing her former newsroom as described in chapter 2, she mentioned that her concerns about the exoticizing coverage of a Japanese plant were ignored and that she was marginalized as a malcontent. Olivia also described her annoyance when her newsroom used a photo of masked Asian Americans in early coverage to visualize the coronavirus despite guidance from the AAJA and her own concerns. Although these criticisms were received well, they were forgotten repeatedly.

Despite pigeonholing being reported frequently in studies of journalists of color and the newsroom, our participants did not seem particularly concerned for the most part. The reason for this is unclear. It could be an artifact of sampling self-identified Asian American journalists, or it could be because Asian American reporters have not had ample opportunities to tell Asian American stories or have prestigious foreign bureau assignments such that they would worry about pigeonholing as concerns about invisibility and misrepresentation are more strongly felt. Perhaps, it is because of the historic invisibility of their racial identifications that assertions of it feel more liberatory than stereotyping. Whatever the reason, there was an active interest in telling Asian American stories from racially activated Asian American journalists in the study. Those who discussed the possibility of tokenizing or pigeonholing understood the risks but felt that the circumstances in their newsrooms provided the space to cover Asian American stories. For instance, Rose said, "I thought about the possibility of tokenizing, especially because I'm the only one covering this beat. But I think the line of whether it becomes tokenism or not, I think that's only crossed depending on the kind of coverage that you produce and also the way the newsroom treats you. I don't feel like my position is being tokenized. They don't treat me as the end-all, be-all for Asian American information in the newsroom." When the newsroom culture is supportive and treats journalists of color as being capable reporters who have the same professionalism and same skill set, then she argues that it is not the stories covered that matter but, rather, the treatment received. Looking to the literature on pigeonholing concerns, reporters' concerns are less because of the stories and communities themselves but, rather, racist attitudes about the value of these stories to the newsroom. It is a question of symbolic capital rather than story type. What insulates some of the reporters is that their reporting is broad enough that reporting about Asian Americans is not experienced as an obligation or a constraint but, rather, as an opportunity. As Clara said, "I don't think they would be treating me like the token Asians in the newsroom. Because I've done a lot of stories that aren't and continued to do stories that aren't related all to race issues and in a lot of breaking news stories. I think I have enough respect in those arenas that I won't be perceived that way." Overall, we found that almost all reporters interviewed have some interest in covering stories about Asian American communities. For those who are not racially identified, their approach to coverage is passive, accepting good stories when available; for those who are primarily ethnically activated, specific moments can produce racial activation that catalyzes interest in telling Asian American stories; and for those for whom racial activation is a persistent feature of identification, they express urgency and place importance on telling these stories. Those ethnic and racial identifications may have been further activated and developed during these times of heightened racial awakening in the United States. From Black Lives Matter to hate crimes against Asian Americans, many individuals are keenly aware of the unfolding tense dynamics of race relations in America. Our participants must have captured that, too, consciously or subconsciously.

Telling Asian American Stories

Because there is an interest in covering Asian America, it is important to ask how that translates into actual coverage in the reporters' everyday work. For instance, some research argues that diversifying newsrooms makes only marginal difference to the actual content of news because of strong socializing pressures and gatekeeping in newsrooms (Sui et al. 2018). For this study, we found that Asian American reporters' motivations for wanting to cover Asian American communities are realized into such efforts as redressing problematic coverage and producing more substantive, nuanced, and diverse coverage.

First, the reporters were well aware of White racial hegemony in the newsroom and recognized that their racial awareness, community belonging, and cultural background are assets to improve and diversify coverage. Implicitly referencing the stereotyped coverage of Asian Americans by non-Asian reporters, Rose said, "It'll help my coverage in terms of not tokenizing a community, but understanding where that might be coming from and why they're having certain problems." Also referencing a deeper knowledge of the community, Jennifer said, "I think being able to tell stories about the experiences of my fellow Asian Americans in a nuanced and extensive way that doesn't just like skim the surface, you know, that goes deep into history, that goes deep into culture, that goes deep into psyche, like understanding how people think and why." While describing her relatively better ability to cover Asian Americans, there is an implied criticism of non-Asian American reporters (likely a reference to White reporters given her criticisms of White newsrooms) that their coverage of Asian American communities is incomplete and superficial because of their lack of awareness of the community.

Pointing to reasons Asian American reporters such as himself are able to produce more nuanced coverage, Ivan said:

> Sometimes you don't have time to go look into your Google search and the history of Asian American, different frames of Asian reticence or the model minority myth; you don't have time to look that up and then Pinterest or you just kind of, it helps to already have that, right? Then, to answer your question, I, I tried to approach it in an organic level. If it is against me, I would say, oh, I'm gonna make sure to put it in, put an angle here just like, going back to my Chinese food story, I guess, just thinking about what authentic Chinese food means or what people, what, what they thought about the exotification of food and their Americanization of food, of other ethnic cultures' foods.

Ivan's deeper knowledge of both Asian American communities and his knowledge of U.S. dominant racist frames of Asian American practices are both leveraged in this response. He has knowledge that helps deepen questions in the moment, and he has a racialized lens that produces new angles to explicitly provide counter-hegemonic frames of Asian American exoticization and difference as well as provide sources with opportunities to directly address dominant cultural tropes.

Other reporters argued that they are uniquely able to find new stories because of their knowledge of Asian American communities. Hannah said, "That's why it's important to have someone that is in the community, that can find those stories that are important and show growth and have actually an accurate representation of the community, which they're not doing right now ... So I needed to push for stories that I felt like weren't just like, ew, Chinese people [laughs]." Her last somewhat joking line reveals that it is not only inaccuracy that is criticized but a particular type of racializing inaccuracy that relies on a dominant understanding of Asian Americans, including in this case entrenched racist discourses of Asian Americans as disgusting (Lee 1999). Because of the ubiquity of COVID-19 during this time, Hannah is also likely reacting to the intersection of discourses about dirtiness as well as Asian Americans as carriers of disease (Le et al. 2020; Leong 2003; Mallapragada 2021; Oh 2020). Although Clara is not seeking to challenge racist tropes, she sees it as less necessary for her to cover general community stories.

> I think of trying to find, I mean, cause we have plenty of people to cover how the virus impacts the public at large, but, yeah, I feel like I can always be looking for ways it's impacting the Asian American community or another specific community that, you know, probably does get underrepresented in

news coverage. Yeah, so definitely, for now, I've got, I'm looking through everything through a wider prism or a narrower one, narrowing in on, yeah, Asian American issues.

Far from being concerned with pigeonholing, Clara seeks to intentionally highlight the experiences of Asian Americans. Importantly, she also links Asian Americans with other marginalized communities to suggest a resistance to model minority narratives of White adjacency and to connect Asian Americans in pan-racial affiliation with Black and Brown Americans, who also bear additional harms because of the compounding inequality associated with COVID-19.

In addition to stories, Ivan and Amy mentioned that they intentionally search to find Asian American sources to include. Ivan said, "I hadn't thought of it like that. No, I think I will, I just try to be a voice, try to get more sources who are, let's say, they are Americans of Asian descent, who they, they consider themselves Asian, and they don't fully embrace the American culture yet. I think that there is that type of source. I think one of the most important things that you can do is reach out to those sources and speak to them, not be lazy." Here Ivan makes a conscious effort to include more Asian (American) sources. Doing so is difficult and may take more time because of the dominance and wide availability of White experts in the source market. But that may be a rewarding activity for Ivan and serve as a venue of oppositional expression like the Black American reporters in Meyers and Gayle's (2015) study, who attempted to use more Black American sources and role models. This practice of inclusion can be understood as an act of resistance.

Although it increases labor for already overtaxed reporters, practicing a politics of representation as gatekeepers is an everyday act of micro-resistance against the White-centrism of news gathering. Amy, in a story of an Asian American business owner, said,

> I think Asian Americans are entrepreneurial, and there are a lot of them that were just flying under the radar because the journalists who are White were not even looking for them. But you know, I think in a lot of ways their story is very similar to a White business owner. I just think it's important that we have an Asian face on it sometimes to just let people know that this person is part of the [community].

In Amy's case, her inclusion of an "Asian face" is an everyday act of resistance that is made necessary because of White reporters' unexamined biases that lead to the exclusion of Asian Americans, whose stories are similar to the human-interest stories White reporters would tell about White members of their community. She also argued that she was uniquely equipped to tell their stories.

> I think the stories that I tell about Asian Americans, I see, I feel that they open up more to me as sources. I sense a sense of comfort that they feel rather than, I guess I'm just comparing it to when I interviewed White people. I don't sense as much of a sense of comfort when they look at me, and so I've just gone towards what I think naturally fits for me as a journalist, which is to tell Asian American stories.

Her ability to include Asian Americans is made more possible because sources are more willing to share their stories with her, someone they trust will understand their experience and write about their lives with more fidelity. Amy also counters the racial distance that her White sources present by leaning into her ability to tell Asian American stories more effectively than her White peers can. It is important to understand that not only do Asian American journalists negotiate the White racial hegemony of their newsrooms but of newsmakers, too.

Similarly, Rose explained that her racial identification improves her reporting by increasing source accessibility and trust. She recounted a story about the misogyny Asian American women experience and how her ability to empathize with her interviewee led to a more emotionally meaningful and an arguably more ethical story.

> Because I could come to the perspective like an Asian woman, I can, I could say, you know, like "I don't know what you're going through personally, but I understand where you're coming from" and also understand that it was a sensitive subject that some people maybe didn't want to talk about or only wanted to talk about with certain caveats. Me being able to say, like as an Asian woman, like I understand where you're coming from really helped people to just open up. I think that's the biggest thing—that people feel more comfortable opening up when the reporter is Asian and you're covering Asian communities.

For stories that carry this degree of sensitivity, it is argued that her subjectivity and compassion matter toward her ability to report more effectively and to tell a more poignant story that dealt with misogyny within an Asian American ethnic community but without problematic generalization or vilification of Asian American communities that implicitly construct White men as superior, a common trope in U.S. media culture (see Hamamoto 1994; Espiritu 2004; Kang 2002).

Another counter-hegemonic practice is efforts to pitch stories that uplift Asian American communities. Talking about the specific context of COVID-19 and the racialized harms to Asian Americans, Hannah said,

> Yeah, I mean, I think it is important because I think we touched on this before, but we make decisions on which voices we wanna uplift, and it's important to

include communities that are non-White into kind of the dialogue about a situation, especially when there is a lot of misinformation coming from, like, a government standpoint, and encourage notes for, you know, prejudice and discrimination on that level, so it was important for me to humanize the issue.

The desire to uplift is a recognition of reporters' discursive power in the cultural terrain. For Hannah, it is seen as a form of balance, a counter-weight to the problematic associations of COVID-19 with race and ethnicity that produced anti-Asian hate and Sinophobia. For Mark, his intentions are to provide platforms for Asian Americans and other people of color to gain cultural capital. Mark said, "And I'm also cognizant to that, like, if you don't, you know, part of it is elevating other voices who are non-White, because if you do that, then they become authorities on their own."

Beyond the goals of including more diverse voices, humanizing and uplifting Asian American communities, and challenging White racial hegemony, the journalists also believed that their racial identification plays a role in how they tell Asian American stories. In other words, their subjectivity matters, thus challenging the foundational assumption of objectivity that detachment necessarily produces better coverage, an assumption that White reporters rarely engage in practice, particularly with race and heritage, but often cite to demonstrate their bona fides as journalists. That is, White reporters claim fidelity to objectivity but do not recuse themselves from covering stories about Europe, White business and political leaders, White celebrities, or predominantly White institutions. This racial double standard attempts to disguise White news as raceless news. Thus, the claims that Asian American journalists are uniquely positioned to produce better news because of their subjectivity, rather than in spite of it, is a fundamental challenge to the objectivity paradigm. Mark stated:

> So, yeah, I mean, I do think it's important that the stories you do choose to tell are the stories that are important and that your own background informs that because, you know, it's not, it's a waste for me to just pretend to be a White male and just write as if I'm a White male. It's a waste. It's like, it's like that's what we're reading, anyway, so we should be writing the stories that haven't been, that are informed by our own perspective and can bring light to, you know, injustices or whatever that, that other, that are, just aren't being covered.

Thus, Mark's standpoint as an Asian American is not a possible drawback but value-added for the newsroom. As he points out, by acknowledging it and using it as a lens to see the world and news, it produces journalism that is more concerned with social injustice and approaches the news from the perspective of the marginalized, linking to journalism's connections to the Fourth Estate by keeping the powerful accountable to everyday citizens and by caring for the least powerful in society. He specifically links this to his own family experience, saying:

> Being the son of immigrants speaks to how I approach my work all the time, so in covering the virus, there was a lot, a lot, you know, this issue of Latinos and Black Americans being disproportionately hit hard by the pandemic is like a really big part of the story. . . . Like the reporters who help shape the narrative every day, in terms of what is the main news story, I can see, in some situations where it can be easy for them to just focus on the numbers and not focus on, on that, that this idea that that's a different story. But in, in my own reporting, because, because I'm very aware of being a non-White person in the U.S. that raising that to the issue, where it is part of the primary news story, that is something that is, is important to me, and I think me being an Asian American or just being a non-White person helps me make sure to elevate that to the point where it's like you have to talk about it. It is an essential part of the story. It's not just a sidebar. It's the story.

Similarly, Dana points out that her background also matters in her reporting.

> I have come to be a lot more accepting of myself and accepting of the fact that I do have certain identity traits that can't be divorced from who I am. I can't change the fact that I'm Asian and that I'm the daughter of a refugee. It's just, it's just the facts, so, and people will write, and I think that I should just come at sources and come at our audience very transparently about that, that I do come from this particular background and that might influence the stories I choose to tell, but in the actual execution of the stories, I will adhere to journalistic practice and be as fair as possible. I do think that I'm fair. I, like any other journalist, come to my reporting from a certain background, and that is true for [name redacted] who is a White man in his fifties. That he, like, that he doesn't get to be described as the neutral point of view. I also, if he is neutral, then I'm also coming at it neutrally. We should just say, we should all acknowledge who we are when we come to our stories.

Dana deconstructs different assumptions in her comments. First, she points out that her subjectivity matters and that her journalistic identity is not separate from who she is. Second, she disentangles the assumption that subjectivity is equivalent to bias by arguing forcefully for fairness, a way to negotiate challenges to objectivity. Thus, her challenge decouples the link between objectivity and fairness by pointing to them as conceptually separate. Finally, she points to the double standard discussed earlier in which only White masculinity occupies a position of neutrality. Of course, this echoes the criticisms of Whiteness that critical Whiteness theorists have advanced—its simultaneous ability to be invisible while also being the standard by which people of color are judged (Dyer 1997; Jackson 1999; Nakayama and Krizek 1995).

Belonging to America

In the mediated terrain, the stereotype of Asian Americans as perpetual foreigners is especially pronounced (Espiritu 2004; Ono and Pham 2009; Fong 2008). Indeed, the stereotype is not only pernicious, it is so entrenched that Robert Lee (1999) argues that Asian Americans have been constructed as an "alien" presence, and it is so persistent that Palombu-Liu (1999) created the discursive construction of "Asian/American" to capture dominant culture's racialized conflation of Asian and Asian American. In this context, it is unsurprising that several reporters chose to tell stories that demonstrate that Asian Americans belong and contribute to the larger society. By doing so, they produce counter-hegemonic meanings. Rose was clearest about having a counter-hegemonic intention by demonstrating that Asian American history and communities also belong to the tapestry of U.S. America.

> I think the more you flood the space with Asian American stories in a mainstream environment, the more that people will understand that Asian Americans, we have our, our histories, just as American as like learning about Christopher Columbus or learning about World War II. It's just that those stories are stories that haven't historically been treated with the same amount of mainstream respect and promotion that they deserve, but there's nothing inherent to those stories that means that they shouldn't, that they didn't deserve that treatment. They deserve to be treated with respect, and they deserve a mainstream audience. All you need is someone who will do that and someone who will do that with an understanding of what these communities are and who they are and who these people are, so I think just, in short, it's just important to talk about these stories because they're American stories, and therefore Americans should learn about them. If we as people of color should learn about White American stories, then there's no reason why White Americans shouldn't learn about Asian American stories.

Importantly, Rose frames the selection of Asian American stories as connected to racial equity, linking Asian Americans in solidarity with people of color and criticizing the White racial hegemony of historical, educational, and popular cultural narratives.

With the racialization of the COVID-19 pandemic, several reporters also mentioned that they pitched stories where Asian Americans are humanized as not a yellow peril "other" but, rather, as constitutive of U.S. society. Hannah, for instance, pitched a story of exceptional belonging.

I pitched my own story because my parents, and I, I'm not as active on WeChat as I probably should be, but my parents use it very often; we talked pretty often as well. So, that gave me the idea for a story about just like grassroots efforts in the Chinese community to kind of in, despite of, you know, racist comments from whether its peers or hearing about racist incidents from their friends or hearing things from the president, how they were, like, you know what? We, we are Americans, we care about our community, and we want to help in any way that we can, and because they have a lot of, like, shipping and export type companies, they were chipping in a lot to get materials, whether it was hospital stuff, or masks or other kinds of PPE [Personal Protective Equipment].

This story highlights below-the-radar charitable giving that demonstrates the contributions Chinese Americans made to their communities despite the virulent racism they were simultaneously experiencing. This suggests that Chinese Americans, and perhaps Asian Americans more broadly, are valuable members of society during a crisis. On the other hand, Clara aimed to demonstrate Asian Americans' everyday belonging: "That's what I aim for, like that's what's in the back of my head, sometimes when I work on these stories, push that idea that you know Asian Americans are just as American as everybody else. Like it's you know, there's no, there's no ideal look to what an American is. You know, that would be more commonplace now." In this way, Clara attempts to normalize Asian Americans as U.S. Americans so that questions of foreignness, exclusion, and demonization do not persist.

For other reporters, their intentions were not to directly challenge the perpetual foreigner stereotype but to diversify coverage as a way to intervene in the White racial hegemony of news coverage. Sophia is one of the only people of color in the newsroom, and she uses her voice to advocate for diverse voices, which humanizes people of color in the community. She said, "I will say, being a person of color in a newsroom has been an asset because I feel like I am more hyper-aware of, I think, when, you know, who we're talking or who you cover, and so I think I generally, I'm usually the one that tells my editors, like, hey, like, let's make sure, you know, when we do a special section about heroes in the [community], we don't just cover White people." Interestingly, they are not only watchdogs as members of the press, but Sophia also becomes a watchdog *of* the press as she influences her White peers to report inclusively. As Dana and Amy point out, not only does this have implications for social equity and fairness, but it also produces richer stories because of the diversity of vantage points.

Really seek a full range of voices, for example, and adhere to journalistic practice. I'm not gonna take shortcuts or lie or obfuscate, but I do come from a certain point of view just by nature of me having a certain background. And that isn't necessarily less true or less valid.—Dana

I took it upon myself at that station to really diversify the voices, to really dig to find people who looked like me, both for my own sense of community and also because I think that it's important that our station has a diversity of voices on the air.—Amy

Indeed, Dana's comment anticipates and defuses the criticism that possessing a particular standpoint leads to worse journalism, as she points out that her reporting seeks truth and is thorough, hallmarks of good journalistic practice that the reporters themselves have articulated. Instead, because of a postmodern belief in multiple truths, seeking diverse perspectives could be understood as improving the truthfulness of a story. Amy also alludes to the professionalism of this choice because finding diverse voices is seen as more, rather than less, difficult as she uses the metaphor of digging, a common discourse in journalism to refer to serious, thorough truth seeking.

While the journalists find it worthwhile to demonstrate Asian American belonging, there was some concern that doing so may make ethnic details too pronounced and thus it may be considered too particularistic. Amy said, "So, in a lot of ways, I think that there wasn't that much difference, but at the same time, yeah, I think I tried not to overexplain things like the importance of family dynamics or, you know, Asian values like taking care of your family, taking care of your elders, and I didn't want to overexplain that in my story and say this person lives with their parents because in Asian American culture, it's important to do that versus putting your parents in nursing home or something." Amy doesn't want to exoticize Asian American experiences. She wants to make them part of the story and normalize them. At the same time, however, Amy, who used to work for a news organization in a suburban area whose audience is predominantly White, needed to address the issue so that it could be more relatable to her majority White audience, which meant omitting some details that are considered too ethnic. Similarly, Ivan tries to pitch Asian American perspectives rather in a strategic way. In a story of Chinese food, he said,

I don't necessarily pitch it in that [Asian-specific] way because sometimes that's not the best way to pitch that story to editors, and that's nothing to say to my editors. It's just a timing thing, right? Rather than saying, "Oh, I'm gonna make this about how there's this, here's this cool Asian culture in this restaurant, and I'm going to pitch it in this way, where I really, really heavily focused on the identity aspect of it," if I say, "Oh, this restaurant made $2 million," they'll [editors] be like, okay, that sounds good to me. Then, you just go [do] that story, and then I could add in my own flavor right and put in that perspective.

In this example, Ivan does not explicitly show an Asian American angle in pitching his story to the editors. As he put it, "I am not gonna go at it from that angle pretending that I was like an 'A' Asian American Studies student." Instead, he places a "different angle," which is business and economics, to the story in order to gain wider approval from the editors and possibly from his White-majority audience. This is an interesting tactic, as it can be both empowering and delegitimating. It is a tactic that achieves a level of resistance against the White normative perspectives in newsroom. At the same time, it can be delegitimating and patronizing, as he has to intentionally avoid putting an emphasis on Asian American experiences, as if the experiences are of a trivial concern. Either way, it would require substantial cognitive effort to do so, suggesting that Asian American reporters have to navigate the White news space with subtlety.

Asian American reporters like Ivan and Amy thus have to walk a fine line: they attempt to elevate Asian Americans' nuanced experiences, but do not want to make them too particularistic and pronounced, which may not fly well in the face of majority non-Asian audiences. So, they have a difficult task of presenting Asian American universality, while pointing to the Asian American specificity at the same time. These two goals appear to be in contradiction, but we argue that universalism and particularism exist as a dialectic. That is, they operate in mutually constitutive tension. This tension navigates the inherent contradiction with alterity. Being a part of a racially marginalized group means that there are simultaneously unique experiences, perspectives, and histories for the community but that these differences do not produce mutually exclusive otherness. Rose pointed to this dialectic that people of color experience.

> I want my work to show that a lot of these issues that I write about are not specific to the Asian community. Like they're not quote unquote Asian issues. They are issues that happened to Asian people and that maybe are more prevalent in certain Asian communities. . . . What I'm saying is that these are larger problems that are happening in our society at large, and then this is how they happen to appear in Asian communities because I think when you get into that rhetoric of these are Asian issues, then people who read those stories might read them and say, "Oh well that's not a problem for me. It's not a problem for the community that I live in." That's absolutely not correct. I'm just showing that this is how it shows up in an Asian community. But this is a larger problem that I'm addressing that you, the reader, should consider how it might happen in your life. So, I think that's my overarching goal. And, I think that's also what most reporters who cover race are also doing.

As Rose explains, social issues journalists cover can be both particularistic and universal. Asian Americans simultaneously belong as fully U.S. American while having some aspects of unique difference. That should be true with other minority groups in the United States. Journalists like Rose then have to capture this dialectic tension and subtleties present in American society. It's a difficult job—balancing and synthesizing universalities and particularities at the same time—but it is a worthwhile job for many Asian American reporters.

Conclusion

This chapter explored the motivations and desires of Asian American reporters for wanting to cover Asian American communities, and how they weave the stories together. We found varying motivations, but, overall, a keen interest in better and more frequent coverage of Asian Americans in the mainstream media. In particular, reporters who possessed racial consciousness demonstrated stronger desires and enthusiasm to elevate Asian American voices. One of the main things they are interested in doing in their coverage is normalizing Asian American experiences because Asian Americans have long experienced the "foreigner" stereotype and been exoticized in the mainstream media. Thus, demonstrating Asian American belonging is an important task for them.

Their effort to achieve more and better coverage of Asian Americans, however, is constricted by the norms and standards of the White dominant newsroom and news market. Facing majority White colleagues, editors, and audiences who often employ colorblind perspectives, they have to confront dominant news logics or act strategically. They do not subvert the White newsroom, but, rather, they push its boundaries. By humanizing subjects with deeper knowledge and including stories of anti-oppression and belonging to America, they attempt to include Asian American voices while maintaining the primary value of truth-telling. They avoid White dominant culture stereotypes and tell all manner of truths that they uncover, including celebratory, sympathetic, hard, ugly, and complex truths about issues affecting Asian American communities. This is what color-conscious news can be—one that seeks to include and understand communities of color not by acting as a booster but by acting as a reporter who reveals truths about the oppressions faced and the oppressions caused by the community the reporter covers. In that sense, the primary difference between reporters of color and White reporters is that White reporters do not have to find ways to tell stories about White society since these stories are already overrepresented as news.

7

COVID-19 and Coping with Gendered Racist Harms

· ·

Covering COVID-19 presents unique challenges to Asian American journalists. Not only do they face the same health hazards as their peers, the ethnoracialization of the disease as the "Wuhan Virus," the "Chinese virus," and "Kung Flu" means that, for some people, Asian Americans are embodied signifiers of the disease. The "racism and xenophobia—especially their latent forms—towards Asian Americans have intensified under the guise of contagion metaphors and erupted in the form of racist speech acts, vicious hate crimes, and inhumane anti-immigration regulations" (Mallapragada 2021, 286). COVID-19's purported origins in Wuhan, China, brought to the surface aversive racism that is linked to the earliest stereotypes of Chinese (and later other Asian) Americans as a "yellow peril" health threat that contaminates White America (Lee 1999; Le et al. 2020b; Mallapragada 2021; Oh 2020). This was present in nineteenth century fears of Chinese Americans as carriers of the bubonic plague and cholera, the irrational fears of monosodium glutamate (MSG) as the cause of "Chinese Restaurant Syndrome" (Kammerer 2018), and the similar vilification of China and Asian/Americans during the SARS scare. With COVID-19, there have been dramatic increases in anti-Asian racism (Kim and Shah 2020) and multiple accounts of individuals in the Asian diaspora in the West who have been verbally and physically assaulted regardless of heritage or family history (Liu 2020).

With the COVID-19 pandemic, there is an opportunity to understand how Asian Americans, as journalists of color, navigate usually discounted racial identities during a time in which their very bodies are racially fraught. This chapter aims to capture this moment by conducting research concurrently with journalists who worked during this time. During the interviews, we were guided by the following question: how do Asian American journalists navigate the racialization of COVID-19 in their newsrooms, in their work in the field, and in response to feedback from viewers, readers, and listeners? In this chapter, we argue that while Asian American reporters generally minimized racist harms, the perception of them and the activation of racialized reflexivity are both gendered. To do so, we briefly discuss the ways our participants minimize racist harms as a means of coping, the gendering of racist harms, and the gendering of racial reflexivity.

The Minimizing of Racist Harms

With the exception of a single reporter, every journalist interviewed denied that they directly experienced racialized harms. Dana, for instance, said, "I haven't run into any, I haven't had any sort of racial experiences as a result of all of the discrimination happening that I'm reading about that's happening all over the country against Asian Americans." In fact, several were apologetic, claiming that they were skeptical about whether their experiences would contribute meaningfully to the research project. Larry's response was typical: "You know, if I have, I can't, you know. And this is why I wasn't sure I was going to be that helpful. I, I can't bring it to mind. If I have, I've forgotten it. Nothing sort of comes to mind. You know, something might have happened, someone made a comment on a story, or, but, boy, I can't think of any particular issue that's come up I can think of. I don't know." The most common reason was attributed to the stay-at-home nature of news work during the pandemic.

> I mean, it's mostly been remote, so it's kind of hard to, you know, gauge whether anyone has certain personal feelings towards me because I happen to be Asian, and I'm covering COVID-19 news.—Kate

> I did not because once [the city] was, like, shelter in place, I essentially didn't leave my home [laughs].—Hannah

> So, it doesn't really affect me too much mostly because we're all working from home now and there's basically no opportunity for me to really experience discrimination from people in the field. It's just not gonna happen.—Brian

> I've not really left my house to do any reporting since March, because, I mean, you probably haven't left your house much either, right? So, my work has been

very phone-based and email-based, which is, I'm very fortunate to be in a position where I can do that.—Nina

It hasn't affected me, but you know I haven't, I haven't really been out in the field reporting that much. . . . In my personal life a little bit, but not in my, not in my reporting.—Rose

Given the frequency of the response, it is clear that Asian American journalists' reduced field reporting minimized work harms. Their work was primarily telephonic, and as English speakers with native fluency, their voices do not carry aural markers of racial difference.

Another less common argument proffered for their lack of exposure to racist harms was the distance their beats provided from COVID-19 coverage. For instance, Larry, who does not work on the city desk, says that he primarily covers uncontroversial, human-interest stories. "But there's, I think there's a, at least in the place where I work, in the team where I work, in the department where I work, there is a reluctance to, to kind of get into issues that will make people uncomfortable." For Kate, despite frequently covering health-related stories, she argues that her stories' medical focus maintains distance. She said, "So, really, it's just been like, okay, these are what the health experts are saying about X, Y, and Z, which is you know what's happening before COVID and then when COVID started happening, that just kind of stayed pretty much the same for the most part." In a time when even seemingly straightforward news has been politicized and ascribed ideological meaning, the quote reads as, perhaps, containing a willful desire to not recognize the proximity to racialized harms.

The possibility of willful denial of harms is also visible in the other common reason for a lack of harms—the makeup of the communities in which they work. For instance, several journalists mentioned that the relatively sizeable population of Asian Americans has insulated them from harm.

There is a very strong Asian presence here, and like I said, we have politicians who represent us who are also Asian and so, it seems to be a level of comfort in general culture here in dealing with Asian people, and yeah, I have not really felt too much of it.—Amy

So, it does, really, I think safety in numbers is a good way to describe it because you aren't singled out, and that's very different than my experience growing up.—Dana

There are a lot of Asians here as well. I never felt uncomfortable approaching people. I actually was more concerned about them, like, whether they be, whether they be uncomfortable by me approaching them.—Rose

Though it is likely true that reporting in communities that have visible Asian American populations does, indeed, assure the reporters, many of the reports of COVID-related anti-Asian hate speech and violence have occurred in cities with significant Asian American populations, such as New York City and the Bay Area (Castañeda 2020; Romaine 2020). On the other hand, Clara believes her isolation from other Asian Americans protected her.

> I think, in my city, it is definitely, you know, there's a growing Asian American community, but we're not, everybody's spread out. I think if I were in San Francisco or New York City, where everyone's on top of each other, I probably would have experienced, I probably would have experienced something. I'm sure of it. You hate to say it, because those cities, you know, have such Asian American communities and, you know, and always pride themselves on being diverse, and yet that's where a lot of people feel emboldened to threaten others.

That the perceived reason for safety from harm is not contingent upon the size or constitution of the Asian American population in the community perhaps points to confirmation biases that support a desire to not see harm regardless of different circumstances.

As Lin (2020, 1415) argues, even when Asian Americans experience racialized discrimination, they often find alternative explanations and "dismiss racialised experiences of inequality as functions of individual bigotry rather than systemic racism or inequality." Indeed, Oyserman and Sakamoto (1997) conclude that Asian Americans are resistant to racism as an explanation for discrimination and will argue for less reasonable and, in some cases, far-fetched explanations, instead. Denying the existence of racist harm is a common coping strategy to minimize and not recognize the psychological harms that are caused (Ahn and Park 2019). It could be because many Asian Americans are socialized in predominantly White spaces as "honorary Whites" to both desire and to not challenge White supremacy (Tuan 1998). White people often interpret Asian American challenges to White racial hegemony as betrayals, which bring strict reprisals.

It could also be because as "middleman minorities" positioned outside the Black-White binary construction of race, we are socialized to believe that it is crass and selfish to talk about anti-Asian harms when we recognize that we are relatively advantaged (Son 2014; Fong 2008). Indeed, second-generation Asian Americans generally do not question White racial logics, including the post-racist belief that racism no longer structures life outcomes and that racism is specific only to overt, racist bigotry (Oh 2015). These raced perceptions of a lack of harm may also intersect with the socialization of newsrooms, which, by and large, operate under White racial logics (Heider 2000) and which expect that our racial identities are inconsequential to news work (Nishikawa et al., 2009).

As such, the White newsroom parallels the socialization of White suburbs and schools, except that it is further reinforced by expectations of "professional" practices that have distorted the scientific notion of objectivity—the reliable demonstration of outside truth through the removal of human interpretation—with a market-based norm of appearing nonpartisan that hides the function of human judgment in news gathering and presentation (Schudson 2003).

Intersectional Harms

Before discussing harms, it is important to reiterate that several participants likely did not experience any harm, conscious or subconscious. Upon further probing, however, it also is apparent that the narrative of a lack of harm is more complicated than it first appears. There were a few accounts of direct harms and several accounts of indirect harms. For instance, in Ethan's and Quinn's accounts, they shared how they were racially associated with the disease. Ethan experienced racialized microaggressions when wearing his mask in public. He said, "Uh, I think, you know, you definitely notice the looks that you get when you wear a mask when you're out reporting. It's a different look than I think my White colleagues get when they're out in the field." As he shares his observation, it is important to point out that he shifts pronouns from "I" to "you." He recognizes the harm to himself but discursively distances from it.

Quinn's account points to the way in which his body carries racialized meanings that both stigmatize and foreignize him:

> At the beginning of the pandemic like mid to late March, I would go out and just do some man-on-the-street interviews, and I would have, like, I had this old man just, just after the interview, who called me up and said, 'Hey, you know, the whole China virus,' called it a China virus and, you know, it's not like he, he could have been a lot meaner, but he was just kind of like, he was just, it was as if he was informing me, me that coronavirus came from China and, you know, like is that necessary?

Despite the racist intentions of the man's association of Quinn, disease, and China, he frames the story in a way that qualifies the insult by saying that it could have been "meaner" and that it was informational in tone. This apologia functions to partially excuse the racist prejudice of the statement. Further, that he refers to the person as an "old man" trivializes the harm by implying its antiquated nature, positioning the man as less relevant to the contemporary and future ethnoscape of the United States.

Rather than direct experience, a few reporters mentioned during our conversations that they have dealt with an increased volume of "hate mail." What is noticeable is that even though there does not appear to be a gendered difference in who receives hate mail, their accounts point to differences in the vitriol of the messages and the experiences of harm. Felix said, "I think pretty much any reporter you talk to can attest to this, but like we get tons of hate mail on a daily basis and a lot of that veers into racist territory, and I can't say that the volume necessarily has gone up since COVID, but it's certainly like every time I do write a story about COVID and anti-Asian discrimination or xenophobia, I will get emails from people screaming about X, Y, or Z based thing. While sharing the story, Felix does not disclose the particular racist messages he receives, which either is a means of diminishing their importance or of coping by forgetting. Instead, he uses language such as "veer," which suggests that "racist territory" is a detour from the main argument rather than the argument itself, thus giving the writer of hate mail the benefit of the doubt as their racism is ascribed to a lapse of judgment rather than motivated hatred. What else is important in the message is that he clarifies that his account is not exceptionable. That is, he is similar to "pretty much any reporter." By making this discursive qualification, he protects himself by interpreting the "hate" as a collectively shared experience regardless of race, but the effect of this interpretation likely diminishes resistance that would protect him from such harms, e.g., speaking to his editors or news director to create email policies. It might become easy to believe, for instance, that a colleague would have said something if it was important since everyone experiences the same harms. It is a universalizing tendency that is apparent in post-racism, which has disproportionate harms for people of color but argues that racist harms are exceptions (Bonilla-Silva 2010b; Herakova et al. 2011).

For women reporters who shared stories of overt racist harms, their anecdotes point to powerful, oppressive messages of racist harm. Yet, even then, Nina begins her account by qualifying hate mail as out of the ordinary. Her story is worth recounting at length.

> Lately, I've been writing about stuff that's a little bit more political than my other stories have been, and, like 1 percent of the feedback I'm getting is racial. Actually, I got this email last week. I'll read it to you. I thought of it when you emailed me. I should stress that this is like, a very rare kind of message I get. . . . A lot of people in the right want to believe that the coronavirus is not that bad. Therefore, we shouldn't shut down. We should, like, send people back to work. We should re-open schools, right? Like this is all, like, an overblown crisis like by the left mainstream media, anyway. So, these scientists have, like, pushed a theory and pushed data saying it's really not that bad, and my story, my stories have investigated them and the problems with their argument. So, as I've been writing more and more about this, these people, I get more, more pushback from the right, so here's like one email I got against, like, a big exception, but that's like a very, this is a very racial one. Okay. So, this was sent last week:

"Here's a tip"—this is so bad. "You're neither intelligent enough nor educated enough to be a reporter that is in no small part due to the fact that you're female, the dumber of the two sexes. You are a f-cking joke. I bet your Asian parents are mortified. I mean, I know your college is circling down the drain, but you still wasted your admission there on that toilet paper you call a diploma. Your life has no value. Kill yourself."

Even in the context of an overtly racist and sexist message, it appears that Nina has been socialized as an Asian American and as a reporter to diminish the harm of this message by referring to it as a more benign "racial" message. Though it might be argued that this discursive move is simply because of the discomfort about talking directly about racism and sexism, we read it as a move to minimize the harm of the message, particularly as she makes the additional discursive move of minimizing harms by describing the message as rare.

In addition, the message Nina has shared is more severe than the stories shared by Felix and Quinn. Tara, on the other hand, was the only reporter to openly point to the harms she encounters.

> Well, I think the rhetoric of the president of the United States is not helping, not just for a journalist but because he doesn't like journalists, but also for people that are, you know, Asian. He calls it a Chinese virus, and I've gotten things like that, you know, like people saying, just online bullies and stuff like saying stuff on my professional pages. Like, go back to China, or like posting these, I had, somebody was like, posting a picture of like COVID with a big, China with a big X on it and posting it on all of my stuff, and I ended up blocking them. I had someone else call me a Communist and told me get out of here, you know, get out of their state or their country or whatever. So yes, it has impacted me because I've, I've gotten things before but never to this extent, more in the last six to seven months than ever in my entire career.

The level of harm for Tara had become serious enough that her newsroom assigned a security detail when she covered conservative rallies. Her double conspicuousness as an Asian American woman and as a reporter have marked her as especially vulnerable in spaces that cultivate anti-Asian hostility (Le, Arora, and Stout 2020), White supremacy (Kelly 2020), and antipathy toward the press. More generally, women reporters of color, especially in broadcast news, are more likely to be harassed (Miller 2020; Miller and Lewis 2020).

In both cases, perhaps because of their double oppressions as racial minorities and as women, the harms experienced are more substantial, yet despite these harms, especially for Asian American women reporters, there is, as mentioned earlier, generally a minimization of racism as harassment. As Hannah mentioned in her interview, hate mail's commonality leads to its normalization.

Byerly and Ross (2006) write that women journalists often deny the harms of sexism in their work. Because of these harms, women journalists cope by avoiding certain topics, disengaging from audiences, and, in some cases, leaving their professions (Chen et al. 2018). To remain requires developing a "thick skin," which might be perceived as a badge of honor but which might also mean that there are few healthy ways of coping with everyday harms and trauma. Together with their racial difference and the hyperfeminization of Asian American women, it likely multiplies harms as Asian American women reporters deal with their double marginalization and the demands to prove themselves as able to deal with the rigors of the profession in a masculinized newsroom.

As Adams (2018) argues, women journalists describe even serious threats casually because abuse and threats occur regularly in their work. As such, it is most likely that racist abuse is so normalized that it only becomes mentioned as a direct example of abuse in severe cases or with further probing. Though the literature does not make it clear whether men journalists of color also face similar abuses or cope similarly, it is likely that there is both commonality and difference. An understanding of hegemonic oppression and coping would suggest that there may be similar patterns of racist abuse but that it would be less severe because men would primarily face racism but rarely the intersection of racism and sexism. The psychological literature on Asian American coping suggests that while both men and women try to trivialize or ignore discrimination (Liang et al. 2007), men do this even more so by relying on "emotion-focused coping strategies," i.e., finding ways to feel better such as believing that they are less discriminated than other people of color, ignoring offenses, and trivializing the harm or the abuser (Kuo 1995). Asian American men are generally uncomfortable expressing feelings about discrimination, particularly with other men because they already have their masculinity questioned in dominant society, and sharing feelings is gendered feminine (Liu 2002). Though Asian American men and women both tend to deal with racism alone (Taylor et al. 2004; Yeh and Wang 2000), women are more likely to use "active strategies" to cope with racism, particularly by leaning on close social support networks for advice (Liang et al. 2007; Kuo 1995).

Connecting the literature on women reporters and coping with abuse and Asian American coping strategies, it might be expected that Asian American reporters are susceptible to generally denying or minimizing racism. Asian Americans do this as a coping practice of navigating White racial hegemony, and this is a socialized expectation of journalists. In addition, denial of structural racism is the dominant mode for understanding race and racism in a larger cultural climate of neoliberally informed colorblindness or post-racism in which racism is relegated to only interpersonal acts of racist bigotry (Bonilla-Silva 2010b; Prashad 2001). Altogether, then, it might create a climate in which denial of racist harms becomes multiply reinforced within broader culture, as Asian

Americans, and in predominantly White newsrooms. It is notable, however, that while there are broad racial similarities in coping strategies, Asian American women are more likely to discuss their emotions and perhaps have more self-reflexivity about racist harms. It is likely that the salience of the attacks against women coupled with different coping strategies explains men's silences and women's discussions of harm. Indeed, only Asian American women reporters mentioned vulnerabilities such as racialized anxiety, depression, and fear that have emerged in a national climate of anti-Asian racism. What is evident is that Asian American men reporters are mostly limited to naming external harms, e.g., hate speech, while Asian American women reporters name both external and internal harms, e.g., sadness, fear.

Clara, in particular, shared complex feelings of anger and sadness. Though Clara did not experience direct racist discrimination in her work, her identification with Asian American victims produced collectively experienced harm: "So, in the last few months really, like [I] would get depressed at times and just exhausted from reading incident after incident. Whether it's in the news article or somebody sharing it in a Facebook post or a tweet about somebody, like even just the littlest thing, like spitting at somebody and telling them to go back to China or that they carry the virus. It just, it was depressing. It still is depressing, and I would, at times, have to say, I can't read the entire story about this because it's just gonna get me mad or sad." Her sense of collective harm was especially visible in her sympathies for Chinese American business owners, who suffered from the ethnic bigotry of patrons, who slipped easily into fears of Chinese Americans as disease carriers (Kim and Shah 2020; Le et al. 2020). Discussing her coverage of Chinatown restaurants, Clara said, "Like they [customers] just would, like, just thinking that if I don't go to a Chinese restaurant, I'm safe. Like that made me sad."

Amy's anxiety was rooted in the early social stigma against mask wearing. Because the mask was strongly associated with Asian Americans, wearing it was a stigma of both disease and racial difference. It became the visible expression of an invisible disease. Its highly charged racial meanings meant that mask wearing for Asian Americans became a marker of bizarreness and threat, transforming the Asian American wearer into a yellow peril danger. She said:

I was worried about somebody doing something to me [at a pro-Trump rally]. People definitely looked at me in a certain way, wearing a mask, and interviewing them. So both Asian American and a member of the media, there's distrust of both right now. I think within those groups, um, and it wasn't a pleasant experience for me and maybe the story wasn't as deep as it could have been.

Of all of the different participants, Amy is the only one who notes that her fears affected her work. Perhaps, because it might not be construed as sufficiently professional and rugged to have the dangers of the field interfere with the quality of the work, no other participant made a similar admission. If this is true, then it means that the journalists have little room professionally to discuss their fears and anxieties. Doing so would question masculine norms of objectivity that require journalists subjugate their humanity to their work. Indeed, in our conversations, journalists predominantly stated that they did not express their concerns with their colleagues. Though the lack of sharing was attributed in part to their socially distanced work, it is also likely that it is because of conformity to professional (masculine) norms.

Jennifer pointed to a specific moment in which her coverage of anti-Asian harms also produced a fleeting moment of anxiety.

> You know, like people spitting at folks, people punching people, like they were keeping track of all that and sort of at the height of all of that, I had to go out and report this piece, and so I remember going to this neighborhood that I go to all the time, like you go there to go to a restaurant or, and to interview a subject, and she was telling me that she had experienced racial attacks in that neighborhood, and I just was like, as I was walking back to my car, I was, like, looking around, you know, making sure like nobody was near me so that no one could accuse me of bringing the Chinese virus or whatever.

The vulnerability in her vignette is poignant and demonstrates that because of the generalized climate of anti-Asian racism and her specific work reporting it, this produced anxiety as she became acutely aware of her racialized body and the associations of diseased threat that it carried and, more importantly, the irrational acts of hatred that it might produce.

For Tara, as mentioned previously, her fears are not only about imagined possibilities but about lived experiences that have, to some extent, created racialized trauma.

> I've covered rallies before, like, Trump rallies, where I've maybe not felt safe because, just because of his rhetoric to Asian, to Chinese people and, and to the virus, and, like, people don't know [my ethnicity], you know, like, to them, I'm a Chinese girl, you know what I mean? Um, so to them, I'm just a yellow-skinned person that maybe doesn't fit in at the rally. So, I've had to worry in that sense, even; I feel like I've never had to worry before. I feel like, now I'm more scared than I have been before when I covered certain topics.

Her use of "yellow-skinned" and "girl" are provocative discursive choices. She is taking on the insults of the racist, sexist speaker to sarcastically mock their racialization and infantilizing sexism. The mocking, however, does not appear to come from a position of dominance but, rather, a position of vulnerability, exposing signs of the trauma caused by racist, verbal abuse.

With expressions of sadness and fear, it is, again, important to emphasize that it is only Asian American women reporters who articulate the emotional harms of the racist abuse. However, when thinking about racial stresses, men also point to these; however, their concerns are largely external whereas women reporters' external stresses bring a recognition of internal stresses. Among the men participants, only Ethan, Quinn, and Felix mention any racialized harms, and, when they did, they qualified and minimized the harms they experience. For instance, Ethan mentioned the incremental toll of reporting on anti-Asian racism.

> I haven't had any explicit threat about I what I do in my reporting. People haven't called me names or anything like that, but, yeah, I mean, I've definitely learned about the bias and stereotype and the hate that we see against the Asian American community. The instances that I've covered and the stories that I've heard, those are very real stories and instances, and, I think it kind of wears on you a bit because you've been hearing the stories and thinking about what things have been like for people like me. It's, it's a lot to think about on a personal basis, so I think it hadn't changed in, in terms of the process of reporting, the work that I do, but it does take a toll on, kind of, you.

Even as he describes these harms, he minimizes them on three separate occasions by using the qualifiers "a bit" and "kind of." It seems, then, to be a way of defending himself against the psychological ramifications of harm and against accusations that his work has worsened. He makes it clear that he does what his job requires, suggesting an idealized, rugged journalistic figure who is emotionally resilient.

Similarly, Sophia claimed that the drumbeat of stories had created exhaustion, but she acknowledges severe emotional harm that would require intention to undo.

> I think this has really been harmful. Well, that just being, constantly reading about other Asian American women, and then again, it brings up times, even though I've not experienced that personally, it does bring up times, like, again, in the past with, like, my editor, when I see those microaggressions with other people, it's easier to identify them to me, and so I've had to come to terms with that. But also, I think it's the realization that we don't have the tools like for mental health, and the Asian American community has not been great about mental health, and that's playing out here, for sure.

Further, Sophia names the causes as microaggressions, hinting at racism, albeit a form of racism that is mildly framed. As Sue et al. (2007) argue, racial microaggressions can cause substantial harm to Asian Americans, and their denial, a common response by Asian Americans, can lead to increased discrimination and psychological pain.

Racial Reflexivity and News Work

Even though Asian American reporters might minimize the racist harms they have experienced in their work, nearly all of the participants became more aware of and reflected more upon their own racial identities and how they matter in their jobs. For participants, the self-reflexivity did not reveal a new understanding of their own racialized lived experiences but, rather, it was used as a mirror to understand or to be reminded of how they are seen by U.S. Americans, who are not racially Asian. This experience of seeing one's self through the eyes of others has clear parallels to W. E. B. DuBois's ([1903] 1989) concept of "double consciousness," being aware of how as people of color, we are seen by White people, leading to a fracturing in which our lives are in tension, navigating between how we are seen and how we see ourselves—our ascribed and avowed identities.

For Ivan, Brian, and Dana, their racial awareness was primarily directed at how others see Asian Americans in this moment, focusing in particular on the role of the Trump administration.

> The big difference between the racism we see now and the racism that existed during Bush and during Obama was that it's so explicit now whereas it was implicit, and it was a dog whistle.—Dana

> You know, it's always Chinese virus. It's always this and that, and as always, you know, you may have seen the news clip from a couple days ago when [CBS reporter] Weijia asked Trump a question, and he spat back at her; you know, that's very, kind of like, almost, almost mocking tone, like, oh, the Chinese virus. . . . So, like, that's really the big change editorially because like it's just never, I've never seen that kind of racist language being used against media, against Asian Americans in this country, and there is such a laughable reaction from the government about it.—Brian

> I think it was comical that President Trump's script got taken a photo of and that reports of, you know, him crossing out coronavirus and putting Chinese flu, if my memory serves me correct, and then reports of the staffers calling the virus Kung Flu. I think, yeah, that, that's comically horrendous, right? It's almost like comic-book villain stuff.—Ivan

In their descriptions of the anti-Asian racism amplified by the Trump administration, they use powerful language to describe the racism as overtly immoral. Brian, for instance, refers to Trump as having "spat back," which figuratively elicits images of the condescension and abuse of spitting at a reporter for being perceived as Chinese. His claim that the government's response is "laughable" does affective repair as it presents the administration in mocking terms, redirecting the condescension of Trump's government back to it. Ivan's discursive juxtapositions are ambivalent. For instance, to refer to Trump's actions as "comically horrendous" and his person as a "comic-book villain" both minimizes the racist harm by positioning Trump as juvenile and laughable, but it also amplifies the immorality of both by discursively constructing Trump as a villain, which together function to mark Trump as a near-evil, but unserious, threat.

Jennifer's awareness of racism was most activated with the cognitive dissonance of racism from progressives.

> There's a clip of a White man in a very progressive neighborhood in the city. He is in what I would call like one of the more gay, it's like one of the neighborhoods known for lots of queer, queer folks, and so, like, you would think that that's like one of the more progressive parts of the city, right? And like he was, he went on this tirade about China and, like, you know, "F-ck you, China, you disgusting, filthy animals, burn to the ground." . . . So, I was looking through his Instagram—his Instagram was open—and he might be a Bernie Sanders supporter. You know what I'm saying? It's just this, like, dissonance there, like this guy is probably as liberal as it gets, and yet, this is what he's saying about Asians, and so, um, I think that's where I was like, okay we need to tell this story . . . look at what still is lurking, you know, in all of the corners of the city.

Unlike Trump, who is expected to be anti-Asian, the progressive gay man's actions punctured the myth that White liberals and progressives are necessarily anti-racist, and Jennifer's use of the word "lurking" to refer to aversive racism that is activated in opportunistic moments suggests covertness, disguise, and harmful intentions.

Reflecting the self-orientation of double-consciousness, several participants mentioned that this moment has generated self-reflexivity. When asked whether COVID-19 activated his racial identity more strongly, Quinn replied, "Yeah, right before March, that definitely happened. Now during the pandemic, I wasn't as attentive, I want to say, as I was back when in February when that happened, because, you know, I wear a mask. Not everyone, but a lot of people also wear masks, so, but, yeah, yeah, pre-pandemic around February, I felt that." Though Quinn's feelings are not articulated, it suggests a self-awareness of the harm that comes from his marked difference, wearing a mask as an Asian American man. For a few women participants, on the other hand, self-reflexivity not only produces self-awareness but makes clear that they are not fully accepted as they view themselves through the eyes of others.

> I just feel like, yes, it's all this COVID stuff has made me more acutely aware of interactions.—Clara

I think I forgot like what looking like, looking Asian means to people until more recently, and I'm like, oh, yeah, no, we're seen as, you know, carriers of the disease, and we're seen as the peril and even though I'm Korean, you know, and so I think I'm, I'm more self-conscious; I'm, I'm a little more vigilant, probably.—Jennifer

I mean, that's the thing that this coronavirus exposed is, like, you know, we've kind of lived our life, I mean we did what we were told in a sense; we were successful; we did everything and worked hard and really, you know, it's kind of just disheartening to know at the end of the day, like, we're still seen as, like, Asian. We're not seen as Americans, and I mean, and that's been a problem politically for, like, decades.—Sophia

Jennifer's use of the phrase "carriers of disease" points to a resentment at the racist yellow peril construction of Asian American bodies as not only diseased but as disease agents and that her post-racial hopes have been punctured by the rhetorical, psychic, and in some cases physical violence of anti-Asian racism. Sophia, likewise, points to a sense of betrayal that the model minority and its integrationist promises have been illusory and that the othering of Asian Americans as a foreign, contaminating presence persists. Though awareness creates additional stresses, it is necessary to protect against racial harm (Tuan 1998; Atkin and Tran 2020). The awareness of Asian racialization can be a trigger to seek community with others who are similarly marginalized and to share stories that legitimate feelings of marginalization as valid (Parker and Song 2009). It can also motivate pan-ethnic associations (Tuan 1998) and activism (Junn and Masuoka 2008).

Perhaps because most participants already are aware of racialization in the United States, they do not describe the types of racial reflexivity that are useful for community-building nor for collective action. Instead, some participants engaged individual agency to change the stories they covered or to change reporting in their specific newsrooms. Clara links her racial reflexivity with her understanding of newsworthiness:

My identity contributes to what I perceive as important. I think it's not just COVID, but just a long history of Asian Americans getting stomped on. But I feel like now more than before, like, people refusing to take it, and I feel like I'd like to contribute to that. I continue to think about how these kinds of stories that impact Asian Americans when they get treated like this.

In her case, it is clear that COVID-19 is not seen as exceptional but, rather, as connected to a history of anti-Asian oppression. For Amy, who had previously worked in unsupportive, White-centered newsrooms, COVID-19 empowered her to have newsroom conversations about anti-Asian racism:

Oh yeah, definitely, I think, I guess the coronavirus in the way that it's positioned Asians as being the main, the target of President Trump's rhetoric has definitely I think, although, um, I don't know. I guess I would say, yeah, on the one hand, I think that people are—maybe if I were to say racism against Asian Americans is real, maybe pre-coronavirus, people would not have believed me as much as they would now because I could very distinctly point to this point in time as being a point of racism against Asian Americans.

Tara, who had previously not seen her racial identity as relevant to her news work, took the sense of legitimation and urgency of COVID-19 and began pitching stories, a practice that she had previously tended to avoid.

I think when COVID really hit is when I started speaking up more and raising more pitches about stories like that because I really saw the impact on Chinese restaurants that were getting less business because people were worried about COVID even though they're cooking food in America, not in China, and I really like felt for those families that own these small businesses, so I called around to a bunch of like, Asian-owned restaurants and things like that. You know, there's a community who were doing a lot of good work by handing out masks and stuff to hospitals, and there was a shortage of masks and so I was connecting with them a lot. So, when COVID hit, I think I started pushing those pitches a lot more than I had before.

Her separation of her racial and professional identities might explain why her coverage was arguably accommodating as she emphasized the social good that Asian Americans are doing rather than highlighting the structural failures of the government or the racist ideologies in dominant culture. This was also true for Ethan, who, while aware of the dominant White culture of his newsroom, is largely unbothered by it. In this sense, the coverage is hardly radical as it chooses a dominant racial frame. Because of its reflection of dominant ideology, the coverage is less controversial and invisible, rendering it "impartial."

Other journalists, whose positions in their respective newsrooms are more secure and their commitments to contesting anti-Asian racism more pronounced, turned their coverage to anti-Asian harms, as well as pro-Asian activities.

I'm like we found, I found a number of people who would experience, maybe not like they were stabbed or anything, but, like, they were verbally assaulted or, yeah, like sort of more smaller aggressions.—Jennifer

On my end, obviously you feel the huge burden to have the right information out there, and I think you do feel some pressure and maybe this was like, an unconscious driver for that grassroot story, but you feel like some pressure to elevate these voices a little bit more urgently than you might normally. I think because it's imminent, right? Like these verbal attacks on a community that you're a part of existing on a somewhat daily basis, and you're getting emails and you're hearing all these incidents. I think it compounds onto and makes the sense of duty a little stronger to write these stories, and to uplift these voices that, you know, sometimes like, you don't really feel that, like, intense drive to do just because you're doing other things that are also very important. So, it does make it like a certain priority level, if that makes sense.—Hannah

All the Chinese restaurants suffered first because people were afraid to go eat there, and I was just, like, really? You know, like, come on. I mean, I went to go interview business owners in an Asian shopping center here. And, yeah, it was painful to see all of them with empty tables at lunch hour, and I felt so bad for them.—Clara

The urgency of the moment leads to efforts to support the community through their work by writing stories that demonstrate anti-Asian harms. With Hannah's use of the word "uplift" rather than a word like "amplify," it suggests that including Asian American sources and perspectives is not only about providing visibility but also about humanizing Asian Americans for her audience. Clara pointed out later in the interview that she also planned to cover whether Asian Americans have sought mental health services to cope with anxiety, depression, and other mental health concerns related to the pandemic in order to produce second-day stories that render Asian Americans sympathetic and help explain the unique challenges they face.

Dana has taken this moment as an opportunity to talk about anti-Asian harms, even when it is not in her news coverage, because she understands it as an obligation to create a more socially just society.

So, the whole notion of Asian, Asianness, the status of Asian Americans as conditional, I think I've been much more outspoken about on Twitter and when I'm speaking on panels, because I can feel it, I can see it, I can name it, and I can label it now. I think I probably felt it as a child, but I didn't know how to name it and give a voice to it, and now I can, and, so, why wouldn't I? I always say we are the ancestors; we need to be setting the examples for the next generations and the world that we want to see because the world that we live in is problematic.

Dana takes a clearly anti-racist perspective, arguing that Asian American acceptance is dependent on the benefits to White racial hegemony, although she takes care not to name White racial hegemony directly. This is a direct challenge to the forever foreigner stereotype, clarifying that Asian Americans' belonging should not be liminal but should be guaranteed. By using the term "ancestor," she positions herself in a strongly affirmative position to create social change and sees her role as a news worker not simply to report news but to create progressive social change for future generations. As such, different reflexive standpoints shape how participants use their pens and microphones as instruments to support Asian American communities and/or to challenge White racial hegemony.

That standpoint is also noticeably gendered. The preponderance of the journalists whose reflexivity during the pandemic led to more supportive coverage that either highlights the contributions of Asian Americans or the harms to Asian Americans are women. This can be explained in two ways. First, it is likely that men's conformity to norms of stoic masculinity reflected in positivist notions of subject-less impartiality makes it less likely or more difficult to desire supportive coverage that goes beyond their ordinary news work. As the literature indicates, because Asian American men's masculinity is questioned in U.S. racial hegemony, Asian American men feel particular pressure to conform to White masculine norms. Second, the psychological literature on Asian American men finds that they are less likely to use active coping strategies than Asian American women when dealing with racist harms. Thus, at least when it comes to improving Asian American representation and conditions in the newsroom, Asian American women are more motivated to be change agents in the newsroom. Asian American women's doubly marginalized positions in newsrooms, their greater likelihood of coping actively, and their greater likelihood of recognizing internal harms produce reflexivity that, in turn, provides limited challenges to White newsroom norms through affirmative, individual-level change in news work.

Conclusion

During COVID-19, Asian American journalists generally claimed that they suffered no racist harms in their work. This appears to be because of a combination of structural changes to news work, socialization to show a tough skin, and post-racist beliefs that construct racism and harms as overt racist bigotry. When harms were discussed more expansively and when probing was done to consider harms that might have been forgotten, Asian American journalists talked about the racist hate mail they receive and the indirect harms of working in this time in which Asian Americans and journalists are vilified because of the political climate in the country. For men, the harms were externalized to insults they heard during their field reporting. For women, the harms included internal harms, the emotional distress of the insults, and the climate in which they lived and worked. The recognition of internal harms produced more reflexivity about anti-Asian racism, which energized stories to humanize Asian Americans in their communities. That women were more reflexive means that women were more likely to be change agents in their (virtual) newsrooms.

That said, we do not mean to advance a gender deterministic argument but, rather, reflect a social reality that leads to reflexive racial activation and action. In other words, there is a confluence of social and psychological conditions that produces self-reflexivity about structural racism in society and in news practice. Journalists of color are activated to produce coverage that humanizes communities of color and, perhaps, if sufficiently motivated, professionally secure, or in a beat or newsroom that allows for it, it can lead to social justice reporting. By drawing upon the tradition of muckraking, journalists, who seek more humanizing coverage and social equity, counter the prevailing practices of "objectivity" that mute journalistic activism and perspective.

Epilogue

● ●

The Kerner Commission in 1967, contrary to the expectations of the Johnson administration, made clear that Black American communities deeply distrust the White perspective of the news, and it argued that newsrooms should engage in self-studies of their coverage, assign regular beats to Black American communities, train reporters to cover Black American communities fairly, hire and promote Black American reporters, dialogue with editors of the Black ethnic press, and make efforts to train Black American journalism students (Byerly and Wilson 2009). Although not directly related to Asian American hiring, training, and coverage, it has become commonly accepted in an increasingly multiracial, multicultural America that the Kerner Commission findings are true for all communities of color. As such, the American Society of News Editors (ASNE) has created targets for newsrooms to match the racial composition of the communities that they cover. Change, however, has been stubborn to arrive, and the ASNE has continually shifted its diversity targets, signaling that it has all but given up hope that these targets can be met (Delaney 2018). Although newsrooms are in an absolute sense more diverse than they were in the more than half a century since Kerner, these gains should be understood relative to the shifting demographics of the nation. To that extent, it can certainly still be argued that, numerically, news is persistently White, particularly in positions of leadership.

The coverage of Black Lives Matter and the racial reckoning in various newsrooms with White editors' claims that Black American reporters cannot cover BLM demonstrations while White American reporters can cover Trump rallies reveals, too, the persistent White perspective of news. With the early news coverage that conflated COVID-19 with Asian and Asian American people and with the hate speech and crimes directed toward Asian Americans, it is all too clear that reporters of color are operating in precarious spaces, where White perspectives are still normative yet hidden as "objective." It is a certain kind of White racial hegemony that understands only White perspectives as fair and not tinted with racial meaning.

For this reason, it is important to call into question the Whiteness of newsrooms. Although it was not our original intention as we set forth to interview Asian American reporters, it became clear quite early that these are stories that need to be told in order to understand newsrooms and their production of the "first draft of history." It is important to understand how reporters of color fit and navigate news that undermines their particular standpoints. It has become apparent through this process that there is a serious dearth of literature that uses qualitative methods to examine news reporters themselves and the role of race in newsrooms. There is only one major scholarly book that studies White American journalists and their news practices (see Heider 2000), and there are only a few journal articles (Meyers and Gayle 2015; Nishikawa et al. 2009; Walker and Anders 2021; Kil 2020). The only other book-length projects are written by former journalists who reflect upon their own experiences and interviews of other journalists (see Newkirk 2000). At the time of writing, there have been no journalistic accounts of Asian American or Latinx American reporters and their experiences navigating the racial waters of newsrooms. It is for this reason that we believe this book matters.

Our project demonstrates the importance of studying racial identity and identification in news work, and we believe it produced a nuanced, contextual understanding of identification—one that is multiply constituted and constructed from available societal discourses. We argue that this is important because it avoids inadvertent but essentializing tendencies of studies, which claim that Asian Americans or any other journalists of color believe or act in particular ways. We have come to understand that there are intra-racial distinctions in the ways Asian American reporters navigate newsrooms, centered largely around the activation of racial identifications. Asian American reporters, just like any Asian American, articulate identification about race differently. However, it does not mean that racial identifications are completely unique to each individual. Rather, they are centered around different *identity positions*— usually uninterested in racial or ethnic identity, ethnically but not racially identified, racially but not ethnically identified, and simultaneously racially and ethnically identified. All of our participants have racial identifications, but, for some, their racial identifications are only activated in particular racializing contexts, such as direct racial abuse. For others, their racial identifications are a persistent, salient part of their everyday identifications and shape their experiences and worldview. Racial activation was the major dividing line around which Asian American reporters differed in response to White newsrooms and their norms.

Asian American reporters who have an activated racial identification are more likely to challenge norms of journalism, such as objectivity, because they understand them as White news values. They also see newsrooms as not only predominantly White but also as normatively and problematically White, so they are more active about making visible Asian American communities. This does not mean that they want to provide flattering, sympathetic coverage but, rather, fair and more complex coverage that uncovers problematic issues and abuses of power within Asian America but that also points to Asian Americans' community engagement and philanthropy. In other words, their goal is to cover the broad range of humanity—good, bad, and indifferent—in Asian American communities just as they do with White American communities. If there is an active purpose, it is simply to make Asian American communities and their issues visible while avoiding racist tropes and stereotypes in their coverage. From this perspective, they believe that the status quo is problematic as its focus on a singular, objective truth is a coded way of presenting a White perspective of truth while hiding the multiplicities of truths in the communities they cover. On the other hand, Asian American journalists for whom racial identification is not salient identify with the White norms of newsrooms and understand it as good journalism. It is, then, racial activation that leads to racial reflexivity that calls into question dominant assumptions of "good" news practice. This racial activation also intersects with gender as Asian American women reporters are much more likely to be racially activated, perhaps because of their double marginalization and/or because of Asian American men's identification with the masculinization of newsrooms, particularly in a society that devalues Asian American masculinity.

Studying Asian Americans, specifically, has revealed important similarities and differences in their experiences in newsrooms compared to Black American peers (there is not enough literature to make other cross-racial comparisons). It is important to remember that in the United States's racial triangulation of Black, Asian, and White, Asianness is often pitted in binary opposition with Blackness. Asianness is gendered feminine; it is presented as obedient and hardworking; it is presented as socially awkward and nerdy; and it is presented as being emotionally void and lacking human quality (Oh 2012; Eglash 2002). The dominance of the model minority stereotype also places Asian Americans in adjacency with Whiteness, whether or not Asian Americans want the distinction of being liminally accepted as "honorary Whites" (Tuan 1998). This means that Asian Americans experience U.S. racial formations differently because of their different function within U.S. racial politics and formations, and this experience of racialization persists in newsrooms, producing somewhat different

responses by Asian Americans as they navigate Whiteness and racial hegemony in their work.

For instance, compared to the description of Black American reporters in
the scholarly literature, Asian American reporters are more ambivalent in their
responses to the Whiteness of the newsrooms. This is likely because White
supremacy is predicated on anti-Blackness; thus it is likely that a greater per-
centage of Black American reporters have salient racial identifications that are
activated frequently. That said, we do not mean to imply that Asian American
reporters are individually ambivalent. Rather, there are comparatively more
Asian American reporters who do not have racially salient identifications, and, as
such, accept and valorize what other reporters describe as White norms.
Again, to clarify, in our study, there were only a handful of journalists for whom
racial identifications are largely unimportant. Another reason for not identifying racially is because Asian Americans can identify ethnically as Asian
Americans' families were often voluntary immigrants who have at least some
nominal connection to the heritages of their ancestors' national origins (Kibria 2002a). Indeed, because Asian American immigration only really opened
since 1965, just two years before the Kerner Commission, Asian Americans are
relatively new immigrants with a large share of first-generation Americans,
which renews transnational ties. Most new arrivals bring with them transnational wealth and settle in suburbs to provide their children with access to the
best schools and proximity to power. For Asian Americans who grow up in
White suburbs, they have proximity to White Americans, forming interracial
friendships, partnerships, and families. Growing up in these suburbs means
affinity with White people but also a sense of racialized isolation.

In and outside of their neighborhoods, because of Asian Americans' femi-
nization, they are also less likely to be viewed as threats, so experiences of racism are less obvious, including alienation, denied promotion, invisibility,
mockery, bullying, and marginalization. Though severe, anti-Asian racism does
not manifest as the same demonizing experiences that put Black lives under
direct threat from federal and state authorities. Indeed, Asian Americans often
blame themselves for their own (racialized) mistreatment because they have
been socialized to view it as a result of their own deficiencies rather than structural and interpersonal racism (Osajima 2007). For all of these reasons, Asian
Americans are less likely to have racially activated identifications. But, it is
important to point out that, nonetheless, the majority of our participants have
racially salient identifications and that they seek pan-ethnic and pan-racial
affinity and solidarity to cope with the precarity, disrespect, and/or sense of
constraint that working in White news produces.

One other way that Asian American reporters differ is that they do not feel
the same pressures to represent their community fairly as Black American

reporters have (Newkirk 2000). This seems to be truer in entertainment media in which Asian American media workers have discussed "sweat reps." The director of *Crazy Rich Asians*, Jon Chu, for instance, described the pressures he felt and placed upon himself to produce a movie that was faithful to Asian American sensibilities (Li 2016). This is, at least, one way in which Asian American reporters are freer from co-racial pressures. Instead, they share with reporters of color a response to White supremacy to accurately and fairly portray Asian American communities. The reasons for wanting Asian American representation are straightforward. What is less clear is why Asian American reporters do not face the same co-racial audience demands that Black American reporters do. Perhaps, it is because Asian Americans experience their lack of visibility most saliently in popular media, where they are deprived of images that are humanizing, cool, trendsetting, or attractive. This would make sense given the conspicuousness of the model minority stereotype, which dehumanizes Asian Americans as passive and socially awkward. On the other hand, Black Americans in entertainment are quite visible, particularly in music, comedy, and sports. By studying Asian Americans, it can eventually lead to cross-racial comparisons that point to the similarity of experiences for journalists of color as well as their differences. It can help to clarify how White racial hegemony functions and how different racial groups are situated within its terrain.

Finally, Asian American reporters differ because they have less discursive space to call into question anti-Asian racism. Though this was not expressed directly in these interviews, the scholarly literature demonstrates that because of the model minority stereotype, Asian Americans' racial grievances are frequently trivialized and even viewed with resentment. Because Asian Americans are expected to be a compliant model minority that buffers White people from accusations of racism, White people frequently interpret Asian Americans' claims of racism with hostility and a sense of betrayal, particularly when Asian Americans align interests or affinities with Black Americans (Kim 1998). Because the model minority had been created to counter claims of racism and specifically Black American calls for structural change, Asian Americans have been positioned in White racial hegemony as targets (Fong 2008). The consequence of this positioning is that Black, Latinx, and Indigenous Americans are sometimes unsympathetic and resent Asian Americans' claims of anti-Asian racism (Jo 2004; Eng and Han 2018). Further, some Asian Americans also internalize the belief that it is more morally correct to advocate for Black, Latinx, and Indigenous communities and colleagues, who they understand as suffering more (Son 2014; Lin 2020). By this reasoning, advocating for Asian Americans, including themselves, is seen as self-interested and dubious. Because of their positioning as "middle man minorities," Asian Americans are frequently disciplined into not voicing their own racialized harms. Whether it is because of wanting to center the experiences of Black, Latinx, and Indigenous colleagues and communities, or because of the dangers of confronting White racial hegemony in the newsroom and in their work, speaking out is fraught. For these reasons, it is important to study Asian American reporters, specifically, as their experience with racialization differs and provides a new vantage point from which Whiteness in news can be examined.

As our participants point out, newsrooms are "White" and this is where we make an intervention in the theoretical study of newsrooms and race. We borrow from Shannon Sullivan's description of the ontological expansiveness of "White space" to racialize the spaces they occupy by practicing conscious and subconscious habits of White privilege and normativity. Indeed, newsrooms remain among the least diverse workplaces in the nation. As such, we argue that the underlying reason for the inability of newsrooms to diversify in ways that approximate the communities they cover is because of the entrenched nature of newsrooms as White spaces. White owners, newsroom managers, columnists, and editors police the boundaries and habits of newsroom practice in subconscious and conscious ways. They determine what news is, define objectivity from their vantage point, and determine who is good enough to enter the newsroom's gates and get promoted. They create the everyday culture that makes these spaces hospitable for White journalists while requiring journalists of color to adjust and to avoid possible pitfalls. Performing fair and complex journalism that aligns with lived experience requires more work and provides rare newsroom rewards and accolades.

We, then, argue somewhat against the more generous interpretation of Heider (2000), who argues that there is incognizant racism that maintains the status quo because of White journalists' lack of investment in meaningful change. We argue, instead, that there is not only a lack of investment in change but a resistance to it that can be intentional as well as subconscious. This perspective of newsrooms as White spaces also aligns with Drew's (2011) conclusions that workshops that unambiguously demonstrated the persistence of Whiteness in a newsroom have had only a momentary impact on White reporters' self-reflexivity and news practices. As Sullivan (2006) points out, subconscious racial habits are not innocent. Indeed, they maintain and cement White privilege in everyday interactions. In addition, we understand newsrooms as masculinist, classist, and heteronormative. As such, newsrooms connect intersectionally to various hegemonies. This does not only construct White racial advantage but masculine, heteronormative, and elitist advantage, as well. These claims support the journalistic books on Black American reporters and newsrooms, such as Newkirk's (2000) *Within the Veil* and historical books such as Carroll's (2017) *Race News*.

The next theoretical implication of our study is to argue for the importance of racial identity positions in newsrooms. It is a bit of a trite claim that journalists of color are not all the same; however, there has been little work to understand the ingroup diversity. When it comes to their views of what it means to be Asian American, they are not wholly unique, but, like with any group, people form "imagined communities" as Stanley Fish (1976) has famously pointed out. The notion of "imagined" here does not mean they are untethered to reality, but, rather, it is a scholarly way of claiming that communities are created based on what people believe to be similarities. Because everyone within the same culture (the larger culture of the United States in this case) draws upon the same discourses in society, we tend to understand the world in ways that are understandable by other people in the culture, clustering into groups who articulate similar discursive positions and forming, as we say, identity positions. Although there are three different identity positions that we identified in this book, what matters for Asian American reporters when it comes to how they perceive and/or challenge White news, is racial activation. All of our reporters have racial identifications, but, for some, they are only activated in contextually specific circumstances, such as racial pride with a sports hero or racial anxiety with direct, overt racism. For others, the Whiteness of newsrooms has led to a persistent activation within the newsroom because of common experiences of marginalization that increase insight and sensitivity to racial harms. We have also found that racial activation intersects with gender as Asian American women are more likely to have salient racial identifications in their newsrooms.

We do not have a definitive conclusion for why this is the case, but the two most likely conclusions are that Asian American women's double marginalization in White masculine spaces leads to more instances of marginalization of which race and gender cannot be easily teased apart. The undifferentiation of these experiences may produce feelings of generalized marginalization that are tied to one or the other identification or, more accurately, to both simultaneously. Thus, Asian American women reporters' more frequent experiences of marginalization lead to sensitize racial activation. The other explanation has to do with Asian American men's devalued masculinity in dominant culture. Because of this, Asian American men sometimes align with hegemonic masculine norms as a way of claiming their worth. In a newsroom that is already masculinized, Asian American men's claims of racial harms would gender them as not tough enough, and because they are already emasculated in dominant culture, there are incentives to claim masculinity and belonging in the newsroom. That might mean a repudiation of feelings, including feelings of racial marginalization.

Our final theoretical intervention is to build upon the existing literature that challenges objectivity as a practice of discovering truth in news. Problems of journalistic objectivity at this point have been well documented. As scholars have argued, objectivity is not achievable, nor is it necessarily desirable. It perpetuates dominant worldviews and the status quo; it is morally irresponsible, as it promotes bystander journalism; and its supposedly neutral and detached stance obscures multiple and nuanced paths to uncovering truth (Glasser 1992; Maras 2013). We advance these criticisms of objectivity by explicitly linking it to White normativity in newsrooms. Objective news reporting practices—claiming neutrality and detachment in news work—is akin to how Whiteness maintains an invisible yet privileged position in society (Dolan 2011). That is, objectivity is steeped in Whiteness, and it hides White racial interests as well as obscures, trivializes, and marginalizes communities of color, both in the newsroom and society. This critique of objectivity as a White norm was supported by the majority of the journalists we interviewed, especially those who regularly engaged in racial reflexivity. As they saw newsrooms as White spaces, they also regarded their chief norm—objectivity—as the main architecture that perpetuates Whiteness in news coverage and in their newsrooms. As such, the racially activated reporters challenged objectivity by advocating for other news norms such as fairness, transparency, and complexity. Some also wanted to acknowledge and incorporate their biases and subjectivities into the structure of their reporting. However, these efforts are not radical, subverting the objectivity paradigm; rather, these acts of rebellion against objectivity are limited by the entrenched discourses and practices of their professions and their respective news institutions—mainstream, commercial organizations that serve largely (imagined) White audiences.

A New Direction

In our discussions with our participants, we learned that descriptions of creating change, or as we might understand from an academic standpoint, resistance, are situated in individual-level change. This reflects common ways of thinking within U.S. dominant culture that are tied to notions of individualism, a common value in the culture largely and in journalistic culture, specifically (Gans 1979). As such, their calls for change are far from radical. They do not call for overturning the system of journalism or its commercial model. They only call for limited structural change, such as more editors of color, news directors of color, and journalism professors of color. Most of their calls are for micro-challenges, such as finding and pitching stories and correcting White journalists' implicit biases and banal racism. What might be more subversive, the rethinking of objectivity, is primarily limited to their own private views of news norms.

However, as we discussed the White space of news, we learned that there are entrenched structural issues that would require structural change. These structural issues include: (1) under-representation in newsrooms and in leadership; (2) hiring and promotion of journalists with similar socioeconomic status and elite education, which produces a monolithic, elite journalistic class that reflects race and class hierarchies; (3) isolation of Asian American reporters in their newsrooms; (4) news' imagined audience as White, which is linked to commercial motivations of news—subscribers and advertisers; (5) White normativity of journalism curricula and faculty; (6) White normative news values, most specifically objectivity, but also news values such as prominence, and news practices such as which beats are assigned and which kinds of crime have the best video; and (7) the White political and economic structure of society that leads to the overreliance of White sources and perspectives in news.

It is beyond the scope of this book to provide specific structural solutions. Indeed, that might constitute an entire book itself. Our own suggestions will most likely be considered trite as journalists and journalism faculty have dedicated considerable energy to considering these intractable problems. That is, indeed, what makes a hegemony effective. It has interlocking systems that are mutually reinforcing. There are no simple solutions. Instead, we point to the need for structural change and incentives that are strong enough to disrupt White news. For instance, there must be mechanisms for making newsroom employment data transparent and incentives that could induce compliance with ASNE goals. There must also be pipelines to find and hire unconventional news workers and to create pipelines into management. Journalism schools must reflect upon their own curricula and adopt a twenty-first century curriculum that not only takes into consideration new technologies but an increasingly multiracial society. In the absence of these changes, pan-racial coalition among journalists of color, including the major associations, such as the Asian American Journalists Association, the National Association of Black Journalists, the National Association of Hispanic Journalists, and the Native American Journalists Association, is critical to agitate for change and to provide solidarity when journalists of color are brave enough to confront White racial hegemony in the profession or in their newsrooms. We hope for a new journalism that values not only diverse faces but diverse perspectives, too.

Acknowledgments

We are grateful for the support that we received that made writing this book possible. Any book requires a system of support that makes the life of the scholar and the author possible. Most importantly, this project relied on the trust and the participation of twenty Asian American journalists, the vast majority of whom responded to an email request from scholars they do not know. They gave us their time and insight into their lives and work. In some cases, they also dealt with the frustrations of technology as videoconferencing sometimes generated hiccups. We are grateful for their trust and, in some cases, their help in recruiting new participants. We hope that we have rewarded their trust with a faithful and insightful analysis of their experiences, and we hope that they find their participation in this project to be a meaningful one that has helped to move forward scholarly and journalistic conversations about Asian Americans in news, in particular, but also the experiences of reporters of color, more generally. We also want to thank the Asian American Journalists Association, which shared our call for participants with its members.

We also are grateful for our respective institutions that have made work on this book project possible. The first author, David, was supported by Ramapo College of New Jersey (RCNJ), and Seong Jae was supported by Pace University, which are our places of employment and which provided institutional resources necessary to conduct research. During these pandemic times, we relied on their institutional relationships with videoconferencing platforms such as Webex and Zoom, respectively, which helped us to collect and transcribe our interviews. In addition, RCNJ provided David with a Faculty Development Fund summer stipend in 2020 to conduct interviews. Without this financial support, data collection would have certainly been slower.

We also would like to thank the National Communication Association's Asian/Pacific American Communication Studies Division for accepting two chapters for presentation and for the constructive feedback that has helped us to improve those chapters for publication and that provided personal support to keep the project moving forward. Further, we are grateful for Jasper Chang, the acquisitions editor at Rutgers University Press, who saw promise in this project and advocated for it, and we are grateful for Carah Naseem, who took over and capably managed the book through completion. It is always difficult to pick up a project in the middle of the process, and Carah made the process seamless and enjoyable. Finally, we would like to thank our families who have given us the time and emotional support needed to complete this project. We hope that our book can make a small contribution to the lives that our children live as Asian Americans.

Notes

Chapter 1   Introduction

1   For our purposes, we understand the label "Asian American" in inclusive ways to include anyone with lived experience in the United States who has heritage ties to Asia. This can include Chinese Americans as East Asian Americans, Filipinx Americans as Southeast Asian Americans, Russian Americans from Siberia as North Asian Americans, Bangladeshi Americans as South Asian Americans, Iranian Americans as West Asian Americans, and Pacific Islander Americans as Asian Americans. For us, what matters primarily is that individual's self-identify as Asian American and having some heritage claim to it. As a practical matter for this study, we only interviewed Asian Americans with East Asian and Southeast Asian heritage ties because of our concern with how they navigated their work when racially associated with COVID-19.

2   It should be noted that Mansfield-Richardson (2000) has published a book about the *coverage* of Asian Americans, which includes survey results from Asian American journalists.

3   The name has since been changed to the American Society of News Editors to better reflect other modes of delivering news.

4   The first author, David Oh, interned at WTVH-TV in Syracuse, New York, and worked for Arirang TV, an English-language cable network in Seoul. The second author, Seong Jae Min, worked for the IHT-JoongAng Daily, a major English-language newspaper in Seoul, and for the United Nations Information Center in Washington, D.C. Newsrooms for English-language Korean outlets are typically led by White managers and editors.

5   According to the 2019 American Society of News Editors (ASNE) diversity survey, Asian Americans make up about 5 percent of news workers (https://www.newsleaders.org/2019-diversity-survey-results). Asian Americans in broadcast news are heavily underrepresented, making up only about 2 percent of the workforce, according to the Radio, Television, Digital News Association survey of 2020 (https://www.rtdna.org/article/2020_research_newsroom_diversity). Both surveys show that Asian Americans in leadership positions are even fewer in

number. According to the 2020 U.S. Census, Asian Americans make up about 6 percent of the population.

6 A conjuncture refers to a contextually specific historical, cultural, social, political, and technological time. It is a concept that underscores cultural studies' commitments to context.

7 We use the example of Euless because none of our participants are from this particular city. The first author was raised there.

Chapter 2 Asian American Reporters' Racial and Ethnic Identifications

1 Pierre Bourdieu ([1977] 2013) coined the term "habitus" to refer to socially constructed patterns of practice that are internalized by people in a society.

2 It should be clarified, however, that we began asking the questions to gain context and did not have early intentions of writing about the reporters' identification beliefs and practices. Because of this orientation to the interview and the participants' own expectations about the interviews, these conversations were relatively short as participants guided many of their answers toward their work as reporters. In some cases, particularly when identifications were not salient features of their everyday lives or the meanings they gave to their news work, the conversations were limited.

3 Imagined community is a concept by (Anderson 1983) which people construct a sense of nation—who belongs and who does not—based on imagined constructions that define and limit membership.

Chapter 4 Navigating White Newsrooms

1 Participants themselves describe their experiences of racist harms with milder language such as racially problematic situations or racialized issues, but we do not use these terms primarily because they are euphemistic. They all point to discrimination that is based on race, whether interpersonal or structural. Racism does not refer to scale but to a harm caused by perceptions of racial difference. We do, however, refer to microaggressions because these are particular kinds of acts, usually discursive, that are subconsciously dismissive to the speaker and only meaningful in the aggregate. It is the pattern and frequency of microaggressions that cause harm rather than the single statement or question.

Chapter 5 What Counts as News

1 Kovach and Rosenstiel's understanding of journalistic roles and missions is comprehensive and thus not easily reduced to a single position. They also updated their views in the most recent edition of the book. Still, one can argue that providing accurate and reliable facts is at the heart of the journalism they espouse.

2 Quote from Trump's press conference on June 5, 2020. Trump said this while touting unexpectedly strong economic indicators.

References

Adams, Catherine. 2018. "'They Go for Gender First': The Nature and Effect of Sexist Abuse of Female Technology Journalists." *Journalism Practice* 12 (7): 850–869. doi: 10.1080/17512786.2017.1350115.

Ahn, Ji-Hyun, and Hyewon Park. 2019. "Dealing with Hate Speech: Voices from Young Koreans Living in Japan." *Asian Journal of Social Science* 47: 677–700.

Alcoff, Linda Martin. 1998. "What Should White People Do?" *Hypatia* 13 (3): 6–26. doi: 10.1111/j.1527-2001.1998.tb01367.x.

Alemán, Sonya M. 2014. "Locating Whiteness in Journalism Pedagogy." *Critical Studies in Media Communication* 31 (1): 72–88. doi: 10.1080/15295036.2013.808355.

Anderson, Benedict. 1983. *Imagined Communities: Reflections on the Origin and Spread of Nationalism*. Revised ed. New York: Verso.

Anderson, Rob, Robert Dardenne, and George Killenberg. 1994. *The Conversation of Journalism: Communication, Community, and News*. Westport, CT: Praeger.

Arana, Gabriel. 2018. "Decades of Failure." *Columbia Journalism Review*, July 26, 2022, https://www.cjr.org/special_report/race-ethnicity-newsrooms-data.php.

Atkin, Annabelle L., and Alisia G. T. T. Tran. 2020. "The Roles of Ethnic Identity and Metastereotype Awareness in the Racial Discrimination-Psychological Adjustment Link for Asian Americans at Predominantly White Institutions." *Cultural Diversity and Ethnic Minority Psychology* 26 (4): 498–508. doi: 10.1037/cdp0000323.

Bachmann, Ingrid. 2019. "Advocacy Journalism." In *Oxford Research Encyclopedia of Communication*. New York: Oxford University Press.

Baldasty, Gerald J. 1992. *The Commercialization of News in the Nineteenth Century*. Madison, WI: University of Wisconsin Press.

Barroso, Amanda, and Anna Brown. 2021. "Gender Pay Gap in U.S. Held Steady in 2020." Pew Research Center.

Bhatt, Archana J. 2003. "Asian Indians and the Model Minority Narrative: A Neocolonial System." In *The Emerging Monoculture: Assimilation and the "Model Minority,"* edited by Eric Mark Kramer, 203–220. Westport, CT: Praeger.

Bhopal, Kalwant. 2018. *White Privilege: The Myth of a Post-Racial Society*. Bristol, UK: Policy Press.

Bonilla-Silva, Eduardo. 2004. "From Bi-Racial to Tri-Racial: Towards a New System of Racial Stratification in the USA." *Ethnic and Racial Studies* 27 (6): 931–950. doi: 10.1080/0141987042000268530.

Bonilla-Silva, Eduardo. 2010a. "Color-Blind Racism." In *Race, Class, and Gender in the United States,* edited by Paula S. Rothenberg and Soniya Munshi, 113–119. New York: Worth Publishers.

Bonilla-Silva, Eduardo. 2010b. *Racism Without Racists: Color-Blind Racism and Racial Inequality in Contemporary America.* Lanham, MD: Rowman & Littlefield.

Bourdieu, Pierre. (1977) 2013. *Outline of a Theory of Practice.* New York: Cambridge University Press.

Boylorn, Robin M., and Mark P. Orbe. 2014. "Critical Autoethnography as Method of Choice." In *Critical Autoethnography: Intersecting Cultural Identities in Everyday Life,* edited by Robin M. Boylorn and Mark P. Orbe, 13–26. Walnut Creek, CA: Left Coast Press.

Budiman, Abby. 2020. "Asian Americans Are the Fastest-Growing Racial or Ethnic Group in the U.S. Electorate." Pew Research Center. https://www.pewresearch.org/fact-tank/2020/05/07/asian-americans-are-the-fastest-growing-racial-or-ethnic-group-in-the-u-s-electorate/.

Butterworth, Michael L. 2007. "Race in 'The Race': Mark Mcgwire, Sammy Sosa, and the Heroic Constructions of Whiteness." *Critical Studies in Media Communication* 24 (3): 228–244. doi: 10.1080/07393180701520926.

Byerly, Carolyn M., and Karen Ross. 2006. *Women and Media: A Critical Introduction.* Malden, MA: Blackwell.

Byerly, Carolyn M., and Clint C. Wilson. 2009. "Journalism as Kerner Turns 40: Its Multicultural Problems and Possibilities." *Howard Journal of Communications* 20 (3): 209–221.

Calafell, Bernadette. 2010. "'Angry Woman of Color': Academic Policing and Disciplining Women of Color in a Post (Fill in the Blank) Era." *Journal of Communication Inquiry* 34 (3): 240–245. doi: 10.1177/0196859910371375.

Calafell, Bernadette Marie. 2007. "Mentoring and Love: An Open Letter." *Cultural Studies ↔ Critical Methodologies* 7 (4): 425–441. doi: 10.1177/1532708607305123.

Campbell, Christopher P. 1995. *Race, Myth, and the News.* Thousand Oaks, CA: Sage Publications.

Carey, James W. 1989. *Communication as Culture: Essays on Media and Society.* Boston: Unwin Hyman.

Carpenter, Julia. 2019. "Layoffs Hit Women and Minorities Hardest. Here's Why." CNN. Accessed October 16, 2021.

Carroll, Fred. 2017. *Race News: Black Journalists and the Fight for Racial Justice in the Twentieth Century.* Champaign, IL: University of Illinois Press.

Castañeda, Leonardo. 2020. "Hundreds of Anti-Asian Hate Incidents Reported in California During Pandemic: 'There Is Not Just a Virus Known as COVID-19, There's a Virus of Racism.'" *The Mercury News.*

Chalaby, Jean K. 1996. "Journalism as an Anglo-American Invention: A Comparison of the Development of French and Anglo-American Journalism, 1830s–1920s." *European Journal of Communication* 11 (3): 303–326. doi: 10.1177/0267323196011003002.

Chang, Iris. 2003. *The Chinese in America: A Narrative History.* New York: Viking.

Charles, Matthew. 2019. "Advocacy Journalism." In *The International Encyclopedia of Journalism Studies* 1–5. Hoboken, NJ: Wiley & Sons.

Charmaz, Kathy, and Linda Belgrave. 2012. "Qualitative Interviewing and Grounded Theory Analysis." In *The SAGE Handbook of Interview Research: The Complexity of the Craft*, edited by Jaber F. Gubrium, James A. Holstein, Amir B. Marvasti, and Karyn D. McKinney, 347–366. Thousand Oaks, CA: Sage.

Chen, Gina Masullo, Paromita Pain, Victoria Y. Chen, Madlin Mekelburg, Nina Springer, and Franziska Troger. 2018. "'You Really Have to Have a Thick Skin': A Cross-Cultural Perspective on How Online Harassment Influences Female Journalists." *Journalism* 21 (7): 877–895. doi: 10.1177/1464884918768500.

Cheryan, Sapna, and Benoît Monin. 2005. "'Where Are You *Really* From?': Asian Americans and Identity Denial." *Journal of Personality and Social Psychology* 89 (5): 717–730. doi: 10.1037/0022-3514.89.5.717.

Chong, Kelly H. 2017. "'Asianness' Under Construction." *Sociological Perspectives* 60 (1): 52–76. doi: 10.2307/26579793.

Cisneros, J. David, and Thomas K. Nakayama. 2015. "New Media, Old Racisms: Twitter, Miss America, and Cultural Logics of Race." *Journal of International and Intercultural Communication* 8 (2): 108–127. doi: 10.1080/17513057.2015.1025328.

Coloma, Roland Sintos. 2012. "White Gazes, Brown Beasts: Imperial Feminism and Disciplining Desires and Bodies in Colonial Encounters." *Paedagogica Historica* 48 (2): 243–261. doi: 10.1080/00309230.2010.547511.

Correa, Teresa. 2010. "Framing Latinas: Hispanic Women through the Lenses of Spanish-Language and English-Language News Media." *Journalism* 11 (4): 425–443. doi: 10.1177/1464884910367597.

Cross, William E. 1978. "The Thomas and Cross Models of Psychological Nigrescence." *Journal of Black Psychology* 5 (1): 13–31. doi: 10.1177/009579847800500102.

DeCook, Julia, and Mi Hyun Yoon. 2021. "Kung Flu and Roof Koreans: Asian/Americans as the Hated Other and Proxies of Hating in the White Imaginary." *Journal of Hate Studies* 17 (1): 119–132. doi: 10.33972/jhs.199.

Delaney, Paul. 2018. "Kerner Report at 50: Media Diversity Still Decades Behind." *USA Today*. Accessed May 23, 2021.

Dennis, Everette E., and John Calhoun Merrill. 1984. *Basic Issues in Mass Communication: A Debate*. New York: Macmillan.

DiAngelo, Robin. 2011. "White Fragility." *International Journal of Critical Pedagogy* 3 (3): 54–70. Accessed August 17, 2015.

Dixon, Travis L., and Daniel Linz. 2000. "Race and the Misrepresentation of Victimization on Local Television News." *Communication Research* 27 (5): 547–573. doi: 10.1177/009365000027005001.

Docan-Morgan, Sara. 2010. "'They Don't Know What It's Like to Be in My Shoes': Topic Avoidance About Race in Transracially Adoptive Families." *Journal of Social and Personal Relationships* 28 (3): 336–355. doi: 10.1177/0265407510382177.

Dolan, Kevin. 2011. "Whiteness and News: The Interlocking Social Construction of 'Realities.'" PhD diss., University of Illinois.

Domke, David, Philip Garland, Andre Billeaudeaux, and John Hutcheson. 2003. "Insights into U.S. Racial Hierarchy: Racial Profiling, News Sources, and September 11." *Journal of Communication Inquiry* 53 (4): 606–623. doi: 10.1111/j.1460-2466.2003.tb02913.x.

Douai, Aziz, and Sharon Lauricella. 2014. "The 'Terrorism' Frame in 'Neo-Orientalism': Western News and the Sunni-Shia Muslim Sectarian Relations After 9/11." *International Journal of Media & Cultural Politics* 10 (1): 7–24. doi: 10.1386/macp.10.1.7_1.

Drew, Emily M. 2011. "'Coming to Terms with Our Own Racism': Journalists Grapple with the Racialization of Their News." *Critical Studies in Media Communication* 28 (4): 353–373. doi: 10.1080/15295036.2010.514936.

DuBois, W.E.B. (1903) 1989. *The Souls of Black Folks.* New York: Bantam Books.

Durham, Meenakshi Gigi. 1998. "On the Relevance of Standpoint Epistemology to the Practice of Journalism: The Case for 'Strong Objectivity.'" *Communication Theory* 8 (2): 117–140.

Dyer, Richard. 1988. "White." *Screen* 29 (4): 44–64. doi: 10.1093/screen/29.4.44.

Dyer, Richard. 1997. *White.* New York: Routledge.

Edwards, Louise, Stefano Occhipenti, and Simon Ryan. 2000. "Food and Immigration: The Indigestion Trope Contexts the Sophistication Trope." *Journal of Intercultural Studies* 21 (3): 297–308. doi: 10.1080/07256860020007458.

Eglash, Ron. 2002. "Race, Sex, and Nerds: From Black Geeks to Asian American Hipsters." *Social Text* 71 (2): 49–64. doi: 10.1215/01642472-20-2_71-49.

Elmore, Cindy. 2009. "Recollections in Hindsight from Women Who Left: The Gendered Newsroom Culture." *Women & Language* 30 (2): 18–27. Accessed July 7, 2021.

Eng, David L., and Shinhee Han. 2018. *Racial Melancholia, Racial Dissociation: On the Social and Psychic Lives of Asian Americans.* Durham, NC: Duke University Press.

Entman, Robert M. 1993. "Framing: Toward Clarification of a Fractured Paradigm." *Journal of Communication* 43 (4): 51–58. doi: 10.1111/j.1460-2466.1993.tb01304.x.

Entman, Robert M., and Andrew Rojecki. 1993. "Freezing out the Public: Elite and Media Framing of the U.S. Anti-Nuclear Movement." *Political Communication* 10: 155–173.

Entman, Robert M., and Andrew Rojecki. 2000. *The Black Image in the White Mind: Media and Race in America,* edited by Susan Herbst and Benjamin I. Page, Studies in Communication, Media, and Public Opinion. Chicago: The University of Chicago Press.

Erikson, Erik H. 1968. *Identity, Youth, and Crisis.* New York: W.W. Norton.

Espiritu, Yen Le. 1992. *Asian American Panethncity: Bridging Institutions and Identities,* edited by Sucheng Chan, David Palumbo-Liu, Michael Omi, Scott Wong, and Linda Trinh Vo, Asian American History and Culture. Philadelphia, PA: Temple University Press.

Espiritu, Yen Le. 2002. "Multiple Identities of Second-Generation Filipinos." In *The Second-Generation: Ethnic Identity Among Asian Americans,* edited by Pyong Gap Min, 19–52. New York: AltaMira Press.

Espiritu, Yen Le. 2004. "Ideological Racism and Cultural Resistance: Constructing Our Own Images." In *Race, Class, and Gender: An Anthology,* edited by Margaret L. Andersen and Patricia Hill Collins, 175–184. Belmont, CA: Wadsworth.

Ferree, Myra Marx, William A. Gamson, Jürgen Gerhards, and Dieter Rucht. 2002. "Four Models of the Public Sphere in Modern Democracies." *Theory and Society* 31 (3): 289–324. doi: 10.1023/A:1016284431021.

Fish, Stanley. 1976. "Interpreting the 'Variorum.'" *Critical Inquiry* 2 (3): 465–485.

Fisher, Caroline. 2016. "The Advocacy Continuum: Towards a Theory of Advocacy in Journalism." *Journalism* 17 (6): 711–726. doi: 10.1177/1464884915582311.

Folkenflik, David. 2020. "Editors Barred a Black Reporter from Covering Protests. Then Her Newsroom Rebelled." NPR.org.

Fong, Timothy P. 2008. *The Contemporary Asian American Experience: Beyond the Model Minority,* 3rd ed. Upper Saddle River, NJ: Pearson Prentice Hall.

Gabriel, John. 1998. *Whitewash: Racialized Politics and the Media*. New York, NY: Routledge.

Gandy, Oscar H. 1994. "From Bad to Worse—The Media's Framing of Race and Risk." *Media Studies Journal* 8 (3): 39–48.

Gandy, Oscar H. 1998. *Communication and Race: A Structural Perspective*. London: Arnold.

Gans, Herbert J. 1979. *Deciding What's News: A Study of CBS Evening News, NBC Nightly News, Newsweek, and Time*. New York: Pantheon Books.

Gee, Buck, and Denise Peck. 2018. "Asian Americans Are the Least Likely Group in the U.S. to Be Promoted to Management." *Harvard Business Review*.

Gilroy, Paul. 1997. "Diaspora and the Detours of Identity." In *Identity and Difference*, edited by Kathryn Woodward, 299–346. Thousand Oaks, CA: Sage Publications.

Gilroy, Paul. 2012. "'My Britain Is Fuck All': Zombie Multiculturalism and the Race Politics of Citizenship." *Identities: Global Studies in Culture and Power* 19 (4): 380–397. doi: 10.1080/1070289X.2012.725512.

Gitlin, Todd. 1980. *The Whole World Is Watching: Mass Media in the Making and Unmaking of the New Left*. Berkeley, CA: University of California Press.

Glaser, Barney G., and Anselm S. Strauss. 1967. *The Discovery of Grounded Theory: Strategies for Qualitative Research*. Chicago: Aldine Publishing Company.

Glasser, Theodore L. 1992. "Objectivity and News Bias." In *Philosophical Issues in Journalism*, edited by Elliot D. Cohen, 176–185. New York: Oxford University Press.

Gonzalez-Sobrino, Bianca, and Devon R. Goss. 2019. "Exploring the Mechanisms of Racialization Beyond the Black/White Binary." *Ethnic and Racial Studies* 42 (4): 505–510. doi: 10.1080/01419870.2018.1444781.

Grieco, Elizabeth. 2018. "Newsroom Employees Are Less Diverse than U.S. Workers Overall." Pew Research Center. https://www.pewresearch.org/fact-tank/2018/11/02/newsroom-employees-are-less-diverse-than-u-s-workers-overall/.

Grossberg, Lawrence. 1996. "Identity and Cultural Studies: Is That All There Is?" In *Questions of Cultural Identity*, edited by Stuart Hall and Paul Du Gay, 87–107. Thousand Oaks, CA: Sage Publications.

Hackett, Robert A., and Yuezhi Zhao. 1998. *Sustaining Democracy?: Journalism and the Politics of Objectivity*. Toronto, ON: University of Toronto Press.

Hall, Stuart. 1991. "Signification, Representation, Ideology: Althusser and the Post-Structuralist Debates." In *Critical Perspective on Media and Society*, edited by Robert K. Avery and David Eason, 89–113. New York: The Guilford Press.

Hall, Stuart. 1996a. "Introduction: Who needs 'Identity'?" In *Questions of Cultural Identity*, edited by Stuart Hall and Paul Du Gay, 1–17. Thousand Oaks, CA: Sage Publications.

Hall, Stuart. 1996b. "New Ethnicities." In *Stuart Hall: Critical Dialogues in Cultural Studies*, edited by David Morley and Kuan-Hsing Chen, 443–451. New York: Routledge.

Hall, Stuart. 2003. "The Whites of Their Eyes: Racist Ideologies and the Media." In *Gender, Race, and Class in Media: A Text-Reader*, edited by Gail Dines and Jean M. Humez, 89–93. Thousand Oaks, CA: Sage Publications.

Hamamoto, Darrell Y. 1994. *Monitored Peril: Asian Americans and the Politics of Representation*. Minneapolis, MN: University of Minnesota Press.

Hamilton, James T. 2004. *All the News That's Fit to Sell: How the Market Transforms Information into the News*. Princeton, NJ: Princeton University Press.

Han, Alan. 2007. "'Can I Tell You What We Have to Put Up With?': Stinky Fish and Offensive Durian." *Continuum: Journal of Media & Cultural Studies* 21 (3): 361–377. doi: 10.1080/10304310701460714.

Heider, Don. 2000. *White News: Why Local News Programs Don't Cover People of Color.* Mahwah, NJ: Lawrence Erlbaum Associates.

Herakova, Liliana L., Dijana Jelaca, Razvan Sibii, and Leda Cooks. 2011. "Voicing Silence and Imagining Citizenship: Dialogues About Race and Whiteness in a 'Postracial' Era." *Communication Studies* 62 (4): 372–388. doi: 10.1080/10510974.2011.588072.

Holling, Michelle A., Dreama G. Moon, and Alexandra Jackson Nevis. 2014. "Racist Violations and Racializing Apologia in a Post-Racism Era." *Journal of International and Intercultural Communication* 7 (4): 260–286. doi: 10.1080/17513057.2014.964144.

hooks, bell. 1984. *Talking Back.* Boston, MA: South End Press.

Iwamoto, Derek Kenji, Nalini Junko Negi, Rachel Negar Partiali, and John W. Creswell. 2013. "The Racial and Ethnic Identity Formation Process of Second-Generation Asian Indian Americans: A Phenomenological Study." *Journal of Multicultural Counseling and Development* 41: 224–239. doi: 10.1002/J.2161–1912.2013.00038.x.

Jackson, Ronald L. 1999. "White Space, White Privilege: Mapping Discursive Inquiry into the Self." *Quarterly Journal of Speech* 85: 38–54. doi: 10.1080/00335639909384240.

Jo, Ji-Yeon O. 2004. "Neglected Voices in the Multicultural America: Asian American Racial Politics and its Implication for Multicultural Education." *Multicultural Perspectives* 6 (1): 19–25. doi: 10.1207/S15327892mcp0601_4.

Junn, Jane, and Natalie Masuoka. 2008. "Identities in Context: Politicized Racial Group Consciousness Among Asian American and Latino Youth." *Applied Developmental Science* 12 (2): 93–101. doi: 10.1080/10888690801997234.

Kammerer, Peter. 2018. "'Chinese Kitchens Are Dirty and MSG Is Bad for You': How Racism Persists in the West, Despite Evidence to the Contrary." *South China Morning Post.*

Kang, Laura Hyun-Yi. 2002. "The Desiring of Asian Female Bodies: Interracial Romance and Cinematic Subjection." In *Screening Asian Americans*, edited by Peter X Feng, 71–98. New Brunswick, NJ: Rutgers University Press.

Kaplan, Richard. 2009. "The Origins of Objectivity in American Journalism." In *The Routledge Companion to News and Journalism*, edited by Stuart Allan. London: Routledge.

Karlsson, Michael. 2011. "The Immediacy of Online News, the Visibility of Journalistic Processes and a Restructuring of Journalistic Authority." *Journalism* 12 (3): 279–295. doi: 10.1177/1464884910388223.

Karmaker, Goutam, and Somasree Sarkar. 2021. "Shannon Sullivan's Perspectives on Transactional Bodies, Racism, and Identity: A Pragmatist Feminist Approach." *Journal of Gender Studies.* doi: 10.1080/09589236.2021.1923465.

Kawai, Yuko. 2005. "Stereotyping Asian Americans: The Dialectic of the Model Minority and the Yellow Peril." *Howard Journal of Communications* 16 (2): 109–130. doi: 10.1080/10646170590948974.

Kellner, Douglas. 1995. *Media Culture: Cultural Studies, Identity, and Politics Between the Modern and the Postmodern.* New York: Routledge.

Kelly, Casey Ryan. 2020. "Donald J. Trump and the Rhetoric of White Ambivalence." *Rhetoric & Public Affairs* 23 (2): 195–224. doi: 10.14321/rhetpublaffa.23.2.0195.

Kiang, Lisa, Melissa Witkow, and Mariette C. Champagne. 2013. "Normative Changes in Ethnic and American Identities and Links with Adjustment Among Asian American Adolescents." *Developmental Psychology* 49 (9): 1713–1722. doi: 10.1037/a0030840.

Kibria, Nazli. 1997. "The Construction of 'Asian American': Reflections on Intermarriage and Ethnic Identity Among Second-Generation Chinese and Korean Americans." *Ethnic and Racial Studies* 20 (3): 523–544.

Kibria, Nazli. 2002a. *Becoming Asian American: Second-Generation Chinese and Korean American Identities*. Baltimore, MD: The John Hopkins University Press.

Kibria, Nazli. 2002b. "College and Notions of 'Asian Americans': Second-Generation Chinese Americans and Korean Americans." In *The Second Generation: Ethnic Identity Among Asian Americans*, edited by Pyong Gap Min, 183–207. New York: AltaMira Press.

Kil, Sang Hea. 2020. "Reporting from the Whites of Their Eyes: How Whiteness as Neoliberalism Promotes Racism in the News Coverage of 'All Lives Matter.'" *Communication Theory* 30: 21–40. doi: 10.1093/ct/qtz019.

Kim, Claire Jean. 1999a. "The Racial Triangulation of Asian Americans." *Politics & Society* 27 (1): 105–138. doi: 10.1177/0032329299027001005.

Kim, Elaine H. 1998. "'At Least You're Not Black': Asian Americans in U.S. Race Relations." *Social Justice* 25 (3): 3–12.

Kim, Grace S., and Tanvi N. Shah. 2020. "When Perceptions Are Fragile but Also Enduring: An Asian American Reflection on COVID-19." *Journal of Humanistic Psychology* 60 (5): 604–610. doi: 10.1177/0022167820937485.

Kim, Janine Young. 1999b. "Are Asians Black?: The Asian-American Civil Rights Agenda and the Contemporary Significance of The Black/White Paradigm." *The Yale Law Journal* 108 (8): 2385–2412.

Kovach, Bill, and Tom Rosenstiel. 2001. *The Elements of Journalism: What Newspeople Should Know and the Public Should Expect*, 1st ed. New York: Crown Publishing Group.

Kumar, Deepa. 2010. "Framing Islam: The Resurgence of Orientalism During the Bush II Era." *Journal of Communication Inquiry* 34 (3): 254–277. doi: 10.1177/0196859910363174.

Kuo, Wen H. 1995. "Coping with Racial Discrimination: The Case of Asian Americans." *Ethnic and Racial Studies* 18 (1): 109–127. doi: 10.1080/01419870.1995.9993856.

Kvale, Steinar. 1996. *InterViews: An Introduction to Qualitative Research Interviewing*. Thousand Oaks, CA: Sage Publications.

Le, Danvy, Maneesh Arora, and Christopher Stout. 2020. "'Are You Threatening Me?': Asian-American Panethnicity in the Trump Era." *Social Science Quarterly* 101 (6): 2183–2192. doi: 10.1111/ssqu.12870.

Le, Thomas K., Leah Cha, Hae-Ra Han, and Winston Tseng. 2020. "Anti-Asian Xenophobia and Asian American COVID-19 Disparities." *American Journal of Public Health* 110 (9): 1371–1373. doi: 10.2105/AJPH.2020.305846.

Lee, Julia H. 2016. "Model Maternity: Amy Chua and Asian American Motherhood." In *Global Asian American Popular Cultures*, edited by Shilpa Dave, LeiLani Nishime, and Tasha Oren, 61–73. New York: New York University Press.

Lee, Robert G. 1999. *Orientals: Asian Americans in Popular Culture*, edited by Sucheng Chan, David Palumbo-Liu, and Michael Omi, Asian American History and Culture. Philadelphia, PA: Temple University Press.

Leong, Russell C. 2003. "Chaos, SARS, Yellow Peril: Virulent Metaphors for the Asian American Experience?" *Amerasia Journal* 29 (1): v–viii. doi: 10.17953/amer.29.1.3342w7n244051178.

Li, Shirley. 2016. "*Crazy Rich Asians*: Director Jon M. Chu Talks Challenges of Finding All-Asian Cast." *Entertainment Weekly.*

Liang, T. H., Alvin N. Alvarez, Linda P. Juang, and Mandy X. Liang. 2007. "The Role of Coping in the Relationship Between Perceived Racism and Racism-Related Stress for Asian Americans: Gender Differences." *Journal of Counseling Psychology* 54 (2): 132–141. doi: 10.1037/0022-0167.54.2.132.

Liebler, Carol M. 1997. "Individual, Organizational, and Social Structural Influences on Newspaper Framing of Civil Disorder." International Communication Association, Montreal, Quebec: May 1997.

Liebler, Carol M., Joseph Schwartz, and Todd Harper. 2009. "Queer Tales of Morality: The Press, Same-Sex Marriage, and Hegemonic Framing." *Journal of Communication* 59 (4): 653–675.

Lin, May. 2020. "From Alienated to Activists: Expressions and Formation of Group Consciousness Among Asian American Young Adults." *Journal of Ethnic and Migration Studies* 46 (7): 1405–1424. doi: 10.1080/1369183X.2018.1495067.

Lipsitz, George. 1998. *The Possessive Investment in Whiteness: How White People Profit from Identity Politics*. Philadelphia, PA: Temple University Press.

Liu, Emily. 2020. Covid-19 Has Inflamed Racism Against Asian-Americans. Here's How to Fight Back. CNN.

Liu, William M. 2002. "Exploring the Lives of Asian American Men: Racial Identity, Male Role Norms, Gender Role Conflict, and Prejudicial Attitudes." *Psychology of Men & Masculinity* 3 (2): 107–118. doi: 10.1037//1524-9220.3.2.107.

Löfgren Nilsson, Monica. 2010. "'Thinkings' and 'Doings' of Gender: Gendering Processes in Swedish Television News Production." *Journalism Practice* 4 (1): 1–16. doi: 10.1080/17512780903119693.

Louie, Andrea. 2009. "'Pandas, Lions, and Dragons, Oh My!': How White American Parents Construct Chineseness." *Journal of Asian American Studies* 12 (3): 285–320.

Lowe, Lisa. 2007. "Heterogeneity, Hybridity, Mulitiplicity: Marking Asian American Differences." In *Asian American Studies: A Reader*, edited by Jean Yu-wen Shen Wu and Min Song, 423–442. New Brunswick, NJ: Rutgers University Press.

Mak, Aaron. 2021. "'Men's Rights Asians' Think This is Their Moment." *Slate*, July 26, 2022, https://slate.com/technology/2021/09/mens-rights-asians-aznidentity-stop-asian-hate-reddit.html.

Malaolu, Patrick O. 2014. "Sources and the News From Africa: Why Are There No Skyscrapers in Nigeria?" *Ecquid Novi: African Journalism Studies* 35 (1): 25–42. doi: 10.1080/02560054.2014.886659.

Mallapragada, Madhavi. 2021. "Asian Americans as Racial contagion." *Cultural Studies* 35 (2–3): 279–290. doi: 10.1080/09502386.2021.1905678.

Mansfield-Richardson, Virginia. 2000. *Asian Americans and the Mass Media: A Content Analysis of Twenty United States Newspapers and a Survey of Asian American Journalists*, edited by Franklin Ng, Garland Studies on Asian Americans. New York, NY: Garland Publishing, Inc.

Maras, Steven. 2013. *Objectivity in Journalism*. Cambridge, UK: Polity.

Massanari, Adrienne, and Shira Chess. 2018. "Attack of the 50-Foot Social Justice Warrior: The Discursive Construction of SJW Memes as the Monstrous Feminine." *Feminist Media Studies* 18 (4): 525–542. doi: 10.1080/14680777.2018.144733.

McCombs, Maxwell. 1997. "Building Consensus: The News Media's Agenda-Setting Roles." *Political Communication* 14: 433–443. doi: 10.1080/105846097199236.

Meyers, Marian, and Lynne Gayle. 2015. "African American Women in the Newsroom: Encoding Resistance." *Howard Journal of Communications* 26 (3): 292–312. doi: 10.1080/10646175.2015.1049760.

Miller, Kaitlin C. 2020. "Harassing the Fourth Estate: The Prevalence and Effects of Outsider-Initiated Harassment Towards Journalists." PhD diss., School of Journalism, University of Oregon.

Miller, Kaitlin C., and Seth C. Lewis. 2020. "Journalists, Harassment, and Emotional Labor: The Case of Women in On-Air Roles at US Local Television Stations." *Journalism*. doi: 10.1177/1464884919899016.

Min, Eungjun. 2003. "Demythologizing the 'Model Minority.'" In *The Emerging Monoculture: Assimilation and the 'Model Minority'*, edited by Eric Mark Kramer, 191–201. Westport, CT: Praeger.

Min, Pyong Gap. 2002. "Introduction." In *The Second Generation: Ethnic Identity Among Asian Americans*, edited by Pyong Gap Min, 1–17. New York: AltaMira Press.

Min, Seong Jae. 2018. *As Democracy Goes, So Does Journalism: Evolution of Journalism in Liberal, Deliberative, and Participatory Democracy*. Lanham, MD: Rowman & Littlefield.

Min, Seong Jae, and John C. Feaster. 2010. "Missing Children in National News Coverage: Racial and Gender Representations of Missing Children Cases." *Communication Research Reports* 27 (3): 207–216. doi: 10.1080/08824091003776289.

Mindich, David T. Z. 2000. *Just The Facts: How "Objectivity" Came to Define American Journalism*. New York: NYU Press.

Mueller, Jennifer C. 2017. "Producing Colorblindness: Everyday Mechanisms of White Ignorance." *Social Problems* 64 (2): 219–238. doi: 10.1093/socpro/spw061.

Nakano, Dana Y. 2013. "An Interlocking Panethnicity: The Negotiation of Multiple Identities Among Asian American Social Movement Leaders." *Sociological Perspectives* 56 (4): 569–595. doi: 10.1525/sop.2013.56.4.569.

Nakayama, Thomas K., and Robert L. Krizek. 1995. "Whiteness: A Strategic Rhetoric." *Quarterly Journal of Speech* 81 (3): 291–309. doi: 10.1080/00335639509384117.

Newkirk, Pamela. 2000. *Within the Veil: Black Journalists, White Media*. New York: New York University Press.

Nishikawa, Katsuo A., Terri L. Towner, Rosalee A. Clawson, and Eric N. Waltenburg. 2009. "Interviewing the Interviewers: Journalistic Norms and Racial Diversity in the Newsroom." *Howard Journal of Communications* 20 (3): 242–259. doi: 10.1080/10646170903070175.

Oh, David C. 2012. "Black-Yellow Fences: Multicultural Boundaries and Whiteness in the *Rush Hour* Franchise." *Critical Studies in Media Communication* 29 (5): 349–366. doi: 10.1080/15295036.2012.697634.

Oh, David C. 2015. *Second-Generation Korean Americans and Transnational Media: Diasporic Identifications*. Lanham, MD: Lexington Books.

Oh, David C. 2020. "Body as Disease." *Journal of Applied Communication Research Online Publication: Communication Interventions* 1: 50–58.

Oh, David C. 2022. *Whitewashing the Movies: White Subjectivity and Asian Erasure in U.S. Film Culture*. New Brunswick, NJ: Rutgers University Press.

Omatsu, Glenn. 2007. "The 'Four Prisons' and the Movements of Liberation: Asian American Activism from the 1960s to the 1990s." In *Asian American Studies: A Reader*, edited by Jean Yu-wen Shen Wu and Min Song, 164–196. New Brunswick, NJ: Rutgers University Press.

Omi, Michael, and Howard Winant. 1994. *Racial Formations in the United States: From the 1960s to the 1990s*, 2nd ed. New York: Routledge.

Ono, Kent A., and Vincent N. Pham. 2009. *Asian Americans and the Media*. Malden, MA: Polity.

Osajima, Keith. 2007. "Internalized Racism." In *Race, Class, and Gender in the United States: An Integrated Study*, edited by Paula S. Rothenberg, 138–142. New York: Worth Publishers.

Owens, Lynn C. 2008. "Network News: The Role of Race in Source Selection and Story Topic." *The Howard Journal of Communications* 19: 355–370. doi: 10.1080/10646170802418269.

Oyserman, Daphna, and Izumi Sakamoto. 1997. "Being Asian American: Identity, Cultural Constructs, and Stereotype Perception." *The Journal of Applied Behavioral Science* 33 (4): 435–453.

Paek, Hye Jin, and Hemant Shah. 2003. "Racial Ideology, Model Minorities, and the 'Not-So-Silent Partner': Stereotyping of Asian Americans in U.S. Magazine Advertising." *The Howard Journal of Communications* 14: 225–243.

Palombu-Liu, David. 1999. *Asian/American: Historical Crossings of a Racial Frontier*. Stanford, CA: Stanford University Press.

Pande, Somava, and Jolanta A. Drzewiecka. 2017. "Racial Incorporation Through Alignment with Whiteness." *Journal of International and Intercultural Communication* 10 (2): 115–134. doi: 10.1080/17513057.2016.1187761.

Park, Jerry Z. 2008. "Second-Generation Asian American Pan-Ethnic Identity: Pluralized Meanings of a Racial Label." *Sociological Perspectives* 51 (3): 541–561. doi: 10.1525/sop.2008.51.3.541.

Parker, David, and Miri Song. 2006. "New Ethnicities Online: Reflexive Racialisation and the Internet." *The Sociological Review* 54 (3): 575–594. doi: 10.1111/j.1467-954X.2006.00630.x.

Parker, David, and Miri Song. 2009. "New Ethnicities and the Internet: Belonging and the Negotiation of Difference in Multicultural Britain." *Cultural Studies* 23 (4): 583–604. doi: 10.1080/09502380902951003.

Perea, Juan F. 1997. "The Black/White Binary Paradigm of Race: The 'Normal Science' of American Racial Thought." *California Law Review* 85 (5): 1213–1258. doi: 10.2307/3481059.

Phinney, Jean S. 1989. "Stages of Ethnic Identity Development in Minority Group Adolescents." *Journal of Early Adolescence* 9 (1–2): 34–49. doi: 10.1177/0272431689091004.

Phinney, Jean S. 1996. "Understanding Ethnic Diversity: The Role of Ethnic Identity." *American Behavioral Scientist* 40 (2): 143–152. doi: 10.1177/0002764296040002005.

Prashad, Vijay. 2001. *Everybody Was Kung Fu Fighting: Afro-Asian Connections and the Myth of Cultural Purity*. Boston, MA: Beacon Press.

Pyke, Karen D. 2010. "What Is Internalized Racial Oppression and Why Don't We Study It?: Acknowledging Racism's Hidden Injuries." *Sociological Perspectives* 53 (4): 551–572. doi: 10.1525/sop.2010.53.4.551.

Reese, Stephen D. 1990. "The News Paradigm and the Ideology of Objectivity: A Socialist at the *Wall Street Journal*." *Critical Studies in Mass Communication* 7 (4): 390–409.

Rivas-Rodriguez, Maggie, Federico A. Subervi-Vélez, Sharon Bramlett-Solomon, and Don Heider. 2004. "Minority Journalists' Perceptions of the Impact of Minority Executives." *Howard Journal of Communications* 15 (1): 39–55. doi: 10.1080/10646170490275747.

Robinson, Sue, and Kathleen Bartzen Culver. 2019. "When White Reporters Cover Race: News Media, Objectivity and Community (Dis)Trust." *Journalism* 20 (3): 375–391. doi: 10.1177/1464884916663599.

Romaine, Taylor. 2020. "NYPD Creates Asian Hate Crime Task Force After Spike in Anti-Asian Attacks During Covid-19 Pandemic." CNN.

Said, Edward W. 1978. *Orientalism*. New York: Vintage Books.

Sanchez, James Chase. 2018. "Trump, The KKK, and the Versatility of White Supremacy Rhetoric." *Journal of Contemporary Rhetoric* 8 (1/2): 44–56. Accessed August 10, 2021.

Schudson, Michael. 1978. *Discovering the News: A Social History of American Newspapers*. New York: Basic Books.

Schudson, Michael. 2003. *The Sociology of News*, edited by Jeffrey C. Alexander, Contemporary Societies. New York: W.W. Norton & Company.

Schudson, Michael. 2018. *Why Journalism Still Matters*. Hoboken, NJ: Wiley.

Scire, Sarah. 2020. A Window into One Newsroom's Diversity Opens, but an Industry-Wide Door Shuts (for Now). *NiemanLab*. Accessed September 15, 2021.

Shafer, Jack. 2010. "Who Said it First?: Journalism Is the 'First Rough Draft of History.'" *Slate*, July 26, 2022, https://slate.com/news-and-politics/2010/08/on-the-trail-of-the-question-who-first-said-or-wrote-that-journalism-is-the-first-rough-draft-of-history.html#:~:text=Many%20journalists%20give%20former%20Washington,first%20rough%20draft%20of%20history.%E2%80%9D

Shafer, Richard. 1993. "What Minority Journalists Identify as Constraints to Full Newsroom Equality." *Howard Journal of Communications* 4 (3): 195–208. doi: 10.1080/10646179309359776.

Shiao, Jiannbin Lee. 2017. "The Meaning of Honorary Whiteness for Asian Americans: Boundary Expansion or Something Else?" *Comparative Sociology* 16: 788–813. doi: 10.1163/15691330-12341445.

Singer, Jane B. 2007. "Contested Autonomy." *Journalism Studies* 8 (1): 79–95. doi: 10.1080/14616700601056866.

Sobande, Francesca. 2019. "Woke-Washing: 'Intersectional' Femvertising and Branding 'Woke' Bravery." *European Journal of Marketing* 54 (11): 2723–2745. doi: 10.1108/EJM-02-2019-0134.

Son, Inseo. 2014. "Partly Colored or Almost White?: Racial Intermediacy and Identificational Ambivalence of Korean Immigrants." *Discourse & Society* 25 (6): 766–782. doi: 10.1177/0957926514536834.

Song, Miri. 2003. *Choosing Ethnic Identity*. Malden, MA: Polity.

Spickard, Paul R. 2007. "What Must I Be?: Asian Americans and the Question of Multiethnic Identity." In *Asian American Studies: A Reader*, edited by Jean Yu-wen Shen Wu and Min Song, 255–269. New Brunswick, NJ: Rutgers University Press.

Steiner, Linda. 2009. "Gender, Sex, and Newsroom Culture." In *The Handbook of Journalism Studies*, edited by Karin Wahl-Jorgensen and Thomas Hanitzsch, 452–468. New York: Routledge.

Strauss, Anselm, and Juliet Corbin. 1998. *Basics of Qualitative Research: Techniques and Procedures for Developing Grounded Theory*, 2nd ed. Thousand Oaks, CA: Sage Publications.

Sue, Derald Wing, Jennifer Bucceri, Annie I. Lin, Kevin L. Nadal, and Gina C. Torino. 2007. "Racial Microaggressions and the Asian American Experience." *Cultural Diversity and the Ethnic Minority Psychology* 13 (1): 72–81. doi: 10.1037/1099-9809.13.1.72.

Sui, Mingxiao, Newly Paul, Paru Shah, Brook Spurlock, Brooksie Chastant, and Johanna Dunaway. 2018. "The Role of Minority Journalists, Candidates, and Audiences in Shaping Race-Related Campaign News Coverage." *Journalism & Mass Communication Quarterly* 95 (4): 1079–1102. doi: 10.1177/1077699018762078.

Sullivan, Shannon. 2006. *Revealing Whiteness: The Unconscious Habits of Racial Privilege*, edited by John J. Stuhr, American Philosophy. Bloomington, IN: Indiana University Press.

Sun, Wei, and William J. Starosta. 2006. "Perceptions of Minority Invisibility Among Asian American Professionals." *Howard Journal of Communications* 17: 119–142. doi: 10.1080/10646170600656870.

Syed, Jawad, and Faiza Ali. 2011. "The White Woman's Burden: From Colonial Civlisation to Third World Development." *Third World Quarterly* 32 (2): 349–365. doi: 10.1080/01436597.2011.560473.

Taylor, Shelley E., David K. Sherman, Heejung S. Kim, Johanna Jarcho, Kaori Takagi, and Melissa S. Dunagan. 2004. "Culture and Social Support: Who Seeks It and Why?" *Interpersonal Relations and Group Processes* 87 (3): 354–362. doi: 10.1037/0022-3514.87.3.354.

Tracy, Marc. 2020. "Top Editor of *Philadelphia Inquirer* Resigns After 'Buildings Matter' Headline." *The New York Times*, Business. Accessed 2021-06-24 22:03:03. https://www.nytimes.com/2020/06/06/business/media/editor-philadephia-inquirer-resigns.html.

Tran, Julia, and Nicola Curtin. 2017. "Not Your Model Minority: Own-Group Activism Among Asian Americans." *Cultural Diversity and Ethnic Minority Psychology* 23 (4): 499–507. doi: 10.1037/cdp0000145.

Trieu, Monica M. 2018. "The 'Isolated Ethnics' and 'Everyday Ethnics': Region, Identity, and the Second-Generation Midwest Asian American Experience." *National Identities* 20 (2): 175–195. doi: 10.1080/14608944.2016.1211998.

Trieu, Monica M., and Hana Lee. 2018. "Asian Americans and Internalized Racial Oppression: Identified, Reproduced, and Dismantled." *Sociology of Race and Ethnicity* 4 (1): 67–82. doi: 10.1177/2332649217725757.

Tse, Lucy. 1999. "Finding a Place to Be: Ethnic Identity Exploration of Asian Americans." *Adolescence* 34 (133): 121–138.

Tuan, Mia. 1998. *Forever Foreigners or Honorary Whites?: The Asian Ethnic Experience Today*. New Brunswick, NJ: Rutgers University Press.

Tuan, Mia. 1999. Neither *Real* Americans Nor *Real* Asians?: Multigeneration Asian Ethnics Navigating the Terrain of Authenticity. *Qualitative Sociology* 22 (2): 105–125. Accessed November 29, 2020.

Tuan, Mia. 2002. "Second-Generation Asian American Identity: Clues from the Asian Ethnic Experience." In *The Second Generation: Ethnic Identity Among Asian Americans*, edited by Pyong Gap Min, 209–237. New York: AltaMira.

Tuchman, Gaye. 1978. *Making News: A Study in the Construction of Reality*. New York: The Free Press.

Varma, Roli. 2004. "Asian Americans: Achievements Mask Challenges." *Asian Journal of Social Science* 32 (2): 290–307. Accessed November 29, 2020.

Vos, Tim P., and Stephanie Craft. 2017. "The Discursive Construction of Journalistic Transparency." *Journalism Studies* 18 (12): 1505–1522. doi: 10.1080/1461670X.2015.1135754.

Waisbord, Silvio. 2009. "Advocacy Journalism in a Global Context." In *The Handbook of Journalism Studies*, edited by Karin Wahl-Jorgensen and Thomas Hanitzsch, 371–385. New York: Routledge.

Walker, Denetra, and Allison Daniel Anders. 2021. "'China Virus' and 'Kung-Flu': A Critical Race Case Study of Asian American Journalists' Experiences During COVID-19." *Cultural Studies ↔ Critical Methodologies*: 1–13. doi: 10.1177/15327 /08621105515.

Wayne, Michael L. 2014. "Mitigating Colorblind Racism in the Postnetwork Era: Class-Inflected Masculinities in *The Shield, Sons of Anarchy,* and *Justified*." *The Communication Review* 17 (3): 183–201. doi: 10.1080/10714421.2014.930271.

Weber, Joseph. 2016. "Teaching Fairness in Journalism: A Challenging Task." *Journalism & Mass Communication Educator* 71 (2): 163–174. doi: 10.1177/1077695815590014.

Woo, Bongki, Dale Dagar Maglalang, Samuel Ko, Michael Park, Yoonsun Choi, and David T. Takeuchi. 2020. "Racial Discrimination, Ethnic-Racial Socialization, and Cultural Identities Among Asian American Youths." *Cultural Diversity and Ethnic Minority Psychology* 26 (4): 447–459. doi: 10.1037/cdp0000327.

Woodward, Kathryn. 1997. "Concepts of Identity and Difference." In *Identity and Difference*, edited by Kathryn Woodward, 1–6. Thousand Oaks, CA: Sage Publications.

Wu, Frank H. 2002. *Yellow: Race in America Beyond Black and White*. New York: Basic Books.

Yamato, Gloria. 2004. "Something About the Subject Makes It Hard to Name." In *Race, Class, and Gender: An Anthology*, edited by Margaret L. Andersen and Patricia Hill Collins, 99–103. Belmont, CA: Thomson Wadsworth.

Yeh, Christine J., and Yu-Wei Wang. 2000. "Asian American Coping Attitudes, Sources, and Practices: Implications for Indigenous Counseling Strategies." *Journal of College Student Development* 41 (1): 94–103. Accessed December 28, 2020.

Yoo, Hyung Chol, and Richard M. Lee. 2005. "Ethnic Identity and Approach-Type Coping as Moderators of the Racial Discrimination/Well-Being Relation in Asian Americans." *Journal of Counseling Psychology* 52 (4): 497–506. doi: 10.1037/0022-0167.52.4.497.

Index

advocacy journalism, 95–97

alien stereotype, 3, 4, 113

Americanness: access to Asian American community and sense of, 32–34; and common immigrant culture, 26; and coverage of Asian Americans, 113–117; and COVID-19, 51, 113–114; in media, 17; and parents, 19; and racial activation, 30–31; strategies for, 17; as White, 17, 19

American Society of Newspaper Editors (ASNE), 2–3, 36, 48, 59, 136, 141, 144

Asian American community: access to and effect on racial identification, 21, 23–24, 32–34; access to and sense of Americanness, 32–34; coverage of, 6–7, 101–109, 132, 138; knowledge of, 108; size of and minimization of harm to journalists, 120–121

Asian American Journalists Association (AAJA), 6, 73, 74, 144

Asian Americans: Asian American term, 147n1; and body, 51; conflation with Asians, 52–53; as wedge/middleman between Black and White, 3, 121, 140. *See also* journalists, Asian American

Asian American studies, 32–33

Asian giant hornet, 105–106

assimilation: and alien stereotype, 3; and gender, 20; and socialization of journalists, 5, 45; toll of, 30; and upbringing in White neighborhoods, 15

avoidance strategies, 58

balance in coverage, 85, 87, 92, 93, 111

bamboo ceiling, 55–56, 59, 62–64

bias: and fairness, 92; objectivity as form of, 85; racial identification and scrutiny for, 81, 86, 89–90, 109

Black Americans: Asian American complicity in anti-Black racism, 28; and Black-White paradigm, 3, 7; treatment of Black sources, 43. *See also* journalists, Black

Black Lives Matter movement, 81, 107, 136

Black-White paradigm, 3, 7

blame for racism on self by Asian Americans, 30, 57, 79, 139

body, Asian, 51

Calafell, Bernadette, 65, 72

career and newsroom as White space: bamboo ceiling, 55–56, 59, 62–64; and class, 42, 43–44, 60–61, 141, 143–144; and devaluation of multiculturalism, 68–69, 78; downsizing, 61; and leaving of field, 5; marginalization and emotional harm, 64–71, 74, 79–80; marginalization and employment, 56–64, 78–79; mentoring, 72–73; pigeonholing, 63, 102, 104, 106–107; and racial activation, 48–49, 56–58, 71–78, 79; salaries and compensation, 37, 55, 58, 60–61, 78

Chalaby, Jean, 83

About the Authors

DAVID C. OH is an associate professor of communication arts at Ramapo College of New Jersey. He studies Asian Americans and media, transnational reception of Korean media, and Korean media and alterity. He is the author of two books, *Whitewashing the Movies* and *Second-Generation Korean American Adolescents and Transnational Media*.

SEONG JAE MIN is an associate professor of communication studies at Pace University's NYC campus, where he studies journalism and political communication. He is the author of two books, *As Democracy Goes, So Does Journalism* and *Rethinking the New Technology of Journalism*. He was a reporter in many news organizations.